The Trickster in Contemporary Film

This book discusses the role of the trickster figure in contemporary film against the cultural imperatives and social issues of modernity and post-modernity, and argues that cinematic tricksters always reflect psychological, economic and social change in society. It covers a range of films, from Charlie Chaplin's classics such as *Modern Times* (1936) and *The Great Dictator* (1940) to contemporary comedies and dramas with 'trickster actors' such as Jim Carrey, Sacha Baron-Cohen, Andy Kaufman and Jack Nicholson.

The Trickster in Contemporary Film offers a fresh perspective on the trickster figure not only in cinema but in Western culture in general. Alongside original film analyses, it touches upon a number of psychosocial issues including sovereignty of the individual, tricksterish qualities of the media and human relationships in the mercurial digital age.

Further topics of discussion include:

- common motifs in trickster narratives
- the trickster and personal relationships
- gonzo trickster and the art of comic insurrection.

Employing a number of complementary approaches such as Jungian psychology, film semiotics, narrative structure theories, Victor Turner's concept of liminality and Mikhail Bakhtin's theory of the carnivalesque, this book is essential reading for students and scholars of film, as well as anyone with an interest in analytical psychology and wider critical issues in contemporary culture.

Helena Bassil-Morozow has been teaching Film, Drama and Literature in various higher education institutions and in private practice for over seven years. Currently she is an honorary research fellow of the Research Institute for Media Art and Design, University of Bedfordshire. She is the author of *Tim Burton: The Monster and the Crowd* (Routledge, 2010).

The Trickster in Contemporary Film

Helena Bassil-Morozow

Routledge
Taylor & Francis Group

LONDON AND NEW YORK

First published 2012
by Routledge
27 Church Road, Hove, East Sussex BN3 2FA

Simultaneously published in the USA and Canada
by Routledge
711 Third Avenue, New York NY 10017

Routledge is an imprint of the Taylor & Francis Group, an Informa business

British Library Cataloguing in Publication Data
A catalogue record for this book is available from the British Library

Library of Congress Cataloging in Publication Data
Bassil-Morozow, Helena Victor, 1978–
   The trickster in contemporary film / Helena Bassil-Morozow.
      p. cm.
   ISBN 978-0-415-57465-5 (hardback) – ISBN 978-0-415-57466-2
(paperback) 1. Tricksters in motion pictures. 2. Tricksters—Cross-cultural
studies. I. Title.
   PN1995.9.T78B37 2011
   791.43'67–dc22

                                                        2011014006

ISBN: 978-0-415-57465-5 (hbk)
ISBN: 978-0-415-57466-2 (pbk)
ISBN: 978-0-203-80221-2 (ebk)

Typeset in Times by Garfield Morgan, Swansea, West Glamorgan
Paperback cover design by Andrew Ward
Printed in Great Britain by TJ International Ltd, Padstow, Cornwall

For Matthew

Contents

Foreword   viii
Acknowledgements   xii

Introduction   1

1   Common Motifs in Trickster Narratives   24

2   The Trickster and Personal Relationships   47

3   The Trickster and the Economic System   86

4   The Trickster and Contemporary Powers   120

5   Gonzo Trickster and the Art of Comic Insurrection   142

Conclusion   179

References   182
Film references   188
Index   191

Foreword

Christopher Hauke

It is all too easy to feel cheated by a book title. Initially raised expectations can be dashed after the first 20 pages. But what you are holding is the reverse of this. What is the opposite of feeling cheated? Being unexpectedly, substantially rewarded, that's what!

The Trickster in Contemporary Film offers so much more than its straightforward title suggests. The book manages to include just about every example of the movie trickster from the expected *Dumb and Dumber* (still hilarious and subversive after innumerable viewings) and Jim Carrey's brilliant performance in *The Mask*, to the unexpected such as Jack Nicholson's films and – a reminder we could not do without – the work of Charlie Chaplin and his *Modern Times*. Before we are made fully aware of the scope of her theme and how far she will extend it, Helena dives straight in to remind us how the trickster 'reflects the human condition, with its ups and downs, and its explosive mixture of the tragic and the comic . . . [while] this is also a book about the psychology and anthropology of failure and success' (p. 2).

The trickster has huge significance for our own modern times, and the cinema screen is the primary site for its projection, 'because cinema tends to be the psychological mirror of society' (ibid.). Helena prepares the ground for us first by going into the anthropology and mythology of the trickster figure as it has appeared across the world and over many centuries. Unlike standard texts on the trickster, her approach is individually carved to her own subject matter, introducing the character of the trickster almost like one would a genre in film. Drawing on examples from all over the world, she covers all the trickster tropes such as boundary crossing, the body and its scatological events, sexuality, the penis and loss of control, and the strange link between the human and the animal, the outraged and the outrageous. Helena is a film scholar who can find and link accurate film examples to the mythological character, but she is also a Jungian film scholar and this is where we hit bedrock. Carl Jung was a psychologist who reckoned all of humanity had ways of seeing and behaving which lay 'beneath' both the conscious mind and the personal unconscious. Myths and characters such as the trickster found in human stories world-wide form part of the evidence for this *collective* unconscious. The trickster is an archetype, part of our unconscious human potential found in everyone and every culture.

Jung discovered the Winnebago trickster stories to be rich in material relevant to the psychology of modern humans. Riding on the carnival trailer that is modern film, *The Trickster in Contemporary Film* offers a new perspective on 'how contemporary film presents the tricky relationship between consciousness and the unconscious in the "civilised" mind' (p. 3). Like many recent texts that use Jungian thinking, Helena is picking up on something that is at the heart of Jung's psychology but has too often been subsumed beneath attention to Jungian psychology purely as a clinical treatment. Central to Jung's psychology is the idea that modern consciousness suffers from an over-reliance on the rational, the linear, the pragmatic and the profitable. This perspective constitutes Jung's 'psycho-political evaluations of modernity and its discontents' (p. 3) as Helena calls it. Our contemporary neurosis is a neurosis of post-industrial, post-Enlightenment, positivistic and capitalist society. Helena acknowledges the post-Jungian Andrew Samuels (who pointed out the link between Hermes, the trickster and the shape-shifting nature of capitalism) when she asserts 'the trickster dwells at the heart of the capitalist system' (p. 3). What could be a better theme than the trickster to explore the wider field of the challenges to modern capitalist life from Julian Assange and WikiLeaks on the internet to films about Andy Kaufman and Sacha Baron-Cohen's real life twisting of realities that equally challenge our idea of what is 'acceptable'. As Helena says, 'The trickster in . . . film is often a metaphor for repressed potentiality, of futurity, of dormant change . . . an intrinsically rebellious and artistic power in the human psyche which saves us from mental entropy and ensures our progress as individuals' (p. 8).

In *The Trickster in Contemporary Film* Helena has delved into the archives and deals us an intertextual hand rich in originality and surprises. She launches off from Kerényi and Radin noting how the trickster's function 'is to add disorder to order . . . to render possible, within the fixed bounds of what is permitted, an experience of what is not permitted' (p. 6). She then contextualises this function within the concept of *habitus* devised by the philosopher-anthropologist Pierre Bourdieu. As a dynamic between the individual and his surroundings, the *habitus* produces individual and collective practices 'deposited in each organism in the form of schemes of perception, thought and action' (p. 9) which are resistant to examination or change and act to the advantage of those who hold power. Helena points out how, 'This view directly taps into the socio-political role of the trickster principle, which is a chaotic, spontaneous force whose primary aim is to challenge the universal influence of the social order' (p. 10). This position is backed up further using the work of Clifford Geertz, Marshall Berman and Zygmunt Bauman involving different versions of postmodern social critique. Historically, using Bakhtin on the '"thousand-year-old develop-ment of popular culture"' (p. 21), Helena asserts that our movies continue the tradition of Cervantes and Rabelais: 'The trickster of modernity is the trickster of the emerging capitalist world – closely associated with the problematic relationship between the individual and society' (p. 22). This is of course another major theme of Jung's – the urge towards individu-ation in every individual and the strain that 'mass man' and conformity puts on the psychological need for personal authenticity. As the book says, 'The trickster's efforts to become a man, and an independent one at that, can be seen as both ludicrous and heroic because . . . natural and social powers will always be impeding the individual's ability to achieve autonomy' (p. 23).

Helena deepens her analysis of the trickster function by incorporating Victor Turner's and van Gennep's understanding of the liminal – from the Latin *limen* for threshold, the locale of the boundary-crossing trickster. As she writes, 'Between the points of "detachment" and "reattachment" there lies a grey middle area of uncertainty, turbulence and chanciness. This is the playground of the trickster' (p. 17). The trickster is the shadow of the conventional character and the shadow of his conventional world as we witness in the characters played by Adam Sandler in *Click* or Rik Mayall in *Drop Dead Fred* or Jim Carrey in *The Cable Guy*. Helena goes into the playground of these films, their scripts and structures, to uncover what they are reflecting back to contemporary audiences of our own world – what needs questioning and what would be possible if things changed. As she says, '"Crossing the boundary", in narrative terms, is the trigger, the beginning of the conflict' (p. 20). Her thematic analysis leads us through discussions of the role of finding love, new ways of connecting and dis-connecting (Helena is a Facebook stalwart!), geeks and *The Social Network* (an insightful discussion of the degree to which movies need to reflect the 'truth' or tell a true story), the trickster as therapist (*Anger Management*), money, the middle classes, the economy and the birth of the Picaro, the gonzo trickster *Borat* and Andy Kaufman – two supremely executed chal-lenges to the 'truth' and the border between fiction and documentary.

As I wrote at the start of the foreword, this book surprises us and gratifies us with its scope, its detail and how, like the trickster himself, it challenges our beliefs about the function of popular culture, in particular, these trickster film 'comedies'. This book tells us how films can speak to us, inform us and enhance our lives – once we have writers like Helena Bassil-Morozow and Carl Jung to guide us. Because this book is also about contemporary society and its values, and the psychological resources we may bring to challenge its 'discontents', Helena Bassil-Morozow asks us to take the trickster seriously. We can laugh and be outraged, but not laugh and simply move on. As she says, 'individuation is mad because raising your voice . . . against "higher powers" is bound to be dangerous . . . the learning path is fraught with errors. Only fools are prepared to leave the safety of the womb/mother/nature/the village/paradise, and "go and seek their fortune"' (p. 23). This is Helena's invitation to us with her book. Be a fool! Leave your safety! But, above all, be prepared to learn.

Christopher Hauke is a Senior Lecturer at Goldsmiths, University of London, an I.A.A.P. Jungian analyst, filmmaker and author of *Jung and the Postmodern: The Interpretation of Realities*; *Human Being Human, Culture and the Soul*; and co-editor of *Jung and Film. Post-Jungian Takes on the Moving Image* and *Jung and Film II. The Return. Further Takes on the Moving Image*, all published by Routledge.

Acknowledgements

I would like to thank Routledge, and particularly my editor Kate Hawes, for helping me make this book possible.

I am grateful to my students who kept asking me difficult questions and making me seek answers to them. I am also greatly indebted to my teachers, Professors Avril Horner and Irina Kabanova, who also asked me difficult questions (only that was much earlier). Finally, I would like to thank Alexey for providing me with criticism and feedback, and Gregory Singh for introducing me to the world of Adam Sandler.

Given my heavy caffeine addiction, a special thank you to everyone working at the Uxbridge branch of Costa for patiently letting me write on their premises!

Permissions

I am very grateful to Routledge/Taylor & Francis for the permission to quote from *The Collected Works of C. G. Jung* (CW), edited by Sir Herbert Read, Dr. Michael Fordham and Dr. Gerhardt Adler, and translated by R. F. C. Hull, London.

I would also like express my deepest gratitude to Association Chaplin, for the permission to quote from *The Great Dictator*.

Introduction

I'd rather write about laughing than crying,
For laughter makes men human, and courageous.
(François Rabelais, *The Life of Gargantua and of Pantagruel*)

There is a grotesque and hilarious scene in Farrelly's comedy *Dumb and Dumber* (1994), in which Harry (Jeff Daniels) announces to his friend Lloyd (Jim Carrey) that their pet parrot Petey's head 'fell off' because 'he was pretty old'. The background of this tragedy is formed of a series of unfortunate events. The pair lost their employment, acquired a mortal enemy and got robbed by a nice old lady – all in the same day. Upon hearing the devastating news, Lloyd runs up to the parrot, looks at it, then turns away in horror and exclaims melodramatically: 'That's it! I've had it with this dump! We got no food, we got no jobs, OUR PET'S HEADS ARE FALLING OFF!'

This mixture of the grotesque, the tragic, the absurd and the comical reflects the true trickster spirit. A beheaded pet bird must be a pretty gory sight, but the audience laughs hysterically at Lloyd's reaction because of his incongruous perception of the incident as the height of God's injustice and unfairness, as the final blow of cruel fate. The scene is amusing because it is both burlesque and grotesque. Its burlesque character lies in the irony-generating tension between 'the low' image of the parrot and 'the high' idea of God's insensitivity towards the little people in a shabby flat whose world is falling to pieces. The frenzied grotesqueness of the joke about the parrot disintegrating due to old age is both callous and politically incorrect, and more so because it comes immediately after the scene with the thieving old lady on a motorised cart, and will later lead to Lloyd sellotaping the head back to the bird's body and then selling it to a blind boy. Civilised human beings are not supposed to find old age, poverty, stupidity, failure, cruelty and death funny. And yet, the viewer laughs at this intrinsically rude and embarrassing scene; the scene which clearly oversteps the boundaries of moral decency.

The principal entertaining qualities of the brothers' Farrelly's master-piece, however, are not limited to the pathetic incompetence of the pro-tagonists. Lloyd Christmas may be silly, naïve and useless, but his outburst at the fate's mistreatment and injustice shows him as a tragic character, a man who feels trapped in his misfortunes, who is looking for a way out of the blandness and invisibility of his existence. Lloyd feels unfree, Lloyd desperately wants a breakthrough, he blames the invisible (in his case social) forces that obstruct his freedom. He rebels, he goes on a quest. It is not his desperation that produces the richest effect (and affect) in the film – it is the cross-country journey that he undertakes, which consists of a series of mishaps, and which, regardless of the final result, is in itself a transfor-mative process. Like Chaplin's Tramp, Carrey's Lloyd treats his audience to a story of marginality, failure, rejection and metamorphosis.

The key element of Lloyd's and Harry's adventures would therefore be *effort* because the pair display idiotic heroism and superhuman stupidity just for the sake of moving away from a dead point. The character of the prankster Lloyd causes a strong reaction in the audience because, as a version of the trickster, he breaks the boundaries of the image and narra-tive, and infects the audience with his essence. He stirs up the mischievous spirit in the viewer. The audience, Mac Ricketts notes, 'are laughing at themselves. [The trickster] endures their ridicule like a suffering saviour, and at the end he saves them, through their laughter' (Ricketts, 1966: 348). In a way, he reflects the human condition, with its ups and downs, and its explosive mixture of the tragic and the comic.

This book is an attempt to outline and explain the enduring presence of the trickster figure in contemporary films, both comedic and non-comedic, whose narratives concern the current state of Western culture. Unavoidably, this is also a book about the psychology and anthropology of failure and success – both in film and in everyday life because cinema tends to be the psychological mirror of society. When researching this book, I realised that it would be impossible to separate Jim Carrey's struggling losers, Jack Nicholson's madmen and rebels, and Adam Sandler's oxymoronic middle-class fools from the world which they inhabit – post-industrial, quickly-changing, tough, competitive, disjointed, technologically advanced. It would also be wrong to analyse Charlie Chaplin's tramps and immigrants separ-ately from the problems of industrial modernity precisely because they are by-products of industrial urban life; they are shaped by it. The world always looks big and scary for the small man, and in today's mercurial lifestyle, with its technology-enhanced communication and complex rules for personal and professional interaction, there are particularly many opportunities for looking like a fool. The trickster lives along the class divisions, in the existential gaps of urban living, in the civilisedly individualistic notion of 'personal space', and in the complex system of social etiquette that effec-tively separates and labels people.

Most importantly – the fool is the one who lacks heroic consciousness, who fails to compete, who fails to succeed in the world which divides people into winners and losers. With the arrival of the 'clean' society all that was competitive and ruthless in human beings has not automatically disappeared. Moreover, the economic system itself feeds on this hidden energy, as ambition is absolutely vital to the system's efficient functioning. The trickster dwells at the heart of the capitalist system for, as Andrew Samuels writes in his book *The Political Psyche*, capitalism by nature is deeply hermetic, constantly changing, adapting and malleable: 'The tale of Hermes is, in many ways, the pattern of our particular socioeconomic epoch which, like him, is a shapeshifter with numerous names to match its myriad presentations: late capitalism, late-late capitalism, post-capitalism, post-Fordism, the information culture (Hermes as messenger), post industrialism, post-modernism, late modernity and so forth' (1993: 88).

The trickster infiltrates the hyper-serious, persona-dominated professional culture and reminds its representatives that even the most successful businesspeople are never protected from failure – the mutable, unstable, tricky world of global capitalism does not guarantee financial safety and security. Even when human beings choose not to notice him, the trickster is very much alive, hidden under the smooth and polite surface of the post-industrial metropolis, and accumulating explosive potential. Applied to our society, the trickster principle defines the interaction between the world of instincts and the world of rational behaviour; between the 'natural' and the progressive. In other words, it describes the pitfalls and heights of being human.

I employ a set of different methodologies to assess how contemporary film presents the tricky relationship between consciousness and the unconscious in the 'civilised' mind. It may feel that the overall spirit of the book is Jungian but I mainly use Jung's 'bigger' concepts – his psycho-political evaluations of modernity and its discontents (mass psychology, the role of instincts in the age of rationality, the psychological effects of technology), his idea of individuation (the process of becoming oneself) and his interpretation of the shadow archetype. To explain the structure of trickster narratives, I adopt Arnold van Gennep's tripartite 'rite of passage' framework, which I use in conjunction with traditional narrative structure theories. Victor Turner's concept of liminality elucidates anthropological value of the trickster principle and helps to understand its enduring presence in art and ritual, both ancient and contemporary. I also enlist the help of post-Jungian theorists (Andrew Samuels, Christopher Hauke), and cultural anthropologists and sociologists (Pierre Bourdieu, Clifford Geertz, Zygmunt Bauman, Marshall Berman) to paint the picture of the post-industrial world.

In the book I use the terms 'trickster principle' and 'trickster' interchangeably. My understanding of them is similar to Jung's distinction between archetypes and archetypal images: the trickster principle is a general concept; a kind of psychological force (both personal and social) that has at its core the dynamic between restraint and breakthrough. By contrast, the trickster is a concrete realisation of the principle: a character or structural element in myth, work of fiction, cinematic narrative – or even in real life. For instance, gonzo-performers such as Sacha Baron-Cohen choose to be mouthpieces of the trickster principle in order to prove the absurdity of mainstream thinking.

The detailed analysis of the trickster's principal traits and qualities is given in Chapter 1. This is not an anthropological, psychoanalytic or literary, but a structural-comparative analysis. In this chapter I am looking across a range of examples from myth, literature, folklore and cinema in an attempt to define the 'traditional' trickster qualities, and to determine their function and meaning in the narratives. The main task of Chapter 1 is to build a more coherent (however paradoxical this task might sound!) picture of the trickster figure from the narrative fragments that exist in world myth, fiction and film.

Chapter 2 delineates the trickster's role in interpersonal relationships and discusses the importance of emotional connection in today's disjointed world. It uses examples from Ben Stiller's *The Cable Guy* (1996), Frank Coraci's *Click* (2006), the Batman trio (Tim Burton's *Batman* (1989) and *Batman Returns* (1992), and Joel Schumacher's *Batman Forever* (1995)) and *The Social Network* (2010).

Chapter 3 looks at the trickster's relationships with money, big corporations, the middle-class culture of professionalism, and the Western cultural emphasis on ambition and achievement. It looks primarily at Carrey's films, including *The Mask* (1994) and *Fun With Dick and Jane* (2005) but also touches upon the issue of 'middle-class anger' discussed in Peter Segal's *Anger Management* (2003) and Ben Stiller's *The Cable Guy* (1996).

Chapter 4 analyses the trickster's dynamic dialogue with today's 'higher powers' – political, social, legal, cultural and economic giants that limit the freedom of the individual. Charlie Chaplin's voiceless tramps (*A Dog's Life* (1918), *The Pilgrim* (1923), *The Great Dictator* (1940)) and Jack Nicholson's social rebels (*One Flew Over the Cuckoo's Nest* (1975), *Chinatown* (1974)) constitute the core of my analysis of this tragic dialogue.

Chapter 5 discusses the general principles behind what I call 'gonzo tricksterism' – a brand of bawdy comedic entertainment in which the boundary between fiction and reality is blurred. It concentrates on the controversial and risqué art of Andy Kaufman and Sacha Baron-Cohen. Their performances are subversive because they challenge (and often scandalise) the public. A gonzo trickster pushes the viewers out of their comfort zone and into the realm of the liminal, destroys their 'objective' complacency and sense of objective reality by presenting them with multiple realities and possibilities. The discussion of gonzo tricksterism is complemented by analyses of Baron-Cohen's films, *Borat* (2006) and *Brüno* (2009).

As pertains to a book discussing the trickster, the boundaries between chapters are not exactly rigid. Themes and motifs travel from one place to another, ideas overlap and amalgamate, and occasionally, the same film crops up in different chapters. Instead of strict systematisation, I analyse the films synchronically. My task in this book is not to create a coherent grid describing all existing types of trickster film, or even to map out the history of trickster film, but to trace its psychological importance for the Western society. I regard the trickster primarily as a psychological principle operating at the personal and collective levels. As such, trickster narratives – mythological, literary or cinematic – help societies understand the concepts of order and change.

Ways of Defining the Trickster

The trickster figure has been variously defined by anthropologists, sociologists, psychotherapists, cultural theorists, writers and film critics. The enemy of boundaries, he resists the narrow framing of definition. Most writers, however, agree that trickster figures, diverse as they are, nevertheless possess a number of common qualities: they are foolish, rebellious, asocial and anti-social, inconsistent, outrageous and self-contradictory. They exist in a kind of cultural, social and psychological limbo, between the states, outside of the conscious world. Thus, Paul Radin states in his prefatory note to the Winnebago trickster cycle that the 'Trickster is at one and the same time creator and destroyer, giver and negator, he who dupes others and is always duped himself' (Radin, 1972: xxiii) while Karl Kerényi calls the trickster figure 'the spirit of disorder, the enemy of boundaries' (Radin, 1972: 185).

Defining the trickster figure involves some serious hermeneutic issues. The trickster is a shapeshifter, he is change personified. The proverbial rolling stone that gathers no moss, he is constantly in a state of transition. As William Hynes rightly notes in his article on mythic tricksters, 'to define (de-finis) is to draw borders around phenomena, and tricksters seem amazingly resistant to such capture, they are notorious border breakers' (Hynes and Doty, 1993: 33). Hynes also writes that the trickster is constantly disassembling and deconstructing mythical trickster figures (1993b: 35). Throughout the long history of 'trickster criticism', this figure has been variously described and analysed as an archetype (Carl Jung; Paul Radin, 1956; Joseph Henderson (Jung and von Franz, 1964); Karl Kerényi, 1956), culture hero (Frantz Boas, 1898; Joseph Campbell, 1959), folklore and mythological character (Paul Radin, 1956; Karl Kerényi, 1956; Robert Pelton, 1980; Edward Evans-Pritchard, 1967; Mac Linscott Ricketts, 1993; Barbara Babcock-Abrahams, 1975), holy Fool (William Willeford, 1969; Enid Welsford, 1936), an important element of the ritual (Victor Turner, 1979, 1992), an anthropological entity (Robert Pelton, 1980; Edward

Evans-Pritchard, 1967; Mac Linscott Ricketts, 1993; Lawrence Goldman, 1998, and many others), a therapeutic phenomenon – a self-healing element in the psyche (Murray Stein, 1993; Miller, 2004), and as a metaphor for the process of change – personal, social, political or any other (Hynes and Doty, 1993; Brian Street, 1972; Mary Douglas, 1968; Victor Turner, 1979; Susan Stewart, 1978).

The importance of the trickster figure for the contemporary Western individual has also not been overlooked. The trickster has been associated with challenging the social order by introducing destabilisation and imbalance into it (Radin, 1956; Douglas, 1968; Street, 1972), described as part of the contemporary political life (Samuels, 1993, 2001), and analysed as an integral element of contemporary media culture (Graham St. John, 2008; Ricki Tannen, 2007; Terrie Waddell, 2009). An interesting angle on the trickster figure is provided by Sheldon Kopp (1974) and Anne Doueihi (1993). Both regard tricksterism as a gonzo activity which can be undertaken by real people and used in everyday lives – to enhance their professions, for instance. In his book *The Hanged Man: Psychotherapy and the Forces of Darkness* (1974) Kopp discusses the shamanic and tricksterish aspects of the psychotherapy profession, while Doueihi describes the highly controversial anthropologist Carlos Castaneda as a scholar-trickster who crossed the boundary between fiction and science (Hynes and Doty, 1993: 201).

This list is by no means exhaustive. The trickster seems to be a complex umbrella term which resists structuralist and any other quasi-scientific interpretation (as William Hynes reminisces, in the process of compiling *Mythical Trickstre Figures*, Laura Makarius lamented the possibility of creating a comprehensive grid of trickster characteristics (1993: 211)), but welcomes methodological plurality and interpretive *différance*. The term 'trickster' is not confined to the world of mythology – Greek Hermes, North American Wakdjunkaga, Coyote, Hare and Raven, African Anansi and Eshu, Sun Wukong of China, Scandinavian Loki, Hodja Nasreddin of the Asian Folklore, Russian Ivan the Fool, etc. – but can be detected in a wide range of psychological, cultural, political, literary and cinematic contexts. Thus, Don Beecher writes that 'today the term "trickster" has become so familiar a designator that an author can refer to the trickster figure in Old Comedy of Aristophanes and in Plautus and Terence as in Renaissance comedy and in contemporary films and literature' (Beecher, 1987, quoted in Hynes and Doty, 1993: 14).

There has been some agreement among the scholars as regards the trickster's cultural role, and his social and psychological significance. The historian of religion Karl Kerényi notes that the trickster's function in an archaic society 'is to add disorder to order and so make a whole, to render possible, within the fixed bounds of what is permitted, an experience of what is not permitted' (Radin, 1972: 185). For instance, the Winnebago cycle jokingly discusses incest, excreta, menstruation and transvestism, while the myths of Hermes and Loki raise the problem of criminal and antisocial behaviour: theft, forgery, deception, conmanship, murder. The folklorist Barbara Babcock-Abrahams puts the trickster in charge of 'the tolerated margin of mess'; he is a creature who constantly behaves in the maximally antisocial manner: 'Although we laugh at him for his troubles and his foolishness and are embarrassed by his promiscuity, his creative cleverness amazes us and keeps alive the possibility of transcending the social restrictions we regularly encounter' (Babcock-Abrahams, 1975: 147).

True, mythological, literary, cinematic, real and psychological tricksters tend to be idiotically and naïvely brave in their denial of obstacles, constraints and limits, and in their refusal to accept authority in all its forms – religious, political, metaphysical, social, scientific. They seem to regard 'order' and 'peace' as forms of stagnation, as lack of movement, death. Ever the enemy of conformity, Ananse of Ashanti mythology plants contradiction among people by scattering around pieces of a man called Hate-to-be-Contradicted (Pelton, 1980: 27). The Yoruba trickster Eshu makes two sworn friends quarrel when he paints one half of his cap white and the other black, and then rides between the two men on his horse so that each of them can only see one side of the cap. The neighbours, naturally, start arguing about the cap's colour (Pelton, 1980: 141). It is tempting to regard Eshu's behaviour as insensitive and malicious warmongering. In fact, what Eshu encourages is not conflict and war but diversity, autonomy and independent thinking. Like all mythological tricksters, he stands between the tyrannical purity of godly order and the uncertain state that is human freedom. He has the power to tip the scales in favour of the humans, in which case the reins, the responsibility for his own destiny, can be handed back to the man. According to Kerényi, the god of thieves Hermes introduces chaos and accident into the Olympian order (Jung and Kerényi, 2002: 68). The troublemaker Loki proudly bears the title of the enemy of the divine powers because his evil deeds can trigger *Ragnarök* – the doom of the gods (Wagnerian 'twilight of the gods', Nietzschean 'twilight of the idols') (Rosenberg, 1994: 223).

The trickster's involvement into the making, shaking and remaking of the social order has attracted psychotherapeutic explanations. In his seminal essay 'On the Psychology of the Trickster Figure', Carl Jung discusses various aspects and qualities of the trickster figure and traces their origin in history and psychology. For instance, Jung emphasises the link between the trickster and the animal kingdom. In his clearest manifestation, the trickster is 'a faithful reflection of an absolutely undifferentiated human consciousness, corresponding to a psyche that has hardly left the animal level' (CW9/I: para. 465). In other words, this archetype is the remainder of an earlier stage of human development; its task is to remind highly conscious and civilized human beings of their animal roots. Jung also notes the trickster's link with the divine. According to Jung, the trickster is 'God, man and animal at once'. As such, he is both 'subhuman and superhuman, a bestial and divine being, whose chief and most alarming characteristic is his unconsciousness' (CW9/I: para. 472). In his description, Jung deliberately clashes the grand opposites, thus placing the trickster at the centre of the conflict, making him the hub, the cause, and the originator of the friction.

Social Structures, Cultural Systems and Human Agency

The issue of human agency – the capacity of human beings to make decisions and choices; to act independently, outside and regardless of the socio-cultural grid in which they are forced to exist – has direct relevance to the trickster figure. Coincidentally, human agency is also one of the central problems of cultural anthropology. Human beings seem to be permanently caught in the developmental tug of war – the process of fission and fusion (which Gregory Bateson termed *schismogenesis*), the rivalry between individual creativity and cultural imperatives (Bateson, 1936: 195–196).

For decades, psychologists and anthropologists have talked about the trickster as conscious or inadvertent promoter of progress. Karl Kerényi discusses him, in the form of Prometheus, as a bringer of knowledge (Radin, 1972: 181), while Mac Ricketts, in his analysis of American Indian culture, calls the trickster 'the symbol of self-transcending mind of human-kind and of the human quest for knowledge and the power that knowledge brings': 'Unlike the shaman, the priest and the devotee of supernaturalistic religion, the trickster looks to no "power" outside himself, but sets out to subdue the world by his wits and his wit. In other words, as I see him, the trickster is a symbolic embodiment of the attitude today represented by the humanist' (Hynes and Doty, 1993: 91).

Ricketts's alignment of the trickster principle with the issue of human agency (and humanism in general) certainly makes sense. Ethnic tricksters tend to be 'inadvertent libertarians' in that they stress the importance of chance, accident, choice, difference, nonconformity, disobedience and other perforators of public order, divinely prescribed lifestyle and communal necessity. Psychologically, the 'release of the trickster' motif may corre-spond to a number of processes in the human psyche: repression, regression and release of trapped psychic contents (in a dream or an outburst of rage, for instance); the dynamics of neurosis; accumulation and eruption of creative energy; the functioning and development of ambition, motivation, inspiration; incentive to overcome the period of stagnation and move on. The trickster in mythology, literature and film is often a metaphor for repressed potentiality, of futurity, of dormant change. As such, the trickster principle is an intrinsically rebellious and artistic power in the human psyche which saves us from mental entropy and ensures our progress as individuals. The trickster principle keeps consciousness alive or, in the words of Andrew Samuels, 'acts as a yardstick and spur to consciousness' (Samuels, 1993: 83). It is a radical force which, in a way, works against the psychic facilities that help human beings to conform, adapt and assimilate. As Robert Pelton notes in *The Trickster of West Africa*, the trickster can be regarded as a 'process designed to *combat* darkness by bringing to light the causes of disorder' (1980: 286).

To outline the dynamic between the individual and his surroundings, the philosopher and anthropologist Pierre Bourdieu devised the concept of *habitus* – 'systems of durable, transposable dispositions, structured structures predisposed to function as structuring structures, that is, as principles which generate and organise practices and representations that can be objectively adapted to their outcomes without presupposing a conscious aiming at ends or an express mastery of the operations necessary in order to maintain them' (Bourdieu, 1977: 53). The *habitus*, Bourdieu argues, is a product of history and 'it produces individual and collective practices – more history – in accordance with the schemes generated by history' (1977: 54). These practices are 'collectively orchestrated without being the product of the organising action of a conductor' and ensure 'the active presence of past experiences, which, deposited in each organism in the form of schemes of perception, thought and action, tend to guarantee the "correctness" of these practices and their constancy over time more reliably than all formal rules and explicit norms' (1977: 53–54). Like some giant wieldy monster, the *habitus* tends to ensure its own constancy 'and its defence against change through the selection it makes within new information by rejecting information capable of calling into question the accumulated information, if exposed to it accidentally or by force, and especially by avoiding exposure to such information' (1977: 60). Its influence ranges from communal to centralised as the human propensity to belong to the *habitus* can be harvested by all kind of leaders, from local to global, from religious to financial and political. The individual, Bourdieu argues, is programmed to take seriously the 'performative magic of the social, that of the king, the banker or the priest' while the institutions, which these leaders represent, exploit the body's readiness to belong to an order (1977: 57). Being part of the homogenous (and forcibly homogenised) *habitus*, agents mould their aspirations according to the ingrained notions of what is and is not 'for us'. Like this, the *habitus* effectively shapes its member's future success in life:

> The relation of what is possible is a relation to power; and the sense of the probable future is constituted in the prolonged relationship with a world structured according to the categories of what is possible (for us) and impossible (for us), of what is appropriated in advance by and for others and what we can reasonably expect for oneself. The habitus is the principle of a selective perception of the indices tending to confirm and reinforce rather than transform it, a matrix generating responses

adapted in advance to all objective conditions identical to or homologous with the (past) conditions of its production; it adjusts itself to a probable future which it anticipates and helps to bring about because it reads directly in the present of the presumed world, the only one it can ever know. It is thus the basis of what Marx calls 'effective demand' (. . . as opposed to 'demand without effect', based on need and desire), a realistic relation to what is possible, founded on and therefore limited by power. This disposition, always marked by its (social) conditions of acquisition and realisation, tends to adjust to the objective chances of satisfying need or desire, inclining agents to 'cut their coats according to their cloth', and so become the accomplices of the processes that tend to make the probable a reality.

(1977: 64)

Biological individuals having the same *habitus*, and therefore being products of the same conditionings, tend to possess similar dispositions and social expectations. One can infer from Bourdieu's position, with its Marxist hue, that human agents are deliberately limited by the 'keepers' of the *habitus* from exploring their possibilities and looking for opportunities, incidental or thought-through. This view directly taps into the socio-political role of the trickster principle, which is a chaotic, spontaneous force whose primary aim is to challenge the universal influence of the social order. The trickster questions any fixed position within the *habitus*, thus questioning its validity and supremacy. It does so by introducing chance and unpredictability into the otherwise stable and rational structure. From the point of view of the trickster principle (or rather, from the point of view of its rebellious human carriers), rationality is the source of unfreedom and inequality because any hegemony is structured and, as a rule, has a 'logical' foundation. The trickster destroys the local power, which offers limited social routes, by introducing into it chaos in the form of plurality of discourses, as well as accidents such as chances and opportunities. The natural, instinctual, unpredictable trickster is the enemy of the structure whose aims are the implementation of 'civilisation' and the blind instalment of social control (through law, tradition, religion, communal ties, cultural patterns, economic circumstances, etc.).

Bourdieu's vision of the *habitus* as a set of social patterns limiting human agency is ideologically similar to Freud's theory of humour. In Freud's view, humour emerged as a defence mechanism protecting civilisation from the overflow of aggressive impulses coming from the unconscious. He argues that 'brutal hostility, forbidden by law, has been replaced by verbal invective' (1977: 102) and 'though as children we are still endowed with a powerful inherited disposition to hostility, we are later taught by a higher personal civilization that it is an unworthy thing to use an abusive language; and even where fighting has itself remained permissible, the number of things which may not be employed as methods of fighting has extraordinarily increased' (1977: 102). Seen in this light, jokes are used by human beings to inoculate the powerful and dangerous instincts. Civilisation has to defend itself against the unconscious; it demands that any demons are kept in check, and humour is one of the most effective means of warding them off.

The influential American anthropologist Clifford Geertz proposed to explore the theme of psychological 'ingrainedness' in one's culture via the notion of control mechanisms created and implemented by it. His view on the subject, however, is more positive than that of Pierre Bourdieu. Geertz argued that culture should not be regarded as 'complexes of concrete behaviour patterns – customs, usages, traditions, habit clusters' – but as a set of 'programs' whose primary purpose is to govern the behaviour of the individual and to ensure complicity and social heterogeneity. Thus, plans, recipes, rules, instructions exist because 'man is precisely the animal most desperately dependent upon such extragenetic, outside-the skin control mechanisms, such cultural programs for ordering his behaviour' (Geertz, 1975: 44). Geertz effectively advocates that human agents need culture to structure and organise their world; that man is in need of readymade symbols and prescribed meanings because they put a 'construction upon the events through which he lives', thereby helping him to 'orient himself within the "ongoing course of things", to adopt a vivid phrase of John Dewey's' (1975: 45). In a way, the rigidity of a given culture is a guarantor of the individual's psychological stability because, undirected by cultural patterns – 'organised systems of significant symbols – man's behaviour would be virtually ungovernable, a mere chaos of pointless acts and exploding emotions'. His experience would be 'virtually shapeless' (1975: 46).

Moreover, without highly particular, defining forms of culture, constrictive, conservative and prison-like as they are, man is incomplete, unfinished. Human beings have psychological necessity to belong to a collective identity – 'Dobuan or Javanese, Hopi and Italian, upper-class and lower-class, academic and commercial' (1975: 49). Only through their culture can individuals attain full completion (cf. Jung's individuation and 'wholeness') because culture is there to fill the 'information gap' between 'what our body tells us and what we have to know in order to function' (1975: 49). Cultural imperatives take the man beyond the narrow frame of his body; liberate him from – or at least, alleviate his dependence – on its intractable, base, brutish and strictly practical functions. In a way, as they grow up and attain more consciousness, human beings exchange one type of prison for another; they grow out of their absolute dependence on the instincts and into the cultural imperatives governing these instincts. In either case, human behaviour is heavily framed.

Geertz's vision of culture as 'completing' the individual and dragging the human child out of the ungovernable animalism of the instinctual runs parallel to the classical idea of the trickster as a culture hero. Paul Radin (1956), Joseph Henderson (Jung and von Franz, 1964) and Joseph Campbell (1968) use the trickster as a symbol of human becoming, and explain the phylogenetic issues of society growing out of its 'bestiality', and gradually introducing social structure, via an extended ontogenetic metaphor. Thus, the Winnebago trickster Wakdjunkaga starts off by being completely unable to control his body and its functions – his hands fight each other, his anus stubbornly does its own thing, and his penis is separated from his body. However, the trickster develops a better awareness of himself and his surrounding towards the end of his journey. One might even say that he 'grows into civilisation'.

Paul Radin, in his analysis of the Winnebago trickster cycle, maintains that the rogue's progress in myth is the metaphor of human development. Civilisation – local Winnebago civilisation – completes him. Radin follows Wakdjunkaga the trickster's development path:

> The cycle begins with an incident found in no other version, namely Wakdjunkaga pictures as the chief of the tribe, giving a warbundle feast on four different days. He, although host and consequently obligated to stay to the very end, is described as leaving the ceremony in order to cohabit with a woman, an act which is absolutely forbidden for those participating in a warbundle feast. On the fourth day he stays to the end and invites all the participants in the feast to accompany him by boat. Hardly has he left the shore when he returns and destroys his boat as useless. At this piece of stupidity some of his companions leave him. He then starts on foot, but after a short time destroys his warbundle and his arrowbundle and finds himself eventually deserted by everyone and alone; alone, that is, as far as human beings and society are concerned. With the world of nature he is still in contact. He calls all objects, so our text tells us, younger brothers. He understands them; they understand him.
>
> (Radin, 1972: 132–133)

The raconteur begins his tale with desocialisation, Radin explains, in order to bring the metaphorical representation of the individual – the fool Wakdjunkaga – to his incomplete, undeveloped self. He is 'still living in his unconscious, mentally a child' which explains why he disrespects the Winnebago cultural canons, lacks the ability to catch fish and cannot control his own hands while they are fighting each other. However, as the tale progresses, Wakdjunkaga acquires more human traits, starts scrutinising and analysing his actions, and the raconteur begins to define his physical appearance and character traits with better precision:

> He is now to be shown emerging out of his complete isolation and lack of identity, and as becoming aware of himself and the world around

him. He has learned that both right and left hands belong to him, that both are to be used and that his anus is part of himself and cannot be treated as something independent of him. He realises, too, that he is being singled out, even if only to be ridiculed, and he has begun to understand why he is called Wakdjunkaga. [. . .] He is now to be given the intestines and anus of the size and shape which man is to have.

(1972: 136)

Moreover, Radin argues, as part of the process of becoming human, the Winnebago trickster becomes aware of his sexuality. The sexual instinct, as the eternal cause of conflict between civilisation and the unconscious, is an important element of culture hero myths. The umbrella theme of the Wakdjunkaga tale is 'the evolution of a trickster from an undefined being to one with physiognomy of man, from a being psychically undeveloped and a prey to his instincts, to an individual who is at least conscious of what he does and who attempts to become socialized' (1972: 136). The reduction of his enormous penis, which he carries on his back, to the human size by a cheeky chipmunk, symbolises the beginning of Wakdjunkaga's 'transition from a generalized natural and procreative force to a concrete heroic human being' (1972: 142). His biological maturity forms the foundation for the full psychical development and social-ethical maturity (1972: 143).

Joseph Henderson postulates that the Winnebago Hare cycle is the logical continuation of the cycle about the foolish Wakdjunkaga (Jung and von Franz, 1964: 104). Both represent different stages of the hero myth. For instance, the development of the Hare's bravery and aggression towards his grandmother ('mother Earth') coincides with his attaining higher consciousness. The Hare slays various animals, and when his grandmother objects to it, he threatens to kill her as well. The Hare growing out of his grandmother's influence represents man gradually acquiring mastery over some aspects of nature – human nature as well as the outside world. 'At the end of his rogue's progress' – Henderson writes – 'he is beginning to take on the physical likeness of a grown man' (Jung and von Franz, 1964: 104). Eventually this lowly, dung-obsessed, lewd, dumb creature learns his own name and develops capability to defend himself against the harsh outside world. The trickster is a gate-opener, and as such he welcomes 'a proper hero' onto the stage.

Carl Jung's psycho-anthropological concept of *individuation* – becoming oneself while also dealing with society's pressures and demands – effectively explores the tension between individual choice and conformist behaviour. According to Jolande Jacobi, individuation is a 'spontaneous, natural process within the psyche' which is 'potentially present in every man, although most men are unaware of it' (Jacobi, 1973: 107). Individuation, however, does not merely mean *finding oneself* – its ultimate aim is somewhat oxymoronic: to create an independent-thinking, unique individual who would at the same be 'a member of collectivity' since the accent in the individuation process is not 'on his supposed individuality as opposed to his collective obligations but . . . on the fulfilment of his own nature as it is related to the whole' (1973: 107). Individuation does not mean some kind of Zarathustrian loneliness but is inevitably bound to social achievement and involvement with one's fellow human beings (CW7: para. 267).

Ever the perceptive auto-anthropologist, Jung applied his individuation theory and its satellites, such as the concept of the shadow, to his study of Western modernity with its political and economic disasters – the First World War, the socialist threat, the fascist ideology, the Holocaust. In regard to moral catastrophes like fascism and worrying political novelties (for instance, the arrival of the 'mass man' dependent on the omniscient State), Jung was particularly interested in the dynamics of compliance and disobedience, in the psychology of the common man, in the degree of honesty in the citizen's blind subscription to state policy. In industrialised societies the State has taken over the natural community as the primary bearer of policy and the force that controls the individual – but how has it changed the individual as an agent, as the shaper of his or her own, unique destiny? Jung wrote that 'the "common man", who is predominantly a mass man, acts on the principle of realizing nothing, nor does he need to, because for him the only thing that commits mistakes is that vast anonymity conventionally known as the "State" or "Society"' (CW8: para. 410). Human beings are characterised by the propensity for imitation (here we can invoke both Lacan and Geertz). Hence, society is organised less by law than by this ability to copy and imitate (or 'emetate', as Andy Kaufman would have said), which is a necessary attribute of successful learning and an inherent part of cultural preservation. According to Jung, certain lazy human beings often abuse this psychological propensity and resort to borrowing traits from public people rather than trying to find their own path (individuate). He writes in the essay titled 'The Relations Between the Ego and the Unconscious':

> . . . we see every day how people use, or rather, abuse the mechanism of imitation for the purpose of personal differentiation: they are content to ape some eminent personality, some striking characteristic or mode of behaviour, thereby achieving an outward distinction from the circle in which they move. We could almost say that as a punishment for this the uniformity of their minds with those of their neighbours, already real enough, is intensified into an unconscious, compulsive bondage to the environment.

(CW7: para. 242)

The essay was published in 1928, before the arrival of television and the full offensive of mass media – i.e., before the advent of the principal simulacra-generating machines which make the problem of mindless imitation significantly worse.

For Jung, the individual's struggle against the binding force of imitation and his desire to differentiate himself from the crowd are tied up with the problem of the collective shadow – the dark force that empowers people and makes them feel as one mind, one being. For,

> identity with the collective psyche always brings with it a feeling of universal validity – 'godlikeness' – which completely ignores all differences in the personal psyche of his fellows. (The feeling of universal validity comes, of course, from the universality of the collective psyche.) [. . .] This disregard for individuality obviously means the suffocation of the single individual, as a consequence of which the element of differentiation is obliterated from the community.
>
> *cuts up penes + bowels*   (CW7: para. 171)

In fact, Jung differentiated between the personal and the collective shadow. The personal shadow, as Jolande Jacobi defines it, is 'a part of the individual, a split-off portion of his being which nevertheless remains attached to him "like his shadow"' (Jacobi, 1973: 109–110). The shadow covers a range of psychological phenomena. According to Jung, it 'personifies everything that the subject refuses to acknowledge about himself and yet is always thrusting itself upon him directly or indirectly for instance, inferior traits of character and other incompatible tendencies' (CW9/I: para. 513). The same phenomenon is labelled *doppelganger* in Freudian psychology, while the literary term is traditionally *the double*. The double takes over the 'daytime' personality, undermining the individual's control over his or her own actions and thoughts.

The collective shadow represents transpersonal evil, and as such is a much more sinister psychological phenomenon. It is an accumulation of personal doubles swayed by the idea *du jour*, and blinded and 'inspired' by the anonymity and emotional puissance of the *participation mystique* (a form of projective identification with the mass into which people are drawn unconsciously, as if 'against their own will'). It is normal for human beings to want to drown their sense of impotence in the grandness and anonymity of the mass. For Jung, who has never underestimated the powerful allure of collectivity, this instinctual force in modern societies is often harvested and orchestrated by political leaders with the help of modern technology. Mass media offers almost unlimited possibilities for goading citizens and modifying their worldview and behaviour. The State, even in its democratic variety, is a self-interested, world-shaping machine whose aim is to limit human agency, not to encourage it. Having witnessed two terrible mass conflicts, Jung argued that the post-Enlightenment rationality was a profound illusion, a superficial cover-up hiding the barely suppressed (psychological) flames of hell. The so-called 'civilised' people are never truly civilised because they tend to stick together, they wish to imitate, they try to be like everyone else – and they invariably look for a unifying power to assist them in this task, be it a local ruler or an almighty State. In his essay 'Psychology and Religion' (1938–40) Jung writes:

> Before the war broke out in 1914 we were all quite certain that the world could be righted by rational means. Now we behold the amazing spectacle of states taking over the age-old totalitarian claims of theocracy, which are inevitably accompanied by suppression of free opinion. Once more we see people cutting each other's throats in support of childish theories of how to create paradise on earth. It is not very difficult to see that the powers of the underworld – not to say of hell – which in former times were more or less successfully chained up in a gigantic spiritual edifice where they could be of some use, are now creating, or trying to create, State slavery and a State prison devoid of any mental or spiritual charm. There are not a few people nowadays who are convinced that mere human reason is not entirely up to the enormous task of putting a lid on the volcano.
>
> (CW11: para. 83)

The collective shadow triggered by the State in an undifferentiated mass of citizens is directly proportionate to the personal shadow, for 'what is called "free will" in the individual is called 'imperialism' in nations; for all will is a demonstration of power over fate, i.e., the exclusion of chance. Civilization is the rational, "purposeful" sublimation of free energies, brought about by will and intention' (CW7: para. 74).

Seen from this angle, the trickster is born out of attempts to suppress the unconscious, out of the idea that all that is outside the rational frame (and outside of the frame of culture) – chance, instincts, bodily processes – should be kept 'under the lid'. The trickster crosses boundaries erected by authorities, however strong and well-built these boundaries are. Excessive repression of the instinctual and the irrational leads to the inevitable over-spillage of unconscious contents. At some point the trickster, who had been long been kept by civilisation squashed in a small space, becomes the collective shadow; transforms into the dark face of instrumental rationality, into the 'other' of the legitimate culture. The culture-hero (the trickster principle) is here to help human beings to balance consciousness with the world of the instinctual, to keep the creative dialogue alive – and not to assist them in shutting down an entire side of their nature. When the trickster rebels against over-regulation of psychic life, the result is proportionately terrible to the pressure applied by the so-called civilisation to the world of the unconscious.

The anthropologist Victor Turner offered a structural solution to the problem of the trickster. He effectively argued that in every culture there are mechanisms for letting off the steam accumulated under 'the lid'.

His idea was that societies allocate special temporal pockets for the release of non-structured, outside-the-frame contents. Rather wisely they decide that, if change is inevitable and if transition is to take place inside a stable order, it would be better for everyone if it happens in a relatively controlled situation. Turner calls situations, events and phenomena that promote change and transition *liminal*. Liminality covers a range of 'trickster behaviours' and reflects the essence of the trickster principle – movement and progress.

Liminality (from Latin *limen* – threshold) was initially mentioned by the French ethnographer Arnold van Gennep in his seminal work, *The Rites of Passage* (1909), and later developed by Turner into a set of concepts. As an anthropological and sociological concept, it means unrest, temporary absence of order, intermediate state. In his discussion of liminality, Turner uses van Gennep's tripartite rite of passage: *separation, transition and incorporation*.

The first phase, *separation*, marks the end of the old state of things and the beginning of a new 'order'. The second phase is the liminal period during which 'the ritual subjects pass through . . . an area of ambiguity, a sort of social limbo which has few . . . of the attributes of either the preceding or subsequent profane social statuses of cultural states' (Turner 1979: 16). The concluding phase is the time of healing of the developmental rift, when 'the ritual subjects' (initiates, candidates, whole communities in social, political or economic transition) return to their new, 'relatively stable, well-defined position in the total society' (1979: 16). Liminal moments are part of healthy life of any social group; for instance, when people are collectively moving from peace to wartime and vice versa, or during calendrical changes. Such moments may or may not involve a status advancement: life-cycle rituals always involve a change of status whereas seasonal celebrations usually don't (1979: 16). Between the points of 'detachment' and 'reattachment' there lies a grey middle area of uncertainty, turbulence and chanciness. This is the playground of the trickster.

According to Turner, the term 'liminality' can refer to 'any condition outside or on the peripheries of everyday life' (Turner, 1975: 47). Liminal states such as, for instance, rites of passage, or liminal events (revolutions, for example) are to be contrasted with stable social and cultural paradigms, while (permanent or temporary) liminal initiates find themselves 'betwixt and between the positions assigned and arrayed by law, custom, convention, and ceremony' (Turner, 1967: 93). Groups of outcast individuals may form *communitas* – a social anti-structure that is 'over and above any formal social bonds' (Turner, 1975: 45). Communitates are not simply upside down 'root structures' or mainstream cultural paradigms with their signs reversed; rather, they are the source and origin of all structures, and at the same time their critique (1975: 202). Monastic life, pilgrimage, bonds of friendship formed among the group of young initiates, contemporary teenage counter-culture movements are all good examples of communitates. Turner links communitas with spontaneity and freedom, while the 'official' structure means 'obligation, jurality, law, constraint and so on' (1975: 49). In this way, the seemingly profane and blasphemous trickster is never too far from the sterile marginality of sainthood.

Turner's analysis of the edges of mainstream culture is useful for the reconstruction of the otherwise erratic, evasive and patchy trickster principle. This principle becomes a form of rebellion, a revolutionary force; a kind of explosive, aggressive, marginal creative energy that appears during transitional periods and drives society out of stagnation. It is an inhabitant, and spokesperson, of liminal situations in which 'new symbols, models, paradigms, etc., arise – as the seedbeds of cultural creativity in fact'. These new symbols then 'feed back into the "central" economic and politico-legal domains and arenas, supplying them with goals, aspirations, incentives, structural models and *raisons d'etre*' (Turner, 1979: 21). However, much as society wants to control liminal moments and guide the initiates through the potentially dangerous period of transition, the trickster principle, being the representative of nature's unpredictability, is a slippery customer.

The Trickster and the Shadow

Cinematic tricksters occupy different positions on what I call the trickster-shadow spectrum, or the scale which 'measures' the extent of malice in the character's playfulness (and the amount of playfulness in the character's cruel and thoughtless actions).

The difference between the trickster and the shadow is very subtle. They can be regarded as two different forms of *doppelganger*, one malicious and evil; the other impish and comical. In fact, the difference, it seems, lies in the perception and in the degree of 'intention' on the part of the trickster when he conducts the action. Whereas the trickster, due to his restricted awareness of himself and his surroundings, is more benign, the shadow's deeds are conscious and premeditated. In a way, they represent two opposing attitudes of human consciousness towards the concept of evil – both in the psyche, and in the external environment. The owner of the inner trickster 'does not notice' the evil because he does not consider himself separated from 'the natural' and 'the instinctive', whereas the shadow is a fruit of guilt, the atavistic, animalistic burden of the civilised person. As such, the shadow is a place of negativised projections, and a waste bin for the unwanted parts of the self. According to Jung, the shadow archetype corresponds to the unconscious man (Diamond, 1991: 97). Following this line of reasoning, the trickster is also 'the unconscious man' – he, too, may represent the 'foolish', basic instinctuality of the unconscious – sexual urges, anger, gluttony, etc.

I have always envisaged the trickster and the shadow as forming a continuous spectrum rather than constituting two separate archetypes.

There is a number of transitory moments where the frontier separating the mischievousness and hostility becomes blurred. Many trickster films contain good examples of this confusion. At the peak of his career Carrey created a bunch of amazingly infantile characters, such as the aforementioned Ace Ventura or Lloyd Christmas. However, even the seemingly innocuous Lloyd has a dark side: for instance, he accidentally kills an ulcer-plagued gangster by feeding him a spicy burger, followed by rat poison. One of Lloyd's other bizarre inspirations consists of taping his dead parrot's head back to its body, and then selling the sellotaped bird to a blind boy. However insensitive this scene may sound in theory, Lloyd's idiotic idea was not meant to be deliberately hurtful. It is a half-digested joke – because the joker does not possess the mental capacities necessary for analysing his actions.

As the shadow grows out of the trickster, it can still retain the light-hearted mischievousness, silliness and some entertaining qualities of a genuine jester. The actor who is often typecast in shadow roles is Jack Nicholson. His 'darkest' characters – Jack Torrance (*The Shining*, 1980), Daryl Van Horne (*Witches of Eastwick*, 1987), Jack Napier (*Batman*, 1989) – are characterised by roguishness and unpredictability. The stupidity of Nicholson's tricksters, however, is counterfeit. These characters are clever, their actions are deliberate, and their thinking shrewd – albeit evil and mad. The Joker, for instance, wears the traditional attire of a clown – motley colours, painted face and a mad smile – but he is more threatening than funny.

However, the line separating the two is easily crossed because the so-called 'civilised mind' looks at the instincts with terrified caution and powerless awe. When the instincts are repressed or blocked, the trickster mutates into the shadow. In other words, the trickster becomes the shadow only when people stop laughing at themselves and start using their rational, civilised and humanistic lifestyle as a protective barrier to ward off the evil spirits of the unconscious. Speaking metaphorically, the trickster keeps access to the unconscious and its creative powers open whereas the shadow, as a split-off figure, symbolises the blockage of morally reprehensible tendencies.

Using Trickster in Narrative Analysis

In this book I use the trickster principle as an umbrella term, as a general basic invariant with the underlying ideas of *effort* and *transition*. The term covers a range of historically and culturally bound trickster figures – clowns, fools, jesters, rogues, everymen, tramps, simpletons, picaros and confidence men. This range is as wide as the variety of trickster behaviours, for the trickster is a fool and a conman at once, fooling others and being tricked in return. His transitionality also explains his pre-civilised, pre-heroic and pseudo-heroic status because civilisation is associated with stability, rationality and order, whereas the trickster is always the one 'outside' – goading, challenging, destroying, and urging it to move on.

If the trickster inhabits the transitional, liminal, unstable middle area of the rite of passage, so is he active in the middle part of the narrative structure skeleton. He is an important part of the story's *gestalt*. The basic narrative structure, originally depicted in the form of a pyramid by the German dramatist and critic Gustav Freytag, consists of *exposition, rising action, climax, falling action* and *denouement* (Thomas, 1999: 73). The exposition ends with an event which Freytag termed *the inciting action* (which is ideologically and structurally similar to Campbell's 'call for adventure' (Campbell, 2008: 41)). The inciting action launches the principal events of the narrative. In the words of Michael Thomas, it occurs 'at the point when the leading character is actually set in motion or where a feeling arises in the character that sets the action in motion. It becomes the chief driving force for all the succeeding action of the play' (Thomas, 1999: 73). This sudden change in the order of things 'forms the transition between the introductory material and the body of the play, and its location in the overall structure helps to shape the emotional dynamics of the entire play' (1999: 74).

The trickster plays a similar function in literary and cinematic narratives. He links the seeming quietness of the exposition to the transformative chain of events that would concern the protagonist during the rising action and climax. In many comedies 'stasis' is the premise. For instance, in *The Mask* (1994), the downtrodden and lonely bank clerk Stanley Ipkiss (Jim Carrey) finds a green mask that turns his boring and uneventful life upside down. Similarly, the hero of *Anger Management* (2003), Dave Buznik (Adam Sandler) bottles up his anger until, one day, he is provoked by a cunning passenger (Jack Nicholson) into a heated conversation with air stewards and security, and subsequently arrested for causing a disturbance onboard the aircraft.

'Crossing the boundary', in narrative terms, is the trigger, the beginning of the conflict. In denouement, we have the completed transformation. Viewed from the narrative analysis angle, the trickster is a narrative element – a character (protagonist, antagonist or secondary), a motif, a plot segment – which triggers structural, and ultimately, transformative, changes in the story by introducing disorder into it. The trickster pushes the protagonist into the 'liminal' phase of the personal or social transformative ritual.

The Birth of the Individual as the Birth of the Trickster

In the films discussed in this book the trickster principle is closely related to the tension and delicate balance between the individual and society; between the cosy darkness of collective anonymity and the birth of individual personality. In his seminal work, *Rabelais and His World* (1965), Bakhtin outlines the birth of modern consciousness – and the birth of our modern conflict between the individual and society. He writes about the rebellious stance of Renaissance authors who, contra the medieval norms of high spiritualism and social rigidity, as well as current demands of literary taste, sourced their inspiration in popular culture and the carnivalesque spirit of folk humour. Rabelais's imagery and narratives, Bakhtin argues, 'are completely at home within the thousand-year-old development of popular culture', a boundless world of humorous forms and manifestations that opposed 'the official and serious tone of medieval ecclesiastical and feudal culture' (Bakhtin, 1984: 3–4). The medieval world had a double aspect – the 'official' and the liminal-carnival (to use Turner's, not Bakhtin's term):

> Carnival festivities and the comic spectacles and ritual connected with them had an important place in the life of medieval man. Besides carnivals proper, with their long and complex pageants and processions, there was the 'feast of fools' (*festa stultorum*) and the 'feast of the ass'; there was a special free 'Easter laughter' (*risus paschalis*), consecrated by tradition. Moreover, nearly every Church feast had its comic folk aspect, which was also traditionally recognized. Such, for instance, were the parish feasts, usually marked by fairs and varied open-air amusements, with the participation of giants, dwarfs, monsters, and trained animals. A carnival atmosphere reigned on days when mysteries and *soties* were produced. This atmosphere also pervaded such agricultural feasts as the harvesting of grapes (*vendange*) which was celebrated also in the city. Civil and social ceremonies and rituals took on a comic aspect as clowns and fools, constant participants in these festivals, mimicked serious rituals such as the tribute rendered to the victors at tournaments, the transfer of feudal rights, or the initiation of a knight.
>
> (1984: 5)

Cervantes, Shakespeare, Rabelais were re-assessing and re-building these traditions, integrating the 'low' into the 'high', while preparing the path for the new authors, characters and literatures of modernity. The carnival moments of anarchy, Bakhtin argues, were 'sharply distinct from the serious official, ecclesiastical, feudal, and political cult forms and ceremonials. They offered a completely different, nonofficial, extraecclesiastical and extrapolitical aspect of the world, of man and of human relations; they built a second world and a second life outside officialdom, a world in which all medieval people participated more of less, in which they lived during a given time of the year' (1984: 5–6). In other words, they sought liminal breakthroughs without challenging either the system or the economic circumstances. The world was immobile, and the opportunities for the individual to reform it were minimal. 'Party-time' allowed a liminal distance, which effectively defamiliarised the official vision of the world, but failed to trigger real change. The mad power of the carnivalesque spirit compensated for the immobility of the system. During the carnival, equality was a form of role-play, a make-believe never destined to become a reality:

> Rank was especially evident during official feasts; everyone was expected to appear in the full regalia of his calling . . . and to take the place corresponding to his position. It was a consecration of inequality. On the contrary, all were considered equal during carnival. Here, in the town square, a special form of free and familiar contact reigned among people who were usually divided by the barriers of caste, property, profession, and age. The hierarchical background and the extreme corporative and caste divisions of the medieval social order were exceptionally strong. Therefore such free, familiar contacts were deeply felt and formed an essential element of the carnival spirit. People were, so to speak, reborn for new, purely human relations. These truly human relations were not only a fruit of imagination or abstract thought; they were experienced. The utopian ideal and the realistic merged in this carnival experience, unique of its kind.
>
> (1984: 10)

The tricksterish 'change' only happened during liminal openings, and it was dreamlike and elusive. Renaissance writers, however, seized upon this wealth of carnivalesque imagery, gruesome, profane and indecent, to deliver their humanist message. Bakhtin remarks that Sancho's role in *Don Quixote* can be compared to 'the role of medieval parodies versus high ideology and cult'. The materialistic glutton Sancho is contrasted to his master Don Quixote's abstract and deadened idealism (1984: 22). Compared to the repressed psyche, the body is alive. Similarly, Rabelais's grotesque-realistic grand opus *The Life of Gargantua and of Pantagruel* (1532–1552) celebrates the 'gay bodily grave', the lower stratum – belly, bowels, earth, sexual organs – thus liberating the man from the narrow-mindedness and tyranny of the spiritual (1984: 22–23).

The trickster of modernity is the trickster of the emerging capitalist world – closely associated with the problematic relationship between the individual and society. Gradually, the trickster becomes an important part of the individuation process. The individuation process itself is an inherent part of the post-medieval world, and literature of modernity has never failed to foreground the importance of the individual and his struggle for the independence from his tribe. Bakhtin writes how already under Cervantes's pen, bodies and objects begin to acquire a private, individual nature, they are rendered petty and homely and become immovable parts of private life, the goal of egotistic lust and possession. This is no longer the positive, regenerating and renewing lower stratum, but a blunt and deathly obstacle to ideal aspirations. In the private sphere of isolated individuals the images of the bodily lower stratum preserve the element of negation while losing almost entirely their positive regenerating force. Their link with life and with the cosmos is broken, they are narrowed down to naturalistic erotic images. In Don Quixote, however, this process is only in its initial stage.

(1984: 23)

Renaissance humanists based themselves on the philosophical ideas of antiquity and rejected the individual-oppressing dogmatic scholasticism of the Middle Ages (with which the trickster fought on the level of popular culture). They mapped out a new world, in which 'individuals in all endeavours are free of a given destiny imposed by God from the outside – free to make their own destiny, guided only by the example of the past, the force of present circumstances, and the guides of their own inner nature' (Perry et al.: 2008: 311). Such individuals are not blindly guided by Providence, but are the products and the shapers of history (2008: 311).

This brings us back to the issue of individuation, of heroic consciousness fighting with its seemingly inhuman instincts, of becoming oneself in a complex modern/postmodern world. The trickster's efforts to become a man, and an independent one at that, can be seen as both ludicrous and heroic because mastery over nature is always relative and transitory while natural and social powers will always be impeding the individual's ability to achieve autonomy. The very desire to become oneself is utopian; it is cheeky, impertinent, rebellious, laughable, crazy. It is the desire to steal the power from the gods (the gods of nature or the gods of society), which, as we know from world mythology, rarely ends well. The culture-hero is, in fact, an oxymoron – he demonstrates to the audience that the very idea of individuation is mad because raising your voice as well as raising your head against 'higher powers' is bound to be dangerous. The idea is utterly stupid. The learning path is fraught with errors. Only fools are prepared to leave the safety of the womb/mother nature/the village/paradise, and 'go and seek their fortune'.

Chapter 1

Common Motifs in Trickster Narratives

[handwritten: Themes/subjects, ideas]

[handwritten: standard typical representation]

Trickster narratives share a number of common motifs which point at a single psychological root and outline the archetypal features of the trickster. Some of the motifs pertain to the structure of the narrative, and some to the trickster figures themselves (cf. Jung's distinction between archetypal patterns ('events') and archetypes ('figures')). Structural elements determine the starting point, progression and outcome of the narrative, and include the trickster or the trickster protagonist being trapped (physically, emotionally or mentally), the trickster or protagonist crossing the dangerous boundary, and the final dissolution of the trickster (his symbolic or physical death). The essentially tripartite structure of trickster narratives matches van Gennep's 'rite of passage' triangle – separation, transition and incorporation.

[handwritten margin: being trapped]

[handwritten margin: recklessness Extravagance Worldliness]

Elements that serve as building bricks of the trickster's figure are his licentiousness, love of freedom, dislike for all types of boundaries, fragmented/flexible body (symbolising his transformative powers), propensity to lie and general dislike of truth, lack of stable identity (for instance, having no name or several names) and erratic behaviour. Other narrative elements are the carnivalesque atmosphere (which indicates the absence of the boundary between 'nature' and 'civilisation', a 'festive' form of Jungian *participation mystique*), scatological references and the invariable presence of animals and pets. Let us have a closer look at these essential ingredients of the trickster narrative.

[handwritten margin: Frank]

[handwritten: vulgar language related to excretory functions]

Being Trapped

[handwritten: Catch me if you can –]

The starting position of the trickster in literary and cinematic narratives is always that of imprisonment, constraint and limitation. When being trapped is one's default position, breaking free becomes the principal goal. Folklore tricksters have to endure various kinds of 'trappedness', from being glued to a tar baby (Brer Rabbit from the Uncle Remus stories) to being turned into a pig by a feminist witch (Odysseus and Circe). In many tales, rogues are overpowered by someone with god-like, or in the very least exceptional, abilities. It requires a Zeus to capture a Prometheus lest the structure of the world should be upset. Prometheus, in Hesiod's version, is riveted by Zeus with shackles and fetters on a pillar, while a 'long-winged' eagle is sent to devour the titan's liver (Hesiod, 2004: 24).

In Scandinavian folklore, the infamous Loki is captured and tied up for arranging the murder of Balder, the second son of Odin. Balder's death is the first sign of Ragnarök approaching, and the gods have to act quickly to stop the onset of chaos. They place a snake above Loki's head, its venom dripping onto his face and causing pain. Although Loki's wife Sigyn is holding a bowl to catch the poison, occasionally she goes off to empty it, and the drops make the prisoner writhe and shudder. His powerful convulsions cause earthquakes (Rosenberg, 1994: 223). As in the case of Prometheus, the victim is immobilised, and the punishment is long, slow and torturous. These are unchanging, monotonous, endless situations, in which, in fact, the core metaphor is *immobilisation*, and the supporting, peripheral symbols, the venom and the eagle, stand for the pain of unrealised ambition. The lack of opportunity to move, progress, change or somehow alter the situation is the actual source of torment here.

The Arabic trickster, Sakr al-Jinni from *One Thousand and One Arabian Nights*, is subjected to a conceptually similar type of punishment. He is an ifrit (an infernal jinn, a cunning fire spirit) who rebels against King Suleiman,[1] is defeated and stuffed into a small bottle, which is then sealed and hurled into the deep ocean. The Jinni is trapped in the bottle for two thousand years, during which time he is 'washed and swashed like a lake squeezed into a cup or a whale squeezed into an egg'. His lengthy entrapment makes him angry indeed. He describes his despair and rage to the poor fisherman who has accidentally caught the copper jar in his net and broken the seal:

> For the first hundred years I swore that if anyone freed me from the copper bottle I would grant him three wishes – however greedy.
> But nobody came.
> For the next two hundred years I swore that if anyone freed me from the copper bottle I would give him and all his tribe everlasting riches.
> But nobody came.
> For the next five hundred years I swore that if anyone freed me from the copper bottle I would make him ruler and owner of all the people of earth!
> But nobody came.
> For the next thousand years I swore . . . and I swore, but now my oaths were terrible. My patience was gone, my fury was bigger than the

1 Suleiman, son of Daud in the Quran; Solomon, son of David in the Bible.

ocean I was floating in. I swore that if anyone freed me from the copper bottle (*unless, of course, it was the all-powerful lord Suleiman*) I would make him the first to feel the scourge of my revenge! My old enemies are long since dead. You will have the honour of standing in their place while I cut you to atoms! I have sworn it.

(McCaughrean, 1999: 35–36)

Sakr al-Jinni's intentions sound serious, but he has no opportunity to realise them. The trickster is tricked by the cunning fisherman into jumping back into the jar, which is then resealed and thrown into the waves. 'The Terror of the Lower Hemisphere', as the Jinni boastfully calls himself, is returned to the underworld where he belongs.

Literary tricksters go one step further than their mythological and folkloric colleagues: instead of portraying and embodying physical immobility (which is a valid but very vague and general metaphor), they accentuate the trickster's desire to progress socially or to break free of social conventions. For instance, the most well-known type of literary trickster is *servus callidus* – the cunning slave, examples of which include Plautus's Pseudolus and Tranio, Carlo Goldoni's Arleccino and Beaumarchais's Figaro. The clever slave/servant has a low position in the social structure, and is forced to stay in his little 'underworld' which is far too constraining for his abilities, projects, and most importantly – for his social ambition.

Similarly, our cinematic tricksters are kept in stifling environments where they accumulate explosive energy: Stanley Ipkiss's green *alter ego* resides within a mask, Beetlejuice (*Beetlejuice*, 1988) is locked inside a small model of a town, and Chip-Larry-Ricardo, the Cable Guy, is altogether shunned by the civilised world. The one who finds the bottle or picks the mask containing the trickster spirit, acquires powerful, but potentially dangerous, abilities. The metaphorical release of the Jinni equals the release of the human potential.

Far from battling a Wotan or a Zeus, contemporary cinematic tricksters clash with more progressive (and secular) incarnates of the principle of determinism, which range from government structures and pernicious ideologies to oppressive bosses at work and despotic family members. For instance, Stu Price (Ed Helms), the unfortunate dentist from Todd Philipps's hit *The Hangover* (2009), becomes accidentally 'enlightened' about his personal life after being drugged by a foolish relative of a friend during a stag trip to Vegas. All aspects of Stu's life are controlled by his domineering girlfriend Melissa (Rachael Harris). Stu is a 'nice guy' who usually avoids risqué things and certainly does not do drugs. The stag night in Vegas turns out to be a complete disaster when the inept brother of the bride, Alan (Zach Galifianakis) spikes the company's Jagermeisters with Rohypnol, mistaking them for ecstasy pills. The next day the groomsmen wake up to a tiger roaring in their bathroom, a baby crying in the wardrobe, and a completely trashed hotel room. Stu is missing a tooth and is wearing a wedding ring. Phil (Bradley Cooper), an immature high school teacher, has a hospital band on his hand. The subsequent quest to find the missing groom, return the tiger to its rightful owner (who happens to be none other than Mike Tyson), and the baby to its mother, transform Stu's views on personal relationships. The tricksterish accident (or Rohypnol, or Alan in the role of the trickster) wrecks his life but eventually proves to be life-changing. When the ordeal is over and Doug is finally married, Stu announces to Melissa that he is leaving her. There are hints in the narrative that he might start a relationship with Jade (Heather Graham), the prostitute he married in Vegas when under the influence of the drug.

Jim Carrey's characters raise their voice against big corporations, media moguls, mafia bosses, police departments and the US legal system. They take on, and often crush in tragicomic battles, the very pillars of modern society: representatives of business, industry, politics, law, media and other creators of rules and imposers of structures. Tim Burton's prominent tricksters – two antagonists (Beetlejuice and the Joker) and a protagonist (Jack Skellington – *The Nightmare Before Christmas*, 2003) – are deeply concerned with the issues of confinement, freedom and power. All three are sketched around Burton's favourite fabula – a man confined in a town which is far too small for his plans and talents. Like the Jinni imprisoned in the bottle, they accumulate the repressed, and therefore tricky and explosive, power of the unconscious. When the time comes, they jump out and wreck enormous havoc on the neighbourhood by pouring their entire reserves of ambition on it at once.

The living space of Beetlejuice, for instance, is limited to a small model town, complete with a cemetery, spooky trees, white suburban houses, grassy lawns and a local saloon. The Maitlands – the couple who were unlucky enough to become ghosts – decide to use his services as a 'bio-exorcist', i.e., they want him to get rid of the annoying Deetzes family who are now occupying their house. The 'undead' Maitlands expect him to 'exorcise' the annoying living intruders. In order to release the 'bio-exorcist', they have to pronounce his name three times. In doing so, they, speaking symbolically, 'announce' his arrival into the world and 'legitimise' the marginalised outcast who is too radical both for the boring land of the living and the bureaucratic world of the dead.

Rik Mayall's character Drop Dead Fred (*Drop Dead Fred*, 1991) lives in a battered music box, which Lizzie Cronin's evil mother eventually wraps in sticky tape – so that Fred cannot escape. When, 20 years later, Lizzie (Phoebe Cates) comes to stay with her mother and opens the locked box, the green spirit jumps out and immediately renews the partisan war against the oppressive and controlling parent. He wakes Lizzie at night and makes her participate in a secret operation which consists of smearing dog mess (any trickster's favourite weapon) over her mother's freshly-cleaned white carpet.

He makes her ruin her immaculate bob haircut by chopping off one side –
because the haircut had been chosen for her by the mother. Certain
'possession' scenes in the film refer to William Friedkin's notorious film *The
Exorcist* (1973) – for instance, when Lizzie starts laughing involuntarily or
suddenly swears at Mrs Cronin. However, the film eschews pure horror
moments, because Lizzie is the principal focaliser and the audience is
allowed to 'see' the parallel poltergeist world. The viewer knows what has
caused the laughter or the swearing fit: the words 'piss off' were actually
meant for Drop Dead Fred, whom Mrs Cronin, unfortunately, could not
see. Meanwhile, the evil mother refuses to pronounce the trickster's name,
apparently thinking that one can exorcise a spirit by 'forgetting' about him
(i.e., repressing him – which can only aggravate the problem and allow him
to accumulate more destructive energy).

Drop Dead Fred also raises his voice for the freedom of the human spirit
from social constructs and conventions. Under his influence, Lizzie completely disgraces herself at a restaurant by pouring water onto the table, then
dropping the glass on the floor and throwing a plateful of spaghetti over her
head – and onto some unfortunate woman. Here, the trickster hijacks a (so
familiar to everyone) situation in which the crisp, tightly structured restaurant discourse is stifling the natural flow of communication. Focalised mostly
through Mickey's eyes (who is Lizzie's love interest), the scene represents
Lizzie as doing something devilishly unpredictable (when her hand disobeys
her, starts shaking and spills the water) – but nevertheless funny.

The most obvious and most basic explanation of the metaphorical
'trapped' state is 'unconscious repression'. Because of his 'repressed' position, the trickster principle ('unconscious contents') accumulates intensive
potentiality, which explodes upon contact with 'conscious reality'. He also
generates mad creativity by sublimating repressed contents. Lizzie's music
box jumps and shakes because Fred cannot wait to be released. Upon his
release, Beetlejuice takes the shapes of various hideous monsters; and the
Loki mask is so powerful that it can 'suck in' Stanley Ipkiss. The king of
delight makers, Jack Skellington becomes 'depressed' when he realises that
his native Town of Halloween is too small for his ghoulish creativity. Jack
feels stifled and acquires a 'longing' for something new. When his scary
artistry explodes all over the Town of Christmas, little children get showered
with ugly presents in the form of snakes, bloodied ducks and angry pump-
kins. The Joker harbours grandiose plans to 'swallow' the entire Gotham
City and control its inhabitants via advertising and media. The feeling of
being suppressed in trickster films is often related to metropolitan (the city is
too big and makes you invisible) and suburban (the town is too small and
does not allow you to develop) issues. Thematically, the motif of being
trapped has to do with the imbalance between the size of the living space and
the proportions of the protagonist's ambition (cf. Hamlet's 'prisons' and
'nutshells' in which he cannot feel like 'a king of infinite space').

Boundary-Crossing

All tricksters have an issue with borders and impediments. Trickster stories are traditionally preoccupied with various ways of transgressing and trespassing – because the archetype designates the budding psyche for which the border between the self and the outer world does not yet exist. For instance, Beetlejuice grabs and kisses Barbara in front of her husband, and then asks him: 'Am I overstepping my bounds? Just tell me.' William Willeford notes that literary and mythological fools love to transgress social and cultural boundaries (Willeford, 1969: 132). Seen in this light, the fool is a borderline figure that 'holds the social world open to values that transcend it' (1969: 137). Morality and politeness belong to the world of human beings, with which the mad and bedraggled anarchist Beetlejuice is not yet fully acquainted. His behaviour is a rebel's way of trespassing the borders of emotional and physical contact, and thus challenging the tyranny of the etiquette.

The trickster's task in narratives is to drag protagonists through a series of transformations, which involve pushing them over the threshold and into the liminal zone, then guiding them through the liminal zone, and, finally, restoring their 'normality' by shoving them over the boundary and into the world of 'reality'. For the duration of the liminal period protagonists have no or limited control over their minds and bodies. They are 'possessed'. Boundaries depicted in trickster films and narratives can be both physical and hypothetical (purely metaphorical).

The trickster principle 'likes' freedom and fluidity, and therefore 'disproves' of partitions separating fantasy from reality (and, when it acts as a creative impulse, it 'removes' the partition between fantasy and reality, the unconscious and consciousness). Charlie Chaplin's films contain good examples of physical borders, erected by society to protect itself from antisocial elements. In *A Dog's Life* (1918) the character of the Tramp lives inside an open air enclosure separated from the rest of the social world by a rotten wooden fence. Chaplin uses the idea of the fence creatively, making this boundary the centre of the conflict between the Tramp and the policeman. In the finale of *The Pilgrim* (1923) the Tramp is left by the sheriff on the border between Mexico and the United States (Turner's 'betwixt and between').

For Carrey's character Carl Allen in *Yes Man* (2008), the threshold separating him from his previous life is his decision, prompted by a self-improvement guru Terrence Bundley ('therapist as a trickster'), to say 'yes' to every opportunity and experience awaiting him in the world. The guru presses him into making a covenant with himself and stop being a 'No Man' (cf. Odysseus telling the Cyclops that his name is 'No man'). During the liminal period of saying 'yes' to everything, the previously reclusive and cautious Carl takes flying lessons, learns Korean language, uses the services of a Persian dating website and accepts an offer of oral sex from his elderly neighbour, Tillie. Saying 'yes' and taking chances seem to be doing magic to Carl's life. His career prospects at the bank improve, he keeps making new friends, and even saves a suicidal man by singing him a song using his newly-acquired abilities to play guitar.

One of the adventures – agreeing to take a tramp to Elysian Park – leads to an acquaintance with a beautiful biker Allison (Zooey Deschanel) who eventually becomes his girlfriend. However, after saying 'no' to his ex-wife's offer of 'getting back together', Carl's luck disappears. Meanwhile, Allison learns about Carl's covenant and begins to doubt the sincerity of their relationship. The film climaxes with Carl hiding in the backseat of Terrence's car, accosting the guru after his 'Yes' seminar and demanding to remove the curse. Carl's behaviour causes a car accident, and both end up in hospital. Both survive the crash (the 'rebirth' motif), and Terrence explains to Carl that the covenant does not exist. The protagonist eventually gets back with Allison – not as a man compelled by a covenant to agree to her offer of moving in together, but as an individual capable of making independent decisions. He explains to her that he loves her but is not ready to move in with her yet. The covenant serves as a threshold *into* and *out* of the liminal zone and encircles a mad but positive experience which turns the protagonist from a 'no man' to a man with a name, a motivated human being capable of changing his life. Like this, Carl is reborn.

The ability to cross the dangerous boundary between the world of the living and the realm of the dead is one of the trickster's most notable qualities. In classical mythology he is even appointed an 'official' psychopomp, a mythical conductor of souls to the nether regions. The Greek Hermes and the Roman Mercurius are psychopomps; in many other trickster stories the right to cross the boundary between life and death is designated as immortality, as the priceless capacity to be reborn many times; as an in-built physical flexibility and ability to take many different forms and wear an endless number of masks. The role of the psychopomp emphasises the trickster's transcendent qualities, among which is the ability to transgress the frontier between consciousness and the unconscious.

The 'psychopomp' aspect of the trickster explains certain bizarre moments in contemporary trickster films. For instance, Beetlejuice is forced to live in limbo – he is stuck between the world of the living and the abode of the dead. The underworld 'bureaucracy' entrusted with keeping the place in order are scared of this anarchic, lawless creature. He just can't rest in peace like all the 'normal' dead people; his incessant mischief, shapeshifting and shouting create havoc. However, he cannot join the world of the living either because he is, in fact, a ghost. By profession he is 'bio-exorcist' which (although the script is never absolutely clear about it) apparently means that he negotiates disputes between the living and the dead; and also solves problems which arise when you are alive but would like to be dead or vice versa. In other words, instead of accepting 'the fate' as it is, or going with the flow, Beetlejuice attempts to create his own rules. Beetlejuice's ostracism is the result of his anarchic 'supernatural' politics; his mindless rebellion against any mediocrity (both worldly and underworldly) and, ultimately, his powerful unpredictability.

Boundary-crossing in trickster narratives symbolises transformative de-normalisation (or de-normalisation for the purpose of transformation). The turbulent change acquired during the liminal period is incorporated into everyday experiences and then used for further development and progression.

The Problem of the Name

The trickster's name (or names) is his passport into the world. Paul Radin links the process of naming, and the name as a concept, to the individual's status in his or her community. He postulates that the Winnebago trickster Wakdjunkaga takes much interest in his name, which translates as 'a foolish one'. 'In Winnebago society' – Radin writes – 'a child has no legal existence, no status, until he receives a name' (Radin, 1956: 135). Throughout his silly adventures, Wakdjunkaga keeps repeating his name to himself as if asserting his – albeit low – existence. For instance, after mistaking a tree stump for a man, he says: 'Yes indeed, it is on this account that the people call me Wakdjunkaga, the foolish one! They are right!' (1972: 134).

A trickster without a name is the one who has not yet had his breakthrough, and the trickster with several names is unsure of his identity – or he does not have a stable identity yet. Michael Keaton's character has two names – Betelgeuse and (its phonetic pronunciation) Beetlejuice. Jim Carrey's character in *The Cable Guy* (1996) alternates between being the anonymous 'cable guy' and having three names (Chip Douglas, Larry Tate and Ricardo). Characteristically fluid in the best trickster fashion, he borrows other people's identities – as well as the names of TV and film characters. The Joker in Tim Burton's *Batman* (1989) also has two names – the 'professional' (the Joker), and the real name, which is Jack Napier. The mad green-faced character from *The Mask* does not appear to have a name at all. Meanwhile, to perform his manic mischief, it borrows the identity of Stanley Ipkiss. Another of Carrey's madmen, Ace Ventura (*Ace Ventura: Pet Detective*, 1994; *Ace Ventura: When Nature Calls*, 1995) wears his name with incredible pride – just like Wakdjunkaga, who proudly announces to the public that he is 'the foolish one'.

The acquisition of a name is psychologically equal in importance to the metaphorical moment of emergence from a restrictive space: a bottle, a sewer, a box, a model town, a womb, a narrow mindset. After digging through Gotham City archives, the Penguin Man dramatically proclaims his new official status to the waiting crowd: 'A penguin is a bird that cannot fly! I am a man! I have a name! Oswald Cobblepot!' He is no longer just an animal (has risen above the animal level) – he is now a Gotham citizen. The name gives him credibility, a face, a social position. It makes him human.

The name makes individuals unique, it makes them visible. The theme of visibility–invisibility in the dark, overpopulated, technology-obsessed urban environment is especially important in trickster films. The spell of the protagonist's invisibility is broken when a radical force (an unconscious one, of course – but exteriorised in the form of a dishevelled madman) makes them behave in an unacceptable and scandalous manner. With the awkward help of Beetlejuice, the Maitlands make the Deetzes notice that there is some 'supernatural activity' going on in their house; while Drop Dead Fred forces Mrs Cronin and Lizzie's cheating husband Charles to admit that 'the girl' has finally grown up.

The Body

Following Radin's and Henderson's argument, the trickster is an incomplete individual, a fluid transitory path from animal to human (Jung and von Franz, 1964: 103–104). An 'undercivilised' creature, he can hardly be expected to be fully responsible for his body's actions. While a fully-fledged individual resists division, the trickster is not entirely aware of his physical and psychological fragmentedness. The aforementioned Wakdjunkaga, for instance, becomes very surprised when different parts of his body behave as if they were autonomous. One night he wakes up and realises that the blanket is missing:

> He sees it floating above him, and only gradually recognizes that it is resting on his huge penis erectus. Here we are brought back again to the Wakdjunkaga whose right hand fights with his left, who burns his anus and eats his own intestines, who endows the parts of his body with independent existence and who does not realize their proper functions, where everything takes place of its own accord, without his volition. 'This is always happening to me' – he tells his penis.
>
> (Radin, 1956: 136)

This, perhaps, explains why in film the trickster's body tends to be presented as a disjointed set of synecdoches (which is achieved by different cinematic means, from animation to framing and camera angles). When Beetlejuice's head suddenly starts spinning on his shoulders, his complaint sounds very similar to Wakdjunkaga's: 'Don't you hate it when that happens?!' Drop Dead Fred's head gets smashed by the fridge door, and he has to 'blow it back into shape'. In yet another scene, his eyes pop out of their orbits when he catches a glimpse under a naughty woman's skirt. There is a very similar 'transformation scene' in *The Mask*: when the green

Frank

man sees Tina Carlyle singing and flirting, his face bursts into hyperbolic grotesquerie – his eyes pop out and his tongue rolls out onto the table. In both scenes, the grotesque effect is achieved with animation.

The trickster principle refuses to respect both moral/social frontiers and physical borders. Put simply, it denies 'reality'. Beetlejuice, for instance, has a truly fluid relationship with his surroundings. He can aptly transform into a giant snake, or turn his hands into giant hammers. However, while playing tricks on other people – like making them sing against their will – Beetlejuice is not entirely aware of himself, his possessions and his surroundings (which would mean 'awareness of reality'). In a scene in the mini-graveyard with the Maitlands, Beetlejuice is fumbling in his pockets for a business card but cannot find it. Instead, he finds a squealing mouse, and passes it on to Barbara, then rummages through his other pocket, finds some dirty dollars, and hands them to Adam. There is an equivalent moment in *The Mask*, in which two policemen search 'the green man' and take various rubbish out of his pockets – big sunglasses, bike horn, bowling pin, mousetrap, a bazooka, etc. There is even a saucy picture of Lieutenant Kellaway's wife, upon the extraction of which from his pocket, the Mask explains to the enraged husband: 'I thought you would have a sense of humour. After all – you married her!'

Meanwhile, the Joker in *Batman*, who is a shadow posing as a trickster, undergoes a set of degenerative physical changes – his face is 'dissolved' in a vat of chemical waste and has to be remade by a black market surgeon. Because he is a shadow, and therefore 'closer' to consciousness than a pure trickster, he is more 'physical'. As a result, his metonymisation is irreversible. After his fatal fall from the top of the Gotham City cathedral, he cannot be 'rebuilt' from fragments. Compared to less shadowy cinematic tricksters – Stanley Ipkiss's *alter ego* (who also falls from the window yet gets up and continues his adventures), Drop Dead Fred (who is 'wiped out' by a lorry but soon reappears), Jack Skellington (falls from the sky but survives), the Joker is already too conscious and darkly human to become resilient in the true trickster fashion. He has to deal with the limitations of the human form. The metonymisation of the trickster emphasises his 'unconsciousness', his inability to attain physical or psychological 'whole-ness'. His lacks the 'conscious' backbone which would allow him to keep parts of himself together, in order, and under control.

Tricksters belonging to the more 'human' type (as opposed to the grotesque and schematic split-off characters like the Mask, Drop Dead Fred or Beetlejuice) also tend to have problems with their bodies as they demonstrate the issues of bodily non-permanence and brokenness in the literal way. Since the alter ego is not split off to form a separate character, the tricksterish protagonists' abilities to transcend their human frame are very limited. When the trickster principle 'hijacks' a human frame, it has to deal with the limitations of the body. Harry Sanborn (Jack Nicholson) in

Something's Gotta Give (2003, directed by Nancy Meyers) is a 63-year-old playboy who has no intention to grow up or acquire a more or less permanent partner. His body, however, betrays his youthful pretensions, and spectacularly breaks down at a very unfortunate moment – just when he is having fun with new girlfriend Marin (Amanda Peet) who is half his age. Harry's heart attack, and the accompanying realisation that his body has become too fragile for mindless fun, influence his decision to seek a more suitable partner.

Two other Nicholson characters – R. P. McMurphy (*One Flew Over the Cuckoo's Nest*, 1975, directed by Milos Forman) and J. J. Gittes (*Chinatown*, 1974, directed by Roman Polanski), do not consider the consequences for their physical selves when embarking on their dangerous anti-authoritarian activities. They are both subdued by the authorities in a brutal way: McMurphy is lobotomised, while the nosy private detective Gittes is beaten up, has his nose broken and receives death threats from his powerful adversary, Noah Cross (John Huston). Their bodies are violated because they have crossed the line into the dangerous territory and disrupted the established order of things – in the first case the life of the oppressive psychiatric hospital, and in the second a well-organised mafia structure. Their one-man rebellion, although irksome for the corrupt politicians and medical tyrants, does not lead to any substantial change or shift in the established scheme of things.

Loss of Control

The issue of control over body and mind has double significance in trickster narratives. On the one hand, the trickster's psyche and body are so fluid that he does not always have control over them. On the other hand, he can play tricks with human beings and cause them to lose control over *their* minds and bodies as well. Tricksters play practical jokes on their victims, but are often deceived and duped in return. This metaphor renders the idea of the interdependence of consciousness and the unconscious. The under-civilised trickster is silly and childlike, and therefore can be easily deceived; but the very adult-like 'consciousness' can become so confident in its over-inflated 'wisdom' and 'maturity' that its vision becomes dangerously narrow. A stagnant vision and loss of perspective makes consciousness vulnerable for the traps set up by the unconscious.

While the human form is fragile, creativity is something that can make it immortal. In his essay on the nature of the creative process, *On the Relation of Analytical Psychology to Poetry*, Jung describes creativity in terms of 'loss of control' and being possessed by 'an alien will'. In this sense, creativity is akin to the trickster taking over the carrier:

They [works of art] come as it were fully arrayed into the world, as Pallas Athene sprang from the head of Zeus. These works positively force themselves upon the author; his hand is seized, his pen writes things that his mind contemplates with amazement. The I work brings with it its own form; anything he wants to add is rejected, and what he himself would like to reject is thrust back at him. While his conscious mind stands amazed and empty before this phenomenon, he is over-whelmed by a flood of thoughts and images which he never intended to create and which his own will could never have brought into being. Yet in spite of himself he is forced to admit that it is his own self speaking, his own inner nature revealing itself and uttering things which he could never have entrusted to his tongue. He can only obey the apparently alien impulse within him and follow where it leads, sensing that his work is greater than himself, and wields a power which is not his and which he cannot command. Here the artist is not identical with the process of creation; he is aware that he subordinate to his work or stands outside it, as though he were – a second person; or as though a person other than himself had fallen within the magic circle of an alien will.

(CW15: para. 110)

It is as if the artist/poet is not 'wholly himself' because he is moved by the creative process. When the focus of interest shifts to the force that moves the creator, 'the poet comes into the picture only as a reacting subject' (CW15: para. 112). He 'appears to be the creative process himself, and to create of his own will without the slightest feeling of compulsion' (CW15: para. 112). The urge to create is sometimes so powerful (operating with 'tyrannical might', as Jung puts it) that it blots out the sense of objective reality in the artist and often ruins his or her life:

The biographies of great artists make abundantly clear that the creative urge is often so imperious that it battens on their humanity and yokes everything to the service of the work, even at the cost of health and ordinary human happiness. The unborn work in the psyche of the artist is a force of nature that achieves its end either with tyrannical might or with the subtle cunning of nature herself, quite regardless of the personal fate of the man who is its vehicle. The creative urge lives and grows in him like a tree in the earth from which it draws its nourish-ment. We would do well, therefore, to think of the creative process as a living thing implanted in the human psyche. In the language of analytical psychology this living thing is an *autonomous complex*. It is a split-off portion of the psyche, which leads a life of its own outside the hierarchy of consciousness. Depending on its energy charge, it may appear either as a mere disturbance of conscious activities or as a supraordinate authority which can harness the ego to its purpose.

(CW15: para. 115)

Creativity, and especially music, is presented in trickster narratives as a way of compelling people to lose their vigilance. Tricksters often mesmerise their victims with song and dance. Wakdjunkaga makes the ducks, whom he is hoping to turn into a nice roasted dinner, sing and dance with their eyes closed. His stomach, he explains, is full of 'bad songs' and it is a long time since he sang any of them (Radin, 1972: 14). While the stupid ducks are dancing to his 'bad songs', the trickster is wringing their necks.

In trickster films the theme of possession is also very popular. Beetlejuice, for instance, hijacks an entire house party, and makes the Deetzes and their cheaply pretentious guests sing and dance to Harry Belafonte's version of 'Day-O' ('Banana Boat Song'). Lydia (Winona Ryder) gets so addicted to the 'out of control' feeling that she asks for more, and in the finale of *Beetlejuice* the Maitlands hypnotise her into singing another of Belafonte's hits, 'Jump in Line'. In a conceptually similar sequence, the Mask performs Desi Arnaz's cheeky 'Cuban Pete', while the crowd of policemen and reporters catch 'the bug', and start dancing and gesturing manically. In Tim Burton's hands, the trickster often becomes a metonymic representative of the creative impulse; he acts as the 'possessing' creative powers. Burton's 'artists' – Vincent Malloy (*Vincent*, 1982), Edward Scissorhands (*Edward Scissorhands*, 1990), Ed Wood (*Ed Wood*, 1994), Willy Wonka (*Charlie and the Chocolate Factory*, 2005)– regard inspiration simultaneously as the curse and the blessing which 'comes from nowhere', and which cannot be easily shaken off. Meanwhile, Batman's wild, and dark, imagination, coincides (and eventually goes head-to-head) with the sadistic fantasies of the Joker.

The Joker practises hypnosis on a very ambitious scale. A shadow pretending to be a trickster, he gathers crowds only to poison them – either with gas, like he does at the Gotham City parade, or via chemically altered cosmetic products. The Joker is also flexible and fluid in the best 'urban trickster' way in that he infiltrates his victims using the powers of media and advertising. Backed by technology, he permeates physical boundaries to get access to people's minds. Poisoned by chemical substances, mauled by plastic surgery, preoccupied with media and absorbed by conceptual art, the Joker is a collective travesty of the body-conscious, image-obsessed American society. Or, rather, he reflects the dark, complacent ugliness of consumer culture. Himself a rotting bunch of synecdoches, he ruins the bodies of Gotham inhabitants in a grimly parodic recreation of mass hysterias and mass obsessions. As Jung writes,

The so-called civilized man has forgotten the trickster. He remembers him only figuratively and metaphorically, when, irritated by his own ineptitude, he speaks of fate playing tricks on him or of things being bewitched. He never suspects that his own hidden and apparently harmless shadow has qualities whose dangerousness exceeds his wildest dreams. As soon as people get together in masses and submerge the individual, the shadow is mobilized and, as history shows, may even be personified and incarnated.

(CW9/I: para. 478)

Whereas the trickster advocates a return to 'nature', the metropolitan shadow uses progress to keep individuals lost and isolated. Some of Carrey's tricksters also embody the dark side of technology as they control the minds and hearts of citizens of the metropolis. For instance, Dr. Nygma/The Riddler (*Batman Forever*, 1995) is a 'mad scientist' whose invention, a mind-controlling TV beam, removes all physical boundaries between himself and the audience. Meanwhile, the Cable Guy – a very lonely man whose only friends are film and TV characters – causes mass TV blackout by jumping onto the satellite dish with intent to die.

The 'hypnotist' may reside 'inside' the protagonist, or, by contrast, become 'split off' and appear in the guise of a separate person (Dr. Buddy Rydell in *Anger Management* (2003); Morty the Angel of Death in *Click* (2006); the self-betterment guru Terrence Bundley in *Yes Man*). Innocuous or demonic, personal or enveloping a whole community, when the trickster's hypnotic power wanes, the protagonist is left with the necessity to make his own choices.

The Trickster Must Die

After the creative, chaotic unconscious energy has been woken up for the purpose of disrupting the stale (personal or social) order, it must go back to its dark wellspring. Depending on the type of the trickster and the genre of the narrative, authors employ various methods of 'killing off' the trickster, from harmless dissolution and successful withdrawal of projection, to suicide and murder.

Structurally, the dissolution of the trickster happens at the end of the narrative, simultaneously with or shortly after crossing the threshold back into 'normality'. If the trickster is 'internal', the protagonist simply loses a set of character traits; when the trickster is projected and externalised, he or she physically disappears. Stanley Ipkiss throws away the green mask once he realises that he does not need to be a walking hyperbole of masculinity in order to win and retain the woman of his dreams. Drop Dead Fred, in one of the final scenes, asks Lizzie to kiss him (psychologically, he is also her animus) and pronounce his name out loud. The name 'switches him off' and he evaporates (rather like a jinny), leaving Lizzie to embrace empty air.

Back at the beginning of trickster cinema, Charlie Chaplin's Tramp traditionally transforms into a more acceptable social being, or is discovered and expelled from society altogether. The Tramp in *A Dog's Life* makes a double exit: he ceases to be a homeless petty thief and leaves the city in order to start a new plentiful life in the country. The last portion of the film, entitled 'When dreams come true', show him as a happily married farmer cultivating his land, enjoying his simple lifestyle and cooing over his dog's newborn puppies. The misadventures of the new arrival to the United States (*The Immigrant*, 1917) end up with Chaplin's character finding a job and getting married, thus overriding his former 'unofficial' status.

Jack Nicholson's tricksters and shadows are often eliminated 'physically'. The Joker is literally broken into pieces; the drunkard ACLU lawyer George Hanson (*Easy Rider*, 1969) is murdered by conservative Louisianian rednecks; Jack Torrance (*The Shining*, 1980) freezes to death in the hedge maze. Some of Nicholson's characters, however, do not die in a brutal manner but are instead 'gently dissolved'. For instance, the annoying Dr. Rydell in *Anger Management*, after messing up the life of the protagonist, a shy and retiring Dave Buznik (Adam Sandler), and successfully driving him to the boiling point, waves his victim goodbye and disappears. Nicholson's character in *Something's Gotta Give*, after experiencing a heart attack, loses his inner trickster, changes his views on life and ceases being a 63-year-old teenager with commitment issues. The heart attack makes him aware of his own mortality and awakens his overdue psychological maturity. He eventually falls in love with a mature woman and, after some doubts, settles down with her.

The trickster's death in the narrative coincides with van Gennep and Turner's notion of the closure of the rite of passage. In narrative terms, the trickster principle is only alive from the end of the 'exposition' and to the moment of narrative climax. He is only alive during the 'liminal period'. The psychological reason for this is that a creature so chaotic, a creature representing the creative-destructive potential of the unconscious, cannot be left 'out in the open', without any regulation or control. For the rest of the time he is brooding underground, like the mischievous Loki in Scandinavian mythology. Used in safe quantities, trickster energy has a therapeutic effect and works with what Jung called the transcendent function, a mechanism which promotes and regulates the vital tension between consciousness and the unconscious (CW6; CW8). As Terrie Waddell proposes,

> The transcendent function might then be thought of as an aspect of trickster when we consider the way it pervades the liminal space as mediator of the dialectical relationship between consciousness and the unconscious. Both these components, however, are beholden to the Self, Jung's overarching regulator of psychic processes, often symbolised in images of wholeness (CW9ii). While itself an archetype, all archetypal

configurations spring from, or are aspects of, this supervisory energy source, that, for the most part, works toward safeguarding the individuation process.

(Waddell, 2009: xiii)

In other words, the trickster's emergence and subsequent dissolution is a necessary part of the individuation process. Jung argues: 'Since life cannot tolerate a standstill, a damming up of vital energy results, and this would lead to an insupportable condition did not the tension of opposites produce a new, uniting function that transcends them. This function arises quite naturally from the regression of libido caused by the blockage' (CW6: para. 824). The trickster's role is prompt and functional; he is a sort of psychological plumber. When the protagonist received a wake-up call, the trickster arrives to clear the blockage.

The Trickster's Licentiousness

The trickster, either in its internal or external, male or female form, tends to be pretty libidinous. As the king of everything natural, instinctual and uncivilised, he cannot overlook the big and important issue of sexual drive. Excretory is the only other bodily function which can rival sex for the first place in the trickster's life. Traditionally, much emphasis in narratives is placed on the size of the penis and the might of the trickster's libido. The trickster gets aroused at the mere thought of sexual contact and is able to have intercourse for hours. His (or her) sexual appetite is insatiable, his energy is measureless. The protagonist, by contrast, is worn out by 'civilisation' and weakened by 'too much thinking'. In trickster narratives, thinking, introspection, shyness and suchlike manifestations of sophistication and good breeding are depicted as harmful and preventing the protagonist from achieving his or her full potential – personal, professional or sexual.

Wakdjunkaga from Radin's rendition of the Winnebago tale is the illustration of the tricky character of the autonomic nervous system. He keeps fighting with his digestive tract and reproductive organs which are personified, metonymised (separated from his body), and generally keep doing 'their own thing'. As a character, Wakdjunkaga is simultaneously a metonymical representative of the autonomic nervous system and its victim, as his budding consciousness is making efforts to 'do something' about the stubborn monsters that are his penis and his anus. Personification of body parts governed by a largely uncontrollable internal system (of which they are mere 'puppets') is yet another version of the umbrella issue which in various forms flags up in all trickster narratives – the issue of human control over the bodily functions. When he gets an unexpected erection which causes his blanket to stick up, Wakdjunkaga addresses his penis in a self-hypnotic, conciliatory manner: 'My younger brother, you will lose the blanket, so bring it back' (Radin, 1972: 18).

Wakdjunkaga's super-sized penis, which, because of its length, is carefully coiled up and deposited in a special box, resists any interference from its owner. Upon seeing the chief's daughter and her friends on the opposite side of the lake, Wakdjunkaga instructs his organ to cross the water and 'lodge squarely in her' (1972: 19). And although the penis prefers doing things its own way, the trickster wins the argument because the organ and his owner are inseparable, representing the oxymoronic mix of cleverness and stupidity typical of the reproductive instinct:

> It went sliding on the surface of the water. 'Younger brother, come back, come back! You will scare them away if you approach in such a manner!' So he pulled the penis back, tied a stone around its neck, and sent it out again. This time it dropped to the bottom of the lake. Again he pulled it back, took another stone, smaller in size, and attached it to its neck. Soon he sent it forth again. It slid along the water, creating waves as it passed along. 'Brother, come back, come back! You will drive the women away if you create waves like that!'. So he tried a fourth time. This time he got a stone, just the right size and just the right weight, and attached it to its neck. When he dispatched it, this time it went directly toward the designated place. It passed and just barely touched the friends of the chief's daughter. They saw it and cried out, 'Come out of the water, quick!'. The chief's daughter was the last one on the bank and could not get away, so the penis lodged squarely in her.
>
> (1972: 19)

Ancient Greek culture also linked the idea of virility to the idea of laughter. Greek comedy actors of the classical age (the fifth century BC) wore costumes that were generally gross and uncouth. People in the audience had nothing against the fact that costumes incorporated, as a basic element, a large leather phallus. This is because, as Richard Green explains, 'the comic performer stands outside the accepted norm, and this is doubtless part of the convention which allows the characters of comedy to behave in ways and to say things which also fall outside the accepted norms of public behaviour' (Easterling and Hall, 2002: 104). Phallus, rather like the contemporary 'middle finger' gesture, was used as a symbol of transgression and defiance.

In Ancient Greece, comedy ignored civilisation, defied the rules, and even openly criticised politics (Aristophanes). Virility in this context means the ability to stand up to oppression and, in a more general sense, to stay alive. It is less about sex per se as it is about libido as Jung understood it – as psychic energy, 'the total force which pulses through all the forms and activities of the psychic system and establishes a communication between them'. It is nothing other than 'the intensity of the psychic process, its *psychological value*, which can be determined only by psychic manifestations and effects' (Jacobi, 1973: 52). Whereas the noble art of tragedy (as it was defined by Aristotle in his monumental work of literary criticism, *Poetics*) depicted men as becoming prey to an assortment of forces beyond their control, from envious gods to thick-headed politicians, comedy insisted on the individual's right to stick his middle finger up at them. This action, of course, is potentially calamitous (as it is foolish to disobey authority), but its dangerousness is part of the appeal. Comedy demonstrated carnivalesque resurrection of the spirit. It proved that the psyche was alive.

Similarly, cinematic trickster narratives seem to be permanently preoccupied with the issue of virility. Tricksters are usually depicted as being oversexed, while their carriers (protagonists) are presented as having low sexual drive. Adam Sandler's comedies replace the problem of low libido with the 'problem of small penis'. Sandler's character in *Click* (2006, directed by Frank Coraci) is a hardworking architect whose workaholism, and the satellite anger problem, are metonymically associated with the inferiority complex which is caused by the inadequate size of his male organ. He cannot stop working because he feels that his family deserves the best. Or rather, in his penis-size-induced frenzy, he unwittingly substitutes emotional connection with material wealth. He uses hard work as an effective penis-enlargement treatment.

Another Sandler character, Dave Buznik from *Anger Management* (2003), directed by Peter Segal) also lets the penis issue control his life. The size of his penis is inversely proportional to the amount of suppressed anger he harbours. Michael and Dave's anger eventually transforms into tricksters (the universal remote control in Michael's case and Jack Nicholson in Dave's), and proceeds to drive their lives to absurdity. In both narratives, the 'problem of the size' exits the private sphere and becomes an extended social metaphor for alpha-maleness and professional success.

Jim Carrey's early tricksters pride themselves on their gargantuan sex drive. Ace Ventura is able to have intercourse for hours on end. The mask man in *The Mask*, unlike its shy carrier Stanley Ipkiss, is bursting with confidence and erotic prowess. Drop Dead Fred is too immature to be interested in sex but he likes to look up women's skirts. Fred's disgusted reaction to all things erotic reflects Lizzie's own immaturity and asexuality. Her emotional development has been hindered by the tyrannical and controlling mother, so the audience is not surprised when this mother (both as Lizzie's inner voice and as the 'real thing') becomes the main target of the trickster's machinations.

The seriously oversexed Harry Sanborn (*Something's Gotta Give*) plays the role of the trickster in the life of the emotionally repressed and exceedingly refined woman author Erica Barry (Diane Keaton). Erica wears virginal pastels and austere polo necks. After her previous relationship failures, she does not trust men and is not planning to enter a relationship – let alone having a love affair with a dangerous and unstable perennial playboy. However, much as the very proper Erica tries to stay away from Harry, his trickster power is enough to turn her life upside down.

The Farrelly Brothers' *The Heartbreak Kid* (2007) develops along a similar line. Ben Stiller's character Eddie is afflicted by a female trickster. An incurable introvert terrified of women, Eddie is lured into marriage by Lila, a scandalously oversexed and bitchy blond. Prior to their wedding Lila is so frail, decent and refined that Eddies deems her to be a good wife material, but during their honeymoon she 'flips' and becomes an argumentative, stupid, sexually insatiable demoness with a very shady past. She is successfully disposed of by the end of the film but her brainlessly boisterous personality leaves an imprint on Eddie's life. After his ordeal, he comes out of his shell and becomes more adventurous. His excessive, oppressive 'thinking' no longer hinders his ability to enjoy life.

The metaphor of hyper-virile penis (or insatiable vagina) covers a wide range of social and personal issues in trickster narratives, but, in essence, it signifies the will to live. It is invariably contrasted with the stale psychological state in which the civilised, urbanised protagonists find themselves after years of spotless rational behaviour and clear thinking.

The Animal Connection

Animals are common guests in trickster narratives. In fact, they symbolise the trickster's connection with the 'underworld' of instincts and animal behaviour. Many mythological and folkloric tricksters are animals, and even when they are not, some association with the animal kingdom is often present. African trickster club boasts a spider (Kwaku Anansi), a hare, and a tortoise; Northern American group includes a raven, a coyote, a rabbit and Wakdjunkaga's numerous animal transformations. The fox is the principal trickster of Russian fairytales; India has the monkey called Hanuman (one of the heroes of Ramayana); the most-known Chinese trickster is also a monkey – the hero of the novel *The Journey to the West* (1590); in Peruvian fairytales the trickster's role is played by a guinea pig; Argentinean folklore has Tokwah who is neither human nor animal; Japanese folktales mention Hare and Badger as cunning transformers.

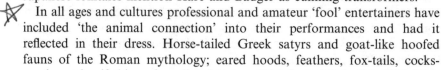

In all ages and cultures professional and amateur 'fool' entertainers have included 'the animal connection' into their performances and had it reflected in their dress. Horse-tailed Greek satyrs and goat-like hoofed fauns of the Roman mythology; eared hoods, feathers, fox-tails, cockscombs and calf-skins of medieval jesters (Welsford, 1936: 123; Willeford, 1969: 3–4); little dogs accompanying circus clowns and participating in clown acts – all these traditional elements emphasise the trickster's role as a culture hero, as a 'mediator' between the world of humans and the 'underworld' of instincts.

On medieval pictures, street and court entertainers are often depicted with animals or wearing all kinds of animal paraphernalia, most famously the eared hood (signifying their relation to the universal symbol of stupidity – the ass). One of the French medieval mock-religious festivals, called the Feast of the Ass (*festum asinorum*) was celebrated in commemoration of the Virgin Mary's flight into Egypt. 'Mary' with an infant was places upon an ass and 'led in great ceremony to the alter where high mass was performed with solemn pomp' (Knight and Lacey, 1825: 264). The whole congregation also sang a blasphemous hymn in his praise. In conclusion of the ceremony, instead of the usual blessing, the priest repeated the braying three times, and the final Amen was also substituted for the same cry (Bakhtin, 1984: 78).

Following Radin's and Henderson's argument, the trickster is an incomplete individual, a fluid transitory path from animal to human (Jung and von Franz, 1964: 103–104). As befits a liminal creature, he is 'stuck in the middle', he is permanently in transition. The trickster, Jung argues, is deserted by his human companions 'which seems to indicate that he has fallen below their level of consciousness' (CW9/I: para. 472). At the same time,

> he is no match for the animals either, because of his extraordinary clumsiness and lack of instinct. These defects are the marks of his 'human' nature, which is not so well adapted to the environment as the animal's but, instead, has prospects of a much higher development of consciousness based on a considerable eagerness to learn, as is duly emphasized in myth.
>
> (CW9/I: para. 473)

Tricksters in cinema share this transitionality with their mythological and folkloric colleagues. It leaves their instincts and their consciousness equally 'unfinished'. Carrey's early tricksters prefer the company of animals to that of humans. For instance, Ace Ventura 'the pet detective' lives in a room full of rescued animals while his estimation of human abilities is condensed in the word 'LUHU-ZEHER'. Lloyd Christmas and his friend Harry, a pair of chronic losers, are attached to their parakeet Petey (subsequently murdered by a gangster), and dream of establishing their own pet store that specialises in worm farms called 'I Got Worms!'. Harry drives a sheepdog van as part of his dog-grooming business 'Mutt Cutts' (he eventually loses all clients due to his careless driving). Both of them envisage their businesses to be organised around animals, not people.

Stanley Ipkiss's only true friend is a little dog named Milo. This friendship effectively emphasises Stanley's immaturity and inability to relate emotionally to human beings. Ipkiss's mad alter-ego, the Mask, occasionally turns into cartoon animals (like he does during the famous scene in the notorious Coco Bongo club, when he becomes excited at the sight of Tina Carlyle singing the very languid *Gee Baby, Ain't I Good To You*). One of Burton's trickster characters, Jack Skellington (*The Nightmare Before Christmas*, 2003) has a small canine companion, Zero the Ghost Dog.

Whenever an animal appears in a cinematic trickster narrative, it usually symbolises the protagonist's psychological immaturity (which makes possible the arrival of the trickster, whether from 'the inside' or 'the outside'). Animals also signify the state of stagnation and subsequent turbulent transition; and narratively – they are harbingers of a crisis.

Poop

Scatological References and Bodily Functions

William Hynes in *Mythical Trickster Figures* (Hynes, 1993b) makes an attempt to explain the trickster's obsession with human excreta:

> all creative inventions are ultimately excreta. Like the mystic who constantly reminds us that no words or doctrinal construct can express adequately the ineffable nature of God, the trickster reminds us that no one creative ordering can capture life. Insofar as an ordering continues to express life, it continues to be viable. If not viable, such orderings will drop away, be replaced with new productions, or these orderings will work to repeal their potential replacements.
>
> (Hynes, 1993b: 216)

The trickster, who hates stagnation and tirelessly creates without envisaging the final result, throws away a lot of by-products and unused ideas – leftovers from his creative process. The very high and elevated idea of the creative process is expressed in trickster tales through scatological imagery. Besides, references to bodily processes are carnivalesque in the sense that they indicate a 'lower consciousness', a consciousness prior to the loss of innocence, the loss of paradise. The trickster is not yet concerned with all the niceties of civilisation, and consequently does not feel shame in the same way human beings are supposed to feel. He has not yet reached the stage when he feels the need to hide his bodily processes from others, therefore he freely burps, farts, belches, hiccups, defecates, urinates and vomits. Obviously, trickster narratives are not all the same and some tricksters (depending on how conscious they are of their actions) do perceive the split between the mind and the body, the civilised 'niceness' and the uncontrollable, stubborn flesh. But generally, the trickster is at one with the world, and at peace with his body – even when this body produces 'dirty' and 'smelly' substances.

Wakdjunkaga's adventures, for instance, include a story of the trickster eating a talking laxative bulb. As he prides himself on being called 'the foolish one', he does not listen to the bulb's warning that eating it would trigger an uncontrollable urge to defecate. The story of the trickster fighting with his own colon is, metaphorically speaking, the story of the stupid mind fighting with the uncontrollable human body which 'knows better'. Predictably, Wakdjunkaga loses the battle with the bulb he has stupidly swallowed:

> 'Well, this bulb did a lot of talking,' he said to himself, 'yet it could not make me defecate.' But even as he spoke he began to have the desire to defecate, just a very little. 'Well, I suppose this is what it meant. It certainly bragged a good deal, however.' As he spoke he defecated again. 'Well, what a braggart it was! I suppose this is why it said this.' As he spoke these last words, he began to defecate a good deal. After a while, as he was sitting down, his body would touch the excrement. Thereupon he got on top of a log and sat down there but, even then, he touched the excrement. Finally, he climbed up a log that was leaning against a tree. However, his body still touched the excrement, so he went up higher. Even then, however, he touched it so he climbed still higher up. Higher and higher he had to go. Nor was he able to stop defecating. Now he was on top of the tree. It was small and quite uncomfortable. Moreover, the excrement began to come up to him.
>
> (Radin, 1956: 26–27)

After his ordeal, Wakdjunkaga ends up covered in his own excrement – which does not embarrass him in the least as he generally is not sensitive or capable of feeling shame. He lacks the necessary capacity for self-reflection.

On-screen tricksters also have a very harmonious, almost paradisiacal relationship with their bodies. Often their 'lowly' behaviour coincides with assault on authority – in fact, excrement and urine are used to symbolically 'defile' authority. Pursued by angered locals, Lloyd and Harry cannot stop the car in order to have a leak, so Lloyd has to use an empty beer bottle. When a policeman spots the bottle on the floor of the car, he accuses Lloyd and Harry of drink driving. In their defence, they let him try the yellow liquid which he spits out in disgust. Jack Nicholson's character in *About Schmidt* (2002) stages a grotesque revolt against his dead wife's orders to urinate sitting down. He is a retired 66-year-old insurance seller who has spent his life doing all the right, safe and clean things which leaves him, deep down, a very angry man dissatisfied with himself, his relatives and his surroundings. The trickster is born (read: the anger escapes) when he discovers a stack of hidden letters from his wife's former lover. The dead (and unfaithful) wife's authority is overrun by the symbolic act of urinating standing up in the most careless and messy manner.

The age-old cheap trick of showing the naked bottom is also popular with tricksters. In search of valuable information about the case on which the pet detective is currently working, Ace Ventura's 'talking bottom' approaches a friendly police inspector with the following phrase: 'Excuse me, may I ass you a few questions?' Throughout the scene Ace and his bottom speak intermittently, with Ace occasionally ordering it to shut up. In the sequel, *Ace Ventura: When Nature Calls*, Carrey's character hides in a giant rubber rhino robot in order to spy on his enemies in the African savannah. Unfortunately, the rhino breaks down and Ace, naked and dishevelled, has to escape through the rhino's rear end. This gross 'butt birth' is the metaphorical epitome of the trickster's silly, grotesque desire to be free; to escape the anonymity and darkness of the unconscious.

Adam Sandler's character in *Click*, armed with his new ability to 'pause' people and manipulate them while they are 'frozen', takes his trousers off and farts into the face of his boss who has unfairly passed him over for promotion. Upon 'awakening' from his hypnosis, the boss is outraged and chokes with disgust. Drop Dead Fred is a 'separated' trickster (as opposed to 'incorporated' ones which share the bodily frame with their human 'carriers', and therefore are more restrained in their actions) and, as 'separated' tricksters go, is more outrageous in his repulsive tricks. He is fascinated with the mucus from his nose, and regularly sticks it onto people's clothes. He is also disgustingly creative in his attempts to over-throw the authority of Lizzie's tyrannical mother. One such escapade includes smearing dog poo all over the matriarch's fresh carpet. Not only are tricksters not afraid of their bodily functions, they also actively use them in their fight with the sterile uptightness of civilisation. Defilement and profanity are their outlets for raw creativity; a breakthrough and productive artistry which rejects all things infertile in their niceness and orderliness.

Chapter 2

The Trickster and Personal Relationships

loss of personal contacts *loneliness in the city* *fleeing*

Contemporary Individuation

Trickster film, especially in its comedic form, concerns itself with emotional aspects of post-industrial lifestyle: the tricky border between professional and personal behaviour, the tough choice between home and work, inconsistency of friendships, and replacement of face-to-face contact with technological surrogates such as the internet. It pays special attention to such satellites of urban life as feeling lonely in a crowd, discerning the 'true', genuine impulse from the myriad of fleeing, disjointed impressions, the difficulty of 'meeting someone' and finding love in the world full of strangers, the danger of being psychologically swept by the power of the mass. It may sound paradoxical, but it deals with the issue of loneliness in the city.

As a rule, trickster protagonists fail to recognise their loneliness. In *The Mask*, Stanley Ipkiss, whose only friends include a TV and a small dog, is hiding his unhappiness behind the façade of politeness and agreeableness (TV set as a substitution for a genuine human connection is a recurring theme in trickster film). Stanley's urban loneliness is overthrown one day by the most hilarious representative of primitive masculinity – the green Mask-man. This wonderful specimen of impulsive bravery acts before he thinks, *Frank* and his method of approaching women is not in the least sophisticated as it consists of grabbing them, spinning them in circles, throwing them in the air (with the intention of catching them a few seconds later, of course) and kissing them so hard that their shoes pop off. Now, that is a perfect, manly, natural and instinctive way to 'connect'. It is far more effective than keeping a respectable distance and approaching the woman of your dreams in a shy and cautious way. Also gone is Stanley's equivocality in dealing with his enemies: instead of silently enduring anything that comes his way, the Mask smashes the car of the guy whose car horn is too loud, eliminates street hooligans with a machine gun, and demolishes the hall in his block of flats just to annoy the evil manageress. For the Mask, unlike for his human carrier, there are no boundaries of propriety between people. Everything is immediate and direct.

immediate + direct

introverts

Interestingly enough, sexual shyness is one of the key problems from which protagonists of the trickster films suffer. Adam Sandler's 'urban professionals' and Ben Stiller's introverts exemplify this issue perfectly. Dave Buznik (*Anger Management*) avoids kissing his girlfriend in public because of a humiliating incident very early in his 'love career'. He also feels embarrassed about displaying any strong or genuine emotions in the presence of other people for fear of exposing his vulnerable side. 'Other people' are potentially hostile strangers (this is how it feels in the metropolitan environment where passers-by are experienced as blurry dots fleeting past at high speed).

What the trickster film is trying to explore is the very modern issue of the appropriate boundaries between the personal and the social. The postmodern individual is forced to individuate (to find the balance between 'yourself' and 'society') in pretty tricky circumstances. Where the First World War had shaken humanity's faith in the ability of scientific rationalism to distinguish right from wrong, and demolished remaining hopes for progressive linearity, the Second World War left the survivors staring into the existentialist void. What does it mean to be human after the Holocaust, after fascist atrocities? Can we, after what had happened, trust the psyche – and especially the collective psyche? Who is God and where had he been during the violent mass conflicts? And what does it take to become the individual in the alienating, disconnecting, fragmenting, lonely atmosphere of the city where everyone is a potential enemy?

Paradoxically, as far as community is concerned, the trickster principle is responsible both for creative unity and destructive fusion. When the 'connection' between these alienated minds finally happens, it can lead either to a wonderful, inspiring unification – or to a most catastrophic sacrifice of individual identities for the sake of the collective machine. Is adhering to the demands of one's *habitus*, regardless of their ethical validity, the correct form of behaviour, or does one have to assert one's personal opinion and moral convictions?

Human beings have now accepted 'the conflict', be it internal or external, psychological or real, as part of their nature. Late modernity, the cultural sociologist Zygmunt Bauman writes in *Liquid Modernity* (2000), is characterised by the realisation that no state of perfection can be reached tomorrow, next year, or even next millennium; that there is no

some sort of good society, just society and conflict-free society in all or some of its many postulated aspects: of steady equilibrium between supply and demand and satisfaction of all needs; of perfect order, in which everything is allocated to its right place, nothing out of place persists and no place is in doubt; of human affairs becoming totally transparent thanks to knowing everything needing to be known; of complete mastery over the future – so complete that it puts paid to all contingency, contention, ambivalence and unanticipated consequences of human undertakings.

(Bauman, 2000: 29)

try as it might

Grafting Bauman's thoughts onto our trickster canvas, it is possible to metaphorically generalise that, try as it might, the Enlightenment project failed to suppress the trickster, and its escape resulted, with disastrous consequences, in large-scale human conflicts in the twentieth century. Since it escaped, it also infected society with its fluidity, fragmentedness, undecidedness, mischief, cruelty and crude survival skills at the expense of others. The trickster is late capitalism (Bauman's 'liquid modernity', post-industrialism) personified.

In addition to the issue of the correlation between the personal and the collective, and the ensuing moral dilemmas, late capitalism throws lifestyle questions at the individual. What it means to be human is only one aspect of the problem. Another question the postmodern individual is trying to answer is what it means to be 'whole' – which, ultimately and inevitably, takes us to the issues of 'reality' and 'truth'. Are emotions, love, relationships, blood ties, sexual encounters, friendships – real in today's world? As Bauman argues, liquid modernity and postmodernity saw orientation points – codes and configurations, patterns and rules of behaviour – becoming flexible, unstable, loose. These patterns

> are no longer 'given', let alone 'self-evident'; there are just too many of them, clashing one another and contradicting one another's commandments, so that each one has been stripped of a good deal of compelling, coercively constraining powers. And they have changed their nature and have been accordingly reclassified: as items in the inventory of individual tasks. [. . .]
>
> Ours is, as a result, an individualized, privatized version of modernity, with the burden of pattern-weaving and the responsibility for failure falling primarily on the individual's shoulders.
>
> (Bauman, 2000: 7)

The more industrial, capitalist, individualised society moves from its communal roots, the more disjointed it becomes. Without the faceless safety of communal living, and without the spiritual, psychological, economic and social support of the ethnic group or clan, the seemingly empowered and independent individual starts to feel rootless, fragile, and ultimately confused by the endless combinatorial possibilities and seductively limitless opportunities of the urban world. In his book *All That is Solid Melts into Air*, the American philosopher Marshall Berman identifies the building blocks of modernity:

need for communal Roots

The maelstrom of modern life has been fed from may sources: great discoveries in the physical sciences, changing our images of the universe and our place in it; the industrialization of production which trans- forms scientific knowledge into technology, creates new human environments and destroys old ones, speeds up the whole tempo of life, generates new forms of corporate power and class struggle; immense demographic upheavals, severing millions of people from their ancestral habitats, hurtling them halfway across the world into new lives; rapid and often cataclysmic urban growth; systems of mass communication, dynamic in their development, enveloping and binding together the most diverse people and societies; increasingly powerful national states, bureaucratically structured and operated, constantly striving to expand their powers; mass social movements of people, and peoples, challenging their political and economic rulers, striving to gain some control over their lives; finally, bearing and driving all these people and institutions along an ever-expanding drastically fluctuating capitalist world market. In the twentieth century, the social processes that bring this maelstrom into being and keep it in a state of perpetual becoming, have come to be called 'modernization'.

(Berman, 1983: 15–16)

Berman also highlights one of the principal dialectical features of modern existence: alongside the great emptiness of values ('God is dead') there exists 'a remarkable abundance of possibilities' (1983: 21). Industrial/post-industrial society is no longer controlling and prescriptive in the way a small community or a tribe are – which means that the 'freed' human beings are made responsible for their own social and financial destinies. In other words, in the capitalist, democratic society people are free to make social and financial choices based on their private interests. Their much-advertised freedom, however, is doubtful. In their assessment of modernity, both Berman and Turner refer to Max Weber's vision of the modern individual as being born into the 'tremendous cosmos of the modern economic order' and trapped in the 'iron cage' of consumerism (Berman, 1983: 27; Weber, 2005: 123). Turner contrasts the anonymity and relative simplicity of communal existence with the individualism and escalating complexity of modern Western lifestyle. He writes:

As societies diversify economically and socially and as particularistic multiplex ties of locality and kinship yield place to a wide range of single-interest relationships between members of functional groups over ever wider geographical areas, individual option and voluntarism thrive at the expense of predetermined corporate obligations. Even obliga- tions are chosen; they result from entering into contractual relations. The individual replaces the group as the crucial ethical point. [. . .]

And, as Max Weber has pointed out, the individual extruded from previous corporate, mainly kin-based matrices becomes obsessed with the problem of personal and individual salvation. The need to choose between alternative lines of action in an ever more complex social field, the increasing weight, as he matures, of responsibility for his own individual decisions and their outcomes, prove too much for the individual to endure on his own, and he seeks some transcendental source of support and legitimacy to relieve him from anxieties about his immediate and ultimate fate as a self-conscious entity

(Turner, 1975: 200)

Without a fixed *habitus* and with so many external influences offering alternative identities (or rather fragments of identities) in its place – TV, newspapers, magazines, advertisements, the shops, the internet – how can one pinpoint the exact boundary between truth and fiction? As Fredric Jameson argues, 'the shift of the dynamics of culture pathology can be characterised as one in which the alienation of the subject is displaced by the fragmentation of the subject' (Jameson, 1991: 14). Since the 'true' subject, the solid subject, the subject who knew exactly who he was, is dead – what is this fluid thing in his place that is breathing and moving?

Fragmentation and the Trickster

Psychological uncertainty invariably leads to anxiety. To quote Bauman once more,

Frank

This kind of uncertainty, of dark premonitions and fears of the future that haunt men and women in the fluid, perpetually changing social environment in which the rules of the game change in the middle of the game without warning or legible pattern, does not unite the sufferers: it splits them and sets them apart. The pains it causes to the individuals do not add up, do not accumulate, do not condense into a kind of 'common cause' which could be pursued more effectively by joining forces and acting in unison. The decline of the community is in this sense self-perpetuating; once it takes off, there are fewer and fewer stimuli to stem the disintegration of human bonds and seek ways to tie again which has been torn apart.

(Bauman, 2001: 48)

A stable (meaning local, not melting-pot global) culture, as Geertz argued, is key to the individuals' ability to interpret the world because it provides them with a knowledge base, ideological orientation and psychological pointers. It also ties their otherwise lonely identity to the mighty unity of the group, thus empowering them and equipping them with a sense of belonging to an establishment which can always support its members – physically, spiritually or emotionally – whatever happens. This is a sense of belonging to 'something bigger'. Overemphasis on this dependence, of course, can potentially lead to the emergence of the collective shadow, complete with *participation mystique*, mass political ritualism and the usual in such cases dissolution of the individual in the mass.

However, the psychological effects of the loss of cultural perspective can be equally devastating. In the world where there is no 'truth', there is also no 'meaning'. 'Our bodies' – Fredric Jameson writes – 'are bereft of spatial coordinates and practically (let alone theoretically) incapable of distantiation' (Jameson, 1991: 48–49). Meanwhile, piecing the fragments of reality together is no mean feat:

> The distorted and unreflexive attempts of newer cultural production to explore and to express this new space must then also, in their own fashion, be considered as so many approaches to the representation of (a new) reality (to use a more antiquated language). As paradoxical as the terms may seem, they may thus, following a classic interpretive option, be read as peculiar new forms of realism (or at least of the mimesis of reality), while at the same time they can equally well be analysed as so many attempts to distract and divert us from that reality or to disguise its contradictions and resolve them in the guise of various formal mystifications.
>
> (Jameson, 1991: 49)

The Industrial Revolution plucked individuals from their native environments and planted them in cities where they acquired the notorious anonymity of mass-producing and mass-consuming organisms. This means that what Jameson calls the 'personal, private style, as unmistakable as your fingerprint', before its final expiration in the world of postmodern fakeness and pastiche, had been an unrealistic, utopian project. Freedom from the tribal *habitus*, which stresses standardised thinking and common identity, has always been no more than an illusion. 'The mass' has always been present in the background; it has been following citizens of industrialised societies like a faithful shadow. Jameson argues that

> not only is the bourgeois individual subject a thing of the past, it is also a myth; it never really existed in the first place; there had never been autonomous subjects of that type. Rather, this construct is merely a philosophical and cultural mystification which sought to persuade people that they 'had' individual subjects and possessed this unique personal identity.
>
> (Malpas, 2001: 27)

In any case, according to Jameson, the features that characterise cultural products in late capitalism are pastiche and schizophrenia. By pastiche he means meaningless imitation of more authentic styles. Like Jung's theory of schizophrenia in modernist texts and paintings, Jameson's use of the word is meant to be descriptive, not diagnostic (Malpas, 2001: 29). Pastiche, Jameson writes, 'is blank parody, parody that has lost its sense of humour: pastiche is to parody what that curious thing, the modern practice of a kind of blank irony, is to what Wayne Booth calls the stable and comic ironies of, say, the eighteenth century' (Malpas, 2001: 25). Meanwhile, the cultural 'schizophrenia', the fragmented consciousness becomes visible when temporal continuities break down and

> the experience of the present becomes powerfully, overwhelmingly vivid and 'material': the world comes before the schizophrenic with heightened intensity, bearing a mysterious and oppressive charge of affect, glowing with hallucinatory energy. But what might for us seem a desirable experience – an increase in our perceptions, a libidinal or hallucinogenic intensification of our normally humdrum and familiar surroundings – is here felt as a loss, as 'unreality'.
>
> (2001: 34)

The culture that is deemed by Fredric Jameson 'schizophrenic' in its hallucinogenic multiplicity and intensity is also described by his British colleague Terry Eagleton as 'depthless, decentred, ungrounded, self-reflexive, playful, derivative, eclectic, pluralistic' (Eagleton, 1996: vii).

Essentially, fragmentedness is a trickster quality – as are the sense of ~~Frank~~ 'unreality', identity confusion, and lack of psychological unity and completeness. Jameson's 'schizophrenia' in the arts, far from being depthless, simply duplicates the trickster's excessive, continuous creativity; his nonstop generating of happenings, situations and narrative fragments; his ceaseless production of texts without envisaging the final result – the process which William Doty, in an attempt to explain the trickster's scatological aspect, metaphorically links to his production of 'excreta'. In fact, there are people who think that most postmodern art, and its visual branch in particular, should be thought of as 'excreta', bearing in mind its disposability and the little effort it takes to produce. This view is not helped by the fact that scatology features prominently in postmodern installations.

The trickster is the mirror reflection of the urban individual who, unlike the misguided 'wholesome' subject of modernity, is searching for a stable *Frank* core (or *the self*, to use Jung's terminology) amongst the scattered fragments of his psyche. The trickster is pre-rational and 'pre-God' while *homo postmodernus* is, allegedly, post-rational and 'post-God', but the result is the same – fragmentedness instead of a solid image, non-linearity instead of rational progressivism, stylistic carnival in the place of sombre realism, the grotesque instead of the objective. The trickster is the unconscious itself, the Bakhtinian carnivalesque, posing a threat to consciousness's truth-seeking, normalising, stabilising, centralising, 'excreta-hiding' and boundary-creating activities. In many ways, the unconscious is that unstable, mischievous – dangerous even – trickster saviour which has the potential to resuscitate the dead subject, to restore it from fragments – at least, partially. Christopher Hauke asserts that

> For Jung, the tension and the contradiction lies between universal mass culture and its denial of the individual, on the one hand, and, on the other hand, the contemporary subject's unrealised access to a conscious relationship or dialectic with the collective psyche which is the potential of each individual. Through the process of individuation, attention is not simply paid to making conscious the repressed elements of the personal unconscious, as in Freud's 'where id was there ego shall be' [. . .] In addition to this, what is aimed for in Jung's psychology is a consciousness of the collective unconscious, not only through its 'inner' imagery but precisely in its projection in the form of mass phenomena. This view acknowledges both the inevitability and the importance of globalisation and the mass but at the same time suggests a method for humanity to gain (not even 'regain' as some conventional views would have it) further human qualities as opposed to the losing of them which the notion of the 'death' of the subject suggests. [. . .] what arises is a new individual-collective dialectic which neither collapses into the mass man, nor into the individual monad.
>
> (Hauke, 2000: 75)

Hauke's view of the postmodern dynamic between the individual and the collective is important for my analysis of the trickster in film. The 'old' unconscious of modernity, Hauke argues, 'has been commodified and absorbed and has no radical edge left'. However, the unconscious as conceived by Jung 'retains the radical challenge by the way it is conceptually maintained at a greater distance from ego-consciousness by Jung's consistent emphasis on the unalterable Otherness' (Hauke, 2000: 75). Hauke gives an example from Jung's *Psychology and Religion: West and East* (CW11), in which Jung insists on the basic untameability of the instinctual. Instead of acknowledging 'the trickster' ('the powers within'), we choose to pretend that our moral selves are fully in control of our actions:

> Always, therefore, there is something in the psyche that takes possession and limits or suppresses our moral freedom. In order to hide this undeniable but exceedingly unpleasant fact from ourselves and at the same time pay lip service to freedom, we have got accustomed to saying: 'I *have* such and such a desire or habit or feeling of resentment',

instead of the more veracious: 'Such and such a desire or habit or feeling *has me*'. . . . we immediately identify with every impulse instead of giving it the name of 'the other', which would at least hold it at arm's length and prevent it from storming the citadel of the ego. 'Principalities and powers' are always with us; we have no need to create them even if we could. It is merely incumbent upon us to *choose* the master we wish to serve, so that his service shall be our safeguard against being mastered by the 'other' whom we have not chosen.

Frank

(Jung, CW11: para. 143)

The alive and untameable trickster representing the powers of the unconscious in a civilised society – and in the postmodern condition whose dreaminess and unreality mimics the patterns of the unconscious – is an integral part of postmodern individuation and postmodern relationships. The trickster thrives on the dissolution of fixed social patterns. This disintegration both hurts the individual and ensures his progress as a unique human being. When the 'social' appears in trickster film, it is usually in the form of an unstoppable 'dark force' of the crowd – a force that is unstructured, unintelligible, destructive (the Joker in Tim Burton's *Batman*, Sacha Baron-Cohen's 'social experiments' in provincial America). The social in the trickster film is an accident, an outburst rather than an established presence. The individual is presented as being lost in the maze of interpersonal and professional relationships because the system within which he is functioning, and on which he depends, feeds on the tensions produced by psychological fragmentation and physical fluidity. As Zygmunt Bauman notes,

> The disintegration of the social network, the falling apart of effective agencies of collective action is often noted with a good deal of anxiety and bewailed as the unanticipated 'side effect' of the new lightness and fluidity of the increasingly mobile, slippery, shifty, evasive and fugitive power. But social disintegration is as much a condition as it is the outcome of the new technique of power, using disengagement and the art of escape as its major tools. For power to be free to flow, the world must be free of fences, barriers, fortified borders and checkpoints. Any dense and tight network of social bonds, and particularly a territorially rooted tight network, is an obstacle to be cleared out of the way. Global powers are bent on dismantling such networks for the sake of their continuous and growing fluidity, that principal source of their strength and the warrant of their invincibility. And it is the falling apart, the friability, the brittleness, the transience, the until-further-noticeness of human bonds and networks which allow these powers to do their job in the first place.

(Bauman, 2000: 14)

Thus, the trickster, reflecting the late-capitalist system, is both the cause of the split and its healer; the one who lacks 'the centre' and the one who, often inadvertently, provides it.

Trickster as a Psychotherapist/Psychotherapist as a Trickster

Cinematic tricksters tend to play the role of inadvertent and dangerous 'psychotherapists'. They heal by irritating the wound and driving the patient to the point of crisis (or catharsis). After catharsis arrives the denouement – time of reflection. Trickster's therapy is the therapy of 'facing the truth' based on the careless exposure of repressed psychic material. Reckless as it is, this kind of therapy 'heals the split' and makes the isolated protagonist connect with others.

In several trickster films – among them *Yes Man* and *Anger Management* – the professional who is supposed to be the specialist on personal problems is actually a cheeky charlatan who turns the life of the protagonist upside down and then denounces responsibility for his actions. In some films a professional therapist makes an incautious move and, like Vicki Rusk in *About Schmidt* (2002), releases a stream of hidden emotions in the accidental 'client', which make him behave in an unpredictable way. Randall Patrick McMurphy (Jack Nicholson) in *One Flew Over the Cuckoo's Nest* (1975) attempts to subvert Nurse Ratched's role as a therapist, and offers an alternative way to cure mental health illnesses. His 'alternative therapy' consists of various acts of civil disobedience (such as escaping from the hospital in a stolen bus), drinking, smoking, gambling and prostitutes.

A therapist in the role of the trickster is an interesting idea. What is therapy, after all, if not release of potentially dangerous, and not often controllable, even within the frame of highly regulated psychotherapeutic discourse, psychic contents? And what about all those much-debated boundaries, all this transference-counter-transference between the therapist and the client? As Sheldon Kopp argues, 'trickery has always been part of the healing process' and 'the savour-healer has his archetypal forerunner in the trickster-hero. At his worst, the shadow of the healer is the charlatan' (Kopp, 1974: 48–52). As a profession, psychotherapy has a shadow because 'the evil underlay of the therapist is that dark brother who sometimes surfaces as the quack or the false prophet. It is a form of corruption, or chronic temptation to a power trip, which the daily personal menace of every honest therapist and to which he must constantly be alert' (1974: 48).

For instance, in *Anger Management*, Dr. Rydell (Jack Nicholson) is entrusted with the task of 'curing' his patient's antisocial behaviour and eliminating his public outbursts of anger. However, Dr. Rydell abuses his position as Dave's psychotherapist in every possible way. He crosses the boundary between the personal and the professional by moving into Dave's house – and even sleeping in his bed. He snores, he farts, he 'unconsciously' puts his hand around his client during sleep. The last boundary between Dave and his shadow is dissolved when Dr. Rydell seduces his girlfriend, Linda (Marisa Tomei). In other words, he does everything to break the shell of artificial niceness, politeness and emotional sterility of Dave's life. He deliberately makes him angry. He deliberately lets the devil out. He makes him face the trickster (or the 'anger monkey' in) before he can move on with his life.

In *Yes Man*, the advice given to Carl Allen by the self-motivation guru Terrence (played by Terence Stamp) to say 'yes' to every experience on one's way radically transforms the protagonist's life. Not all changes triggered by the 'yes' experiment, however, are positive. Terrence's advice derails Carl's life and it spirals out of control. Venturing outside the structured, rational frame of therapeutic discourse (as well as the ritualised frame of everyday life) and flirting with all things random, accidental, unconscious, is bound to end in some kind of disaster – and it does when Carl cannot stop the string of misfortunes caused by his refusal to sleep with his bitchy ex-wife. Since he broke the 'yes' covenant, he is now being punished by some supernatural forces. The man on stage, the God-like persona of the guru is far more powerful than the no-man who feels lost and who, at this stage of his life, needs guidance. Terrence uses the moment of Carl's weakness to make an impression on the audience and hectors him to make a covenant with himself. Like a charlatan-hypnotherapist, he abuses his power for 'showbiz' purposes when he announces that Carl says '"no" to life, and therefore "no" to living'. Terrence, the careless healer, initiates the process of personal change in the client but forgets to monitor it or bring it to a closure. Carl's metamorphosis is left unsupervised, uncontrollable and pretty much on autopilot. Similarly, the tricksterish Larry-Ricardo (Jim Carrey) in *The Cable Guy* parodies a therapist when he whispers, in an attempt to calm down an outraged 'client' whom he was trying to 'cure' from his 'loneliness': 'Come on now . . . this is where the healing begins . . . come on . . . come on . . .'. Steven the 'patient' (Matthew Broderick) is so disgruntled because the 'therapist' had stolen his girlfriend, befriended his parents with the aim of playing the game of 'porn password' with them, had given him the present of stolen goods and sent him a pretty prostitute under the disguise of a genuine love interest.

The hallmark qualities of the trickster principle – loss of boundaries, loss of control over one's psychic processes, release of unconscious contents, framing and finalisation of trickster activities – are very similar to the stages of transition in psychotherapy. The trickster is a close relative of the therapist; moreover – he is his faithful shadow. At the same time, they are close rivals as both offer to cure the lonely urban individual, separated from his tribe, from 'godlessness' and loss of meaning. And both aim, rather paradoxically, to restore wholeness and heal psychological fragmentation by shattering the patient's (protagonist's) current view of life.

Liminal and Liminoid

Turner discerns between *liminal* and *liminoid* ritual phenomena. This division, although artificial, is nevertheless important for our analysis of personal and collective tricksters.

Although Turner does not use the actual word 'modernity', liminality can be matched with pre-modern existence, whereas liminoidness clearly belongs to modernity and postmodernity. Or, rather, it an inevitable by-product of modernity and its preoccupation with creative individualism and artistic independence. Whether the phenomenon is liminal or liminoid is determined by the degree of its author's anonymity. Turner used the term liminality primarily to describe transitional periods in pre-industrial societies. According to him, liminality is closely connected with collective celebration and communal (not individual) creativity. Liminal moments tend to be 'collective, concerned with calendrical, meteorological, biological, or social-structural cycles and rhythms, or with crises in social processes, whether these result from internal adjustments, external adaptations, or unexpected disasters (earthquakes, invasions, plagues, and the like)' (1992: 56).

By contrast, liminoid phenomena, although they may also be collective (theatre and concert visits, big sports events, mass spectacles), are nevertheless 'produced by known, named individuals'. In other words, a liminoid event or artefact is usually a one-off product of individual creativity or small constellation of creativities. Liminoid products are not cyclical but continuously generated; tend to be more idiosyncratic, quirky, radical and subversive than liminal phenomena (which are 'generalised and normative'); develop 'outside the central economic and political processes' and are 'plural, fragmentary, and experimental' (1992: 56–57). Liminoid phenomena 'flourish in societies of more complex structure. They are not cyclical but intermittent, generated often in times and places assigned to the leisure sphere' (1977b: 50–51, quoted in St. John, 2008: 133).

Jungian thought, which has always been preoccupied with modernity and its consequences, provides parallel ideas on the nature and functions of contemporary creativity. In his book on the psychology of creativity, *Art and the Creative Unconscious* (1959), Erich Neumann also discusses artistic experimentation in relation to psychological and social fragmentedness. Neumann wrote extensively on the connection between the psychological state of modern man and the developments in the arts and humanities. His ideas concerning the sidelined, de-collectivised, privatised role of creativity in industrial societies run parallel to those of Turner:

With the growth of individuality and the relative independence of consciousness, the integral situation in which the creative element in art is one with the life of the group disintegrates. An extensive differentiation occurs; poets, painters, sculptors, musicians, dancers, actors, architects, etc., become professional groups, practicing particular functions of artistic expression. The majority of the group, it would appear, preserves only a receptive relation, if any, to the creative achievement of the artist.

(Neumann, 1959/1974: 88)

The result of the isolation of the creative sphere from the receptive group, Neumann argues, is not good for the psyche of the artist. The artist, as the mediator of the unconscious, has to bear the psychological burden of dealing with it, and shaping it into particular forms: 'the creative man is the instrument of the transpersonal, but as an individual he comes into conflict with the numinosum that takes hold of him' (1959/1974: 98). As examples, Neumann mentions classic modernist painters and writers: Klee, Chagall, Dali, Van Gogh, James Joyce. When the cultural canon, with its manifest prescriptivism, starts to disintegrate (as happened in modernism), the form of the outside world gets shattered, and learnable artistic technique ceases to exist (1959/1974: 117). The artist is presented with a world in ruins, the distorted, grotesque, shapeless world which he then has to depict as it is, or try to present it as more wholesome. The artist is left alone with the demons.

Certain authors, however, disagree with the strict division that Turner placed between liminal and liminoid experiences. For example, Sharon Rowe in an article about modern sports argues that Turner's classification of sporting events as a liminoid (and hence meaningless) phenomenon is wrong. She writes that liminoid phenomena also offer an opportunity for society to 'rejuvenate itself with new values and new relational patterns' because they contain 'ludic essence' which is indispensable to sport and 'as aspects of the ludic dimension of modern society, sporting events are critical to the role liminality plays in our collective reflexivity and in supporting a context for metacommunication' (Rowe, 2008: 129). In other words, a football match still contains ritual legacy and is rendered meaningful for the fans by the very fact that during it they feel united, they are overwhelmed by affect, they possess a sense of belonging; as a mass and as a group they go through a powerful transformative experience. During the match they are also forced to accept everything that happens on the pitch as it comes because, like the powerless attendees of a liminal ritual, the power to plan, manage and direct the event is taken out of their hands. Passivity and affect characterise sporting events today.

Mihai Coman discusses the presence of the liminal and the liminoid in media events. Media provides ritualistic space for individual transformation, and rituals control social change. Media is also a form of 'acceptable disorder' (which characterises liminal events), as well as an 'official' form of interruption of everyday life. Coman maintains that 'liminality has become an ideal vehicle for defining both media production and media consumption, best fit to represent the symbolic interruption in daily life and the opportunity for detachment, reflection and challenging social structures that media consumption entails' (Coman, 2008: 97).

The 'liminoidness' and superficiality of mass media and other products of individual creativity is debatable. Although TV programmes are made by named authors and viewed by individuals separated from each other by physical boundaries, the resultant experience can still be regarded as collective; it is a ludic-ritualistic happening. As Gregor Goethals argues, certain programmes, such as nightly news, are a 'shared perception of order and events': 'This collective viewing provides community solidarity since countless citizens are exposed to identical explanations of current realities' (Goethals, 1981: 25). Mihai Coman notes that, besides regular news, there are other 'rhythmic' mass media products that configure ritualistic viewing behaviour: crime dramas, soap operas (and now, I must add, also reality TV shows) (Coman, 2008: 97). The result is a synthesis of uniqueness and commonality in media rituals (2008: 97). This tendency is even more pronounced in cinema viewing because cinema, akin to theatre, is primarily a collective experience – a projective-introjective exchange with a significant affective and individuating potential.

Luke Hockley draws parallel between watching a movie in the cinema and Jung's concept of *participation mystique* – a form of projective identification in which personal and collective identities momentarily fuse (Hockley, 2007: 27). Trickster film often places technology into the heart of the narrative, thus emphasising its mercurial qualities. The media has the ability to unite people and to influence minds; technology both separates human beings and connects them in new ways. Akin to Jung's collective unconscious, it provides potential for mass interaction and virtual places where 'minds can meet'. As Hockley rightly notes, contra Jung's own view that technology is bound on disconnecting us from ourselves,

> the technical world of mass media comes to be part of a mythological space, a space which is as likely to the recipient of unconscious projections as any other person, object, place and so on. Interestingly, and crucially different to the environment of individual clinical analysis is that these fantasies are played out on a global scale as shared anxieties, hopes, frustrations and fears.
>
> (Hockley, 2007: 114–115)

Turner's 'liminoid' phenomena not only combine uniqueness and commonality but also possess a curious combination of connectedness and isolation. The viewers/ritual participants are separated yet they are united by the information they internalise and the entertainment they consume. Such a split is characteristic of the entire postmodern culture and makes the ideal playground for the trickster who thrives in 'liminoid' areas: mass media, the internet, cinema, music, dance and club culture, sports, etc. If the 'liminal' trickster is the trickster selected and controlled by the law-giving part of the community, the 'liminoid' trickster is picked by the individual consumer. However, the 'mass participation', ludic character of the trickster remains intact because liminoid phenomena are still determined by popular choice. Mass entertainment is not about high quality content – it is about mid-and-lowbrow but highly consumable products. This perfectly reflects the *a priori* anti-intellectualism and a-intellectualism of the trickster.

Tricksters in contemporary trickster film mirror society's 'liminoidness' and even more – they embody it. They are born out of individual curiosity and individual rebellion, fed on media and cinema; they use technology to play tricks on people. Cinematic tricksters often live inside the cracks of information society, along communication barriers and psychological borders between people unthinkable in communal living but prevalent in an individualistic society with its family breakdown and reliance on technological means of contact rather than direct physical and emotional connection. They utilise the media's zombifying and soul-collecting talents for their own (malicious, misguided, well-intended, mischievous) purposes.

'Somebody to Love'

One of the principal issues the protagonist of the trickster film faces is the inability to connect with his fellow human beings. Urban lifestyle, because it places much value on individual survival and relies on technological means of communication, does not exactly promote friendship, trust and communal effort. Urban relationships, Georg Simmel argues, are shaped by the market economy. His assessment of the urban psyche influenced by the economic forces of industrial modernity was written in 1903, but is still perfectly applicable to post-industrial lifestyle. Productivity and professionalism are placed above all things impulsive, emotional, 'close'. 'To connect' means to connect on the superficial level, keeping a safe distance from 'the stranger'. Emotional life is squeezed into the frame of the fast-paced, hyper-efficient lifestyle. Simmel writes in *The Metropolis and Mental Life*:

> The metropolis has always been the seat of the money economy. Here the multiplicity and concentration of economic exchange gives an importance to the means of exchange which the scantiness of rural commerce would not have allowed. Money economy and the dominance of the intellect are intrinsically connected. They share a

matter-of-fact attitude in dealing with men and with things; and, in this attitude, a formal justice is often coupled with an inconsiderate hardness. The intellectually sophisticated person is indifferent to all genuine individuality, because relationships and reactions result from it which cannot be exhausted with logical operations. In the same manner, the individuality of phenomena is not commensurate with the pecuniary principle. Money is concerned only with what is common to all: it asks for the exchange value, it reduces all quality and individuality to the question: How much? All intimate emotional relations between persons are founded in their individuality, whereas in rational relations man is reckoned with like a number, like an element which is in itself indifferent. Only the objective measurable achievement is of interest. [. . .] In the sphere of the economic psychology of the small group it is of importance that under primitive conditions production serves the customer who orders the good, so that the producer and the consumer are acquainted. The modern metropolis, however, is supplied almost entirely by production for the market, that is, for entirely unknown purchasers who never personally enter the producer's actual field of vision. Through this anonymity the interests of each party acquire an unmerciful matter-of-factness; and the intellectually calculating economic egoisms of both parties need not fear any deflection because of the imponderables of personal relationships.

(Schwartz and Przyblyski, 2004: 52)

The urban professional has no time for cultivating friendships and relationships. As a result, they tend to be sporadic, non-linear and predominantly work-based. In the city, the liminal is not incorporated into everyday life in the form of a ritual; instead, it is pushed onto the outskirts of existence – organised crime, mass action, mass panics. People tend to 'connect' and 'join' in a hysterical, sudden, uncontrollable rather than 'natural' way. Loneliness, which stems from the chronic professionalisation of relationships, is a companion of the cosmopolitan individual. This lack of continuity, this sporadic and disorganised character of personal life, inevitably give birth to the trickster. Simmel's 'unmerciful matter-of-factness', try as it might, does not eliminate the emotional impulse within. It can only hope to disguise it. The merciless impulse breaks free, often choosing the most inappropriate moment for its escape.

Liminal

The Cable Guy (1996)

Ben Stiller's *The Cable Guy*, an often misunderstood comedy, explores the issues of urban isolation and 'stranger danger'. The film's protagonist is Steven Kovacs, a nice and polite town planning consultant, who is suddenly faced with loneliness after being left by his girlfriend. 'The trickster trigger' –

the failure of Steven's relationship with Robin (Leslie Mann) – is left outside the narrative's frame and the film starts with Steven's arrival into a new flat. Television in the flat is not working properly, and he has to call a cable guy. In fact, the arrival of the Cable Guy is a loose parody of Hitchcock's *Psycho* (1960) which has since then become commonplace in the horror film genre. Steven, who has been waiting for the Cable Guy for four hours, is taking a shower when his door buzzer goes mad. As Steven is the focaliser, the camera is *inside* the shower, focusing on his head, so the audience has no chance to see what is happening behind the curtain. Showers in contemporary cinema have become metaphors for urban vulnerability and exposure. This initial association, culminating in the birth of the dark trickster, sets the tone for the relationship between Steven and his weird friend. Steven has the double role of the projector and the victim while the trickster is both the aggressor and the betrayed. Similarly to *Anger Management*, Steven's unpalatable aggression is split off into a separate figure, and regarded with both horror and fascination. All the features that Steven does not want to see in himself – rudeness, bad manners, 'porn talk', exhibitionistic virility, extreme emotional openness – are accumulated in Larry-Ricardo. This means that, like Dave Buznik (*Anger Management*), he associates them with 'working class people'.

Despite the initial scare, the cable specialist who arrives to mend Steven's TV is simple-minded, very open and overtly friendly – even clingy. So clingy, in fact, that Steven feels very uncomfortable. His problems with the Cable Guy stem from the latter being totally oblivious to social, cultural and personal boundaries. The man is rough and rude; he does not hide his emotions, speaks loudly, and says stupid jokes such as 'by the way, you might want to put on a bathing suit 'cos you will be channel surfing in no time'. He does not seem to understand that it is inappropriate for a man of his social station to try and befriend someone whose interests and job prospects belong to a higher stratum of society.

But worst of all, the Cable Guy easily crosses the boundary (almost sacred in post-industrial societies) between the personal and the professional, by engaging into 'personal talk' with Steven. He intrudes into Steve's privacy when he guesses, creepy-detective style that 'your lady kicked you out. [. . .] Smells like heartbreak to me'. To this Steve, who feels uncomfortable about the stranger meddling with his affairs, replies: 'I really don't want to discuss it with you. Would you just install my cable, please?' The intruder is 'the other' (in this case, primarily the social other) who behaves unpredictably, is psychically threatening, makes semi-sexual remarks and deliberately toys with phallic symbolism (he dramatically inserts a very long drill bit into the drill chuck, and then tenderly strokes the wall looking for a perfect place to insert his tool). When Larry-Ricardo is in the room, Steven instinctively draws the folds of his bathrobe close together to make sure that no parts of his body are showing.

Stranger danger

Unlike in small communities where people know each other, everyone is a stranger in the city. Everyone is potentially dangerous and viewed with suspicion. In the fast-paced environment there is no time to develop any considerable trust. The Cable Guy is the perfect embodiment of the 'stranger danger' phenomenon. In his review of the film, Richard Schickel writes:

> He will organize a merry game of 'porno password' with your parents, supply you with a prostitute when you're horny, beat up a rival trying to make time with your estranged girlfriend. Beware the cable guy bearing gifts. Indeed, beware anyone emerging out of the hostile anonymity of modern city life who is too anxious to assuage your anomie. If bitter experience has taught our paranoia anything, it's that excesses of accommodation are all too often aggression's most winsome disguise.
>
> (*Time*, 17 June 1996)

The Cable Guy is the protagonist's shadow, and, as such, simply mirrors the principal features of the middle-class professional. His loneliness only reflects the loneliness of the antagonist whose personal life is a failure, and who lives on his own. Ideally, Steven would like to deny his despondency – or the fact that it serves as a basis for his 'similarity' to the Cable Guy. The only level on which these two representatives of the middle and working class are equal is emotional. But emotions are downplayed in the metropolitan lifestyle: suppressed, forgotten, lost, replaced and sublimated. The theme of *doppelganger* in *The Cable Guy* is intertwined with the theme of urban disconnectedness, suspicion, and the tragic impossibility of genuine human understanding.

Comedic and simplified as this narrative is, it nevertheless makes all the correct psychological 'moves'. The scriptwriter Lou Holtz Jr. traces the roots of brokenness of the metropolitan individual to childhood and relationships within the family. Chip-Larry-Ricardo's family is dysfunctional. He does not have a father, and his mother (who, supposedly, worked as a prostitute) left him for hours on end planted in front of the TV. As a result of this 'television parenting' Larry-Ricardo failed to develop a perceptible sense of identity, instead imbibing images of various celebrities, TV personalities and cartoon characters. As a shadow of the urban dweller, he demonstrates the personality-destroying consequences of psychological dependency on the media.

The Cable Guy's 'TV parenting' can also be read as a metaphor for the postmodern 'lack of base'. On the allegorical level, Larry-Ricardo is the postmodern condition personified: demonstrating multiple personalities, displaying lack of stable identity, and suffering from a perceptible lack of trust in the outside world. Moreover, what on the allegorical level looks 'postmodern', on the 'personal' level transmogrifies into tendencies usually associated with borderline personality disorder: the Cable Guy fluctuates between hyperbolised agreeableness on the one hand, and uncontrollable aggression on the other; between closeness and distance; between desire to please and desire to kill. He is lonely and sees the world in fragments – or, rather, in media instalments. Surrounded by disjointed images, he is pining for some kind of emotional connection. His lack of stable core, the lack of a firm vision of the world can be traced back to his 'parentlessness' (the postmodern 'absence of God'). In fact, the emotional connection becomes for the Cable Guy the metaphor for personal wholeness; a semi-religious pursuit for the self. In the media-created world of disconnected images, phrases, jokes, pictures, fake emotions and make-believe tears, he wants a genuine friendship. The desire for 'genuineness' is what makes him cross the line between personal and professional, legal and illegal, love and hate.

It is not surprising, then, that this personification of the 'postmodern condition' becomes the trickster in the life of the urban professional. It also natural that 'the postmodern trickster' is put in charge of the technology that connects the contemporary individual to the outside world, and to other individuals. Television is paradoxical in that it is both the destroyer of 'wholeness' and the potential healer of 'the split'. On the one hand, it is an 'unreal' space where floating fragments of someone else's experiences and fictional narratives bump into each other without ever constructing a coherent picture of the world. It is a space filled up with endless invariants of the 'truth'. There is no 'reality' – only a subjective, unverifiable version of it. As Jean Baudrillard famously argued in his essay *The Gulf War: Is It Really Taking Place?*:

Just as the physical or the screen of the psyche transforms every illness into a symptom (there is no organic illness which does not find its meaning elsewhere, in an interpretation of the ailment on another level: all the symptoms pass through a sort of black box in which the psychic images are jumbled and inverted, the illness becomes reversible, ungraspable, escaping any form of realistic medicine), so war, when it has been turned into information, ceases to be a realistic war and becomes a virtual war, in some way symptomatic. And just as everything psychical becomes the object of interminable speculation, so everything which is turned into information becomes the object of endless speculation, the site of total uncertainty. We are left with the symptomatic reading on our screens of the effects of the war, or the effects of discourse about the war, or completely speculative strategic evaluations which are analogous to those evaluations of opinion provided by polls.

(Malpas, 2001: 64)

On the other hand, television is a liminal 'space' without boundaries, a space where groups of lonely, separated urban individuals (deeply suspicious of each other) are united by the fact that they receive, and process, the same information. Within this space the individuals are grouped according to their interests and hobbies. They are involved in the same narratives. Information as a 'common base' is, of course, a dangerous concept because this is when the fragmenting and uniting trickster can easily turn into the collective shadow. In this sense, diversity (destabilising as it is) is better than mass psychological influence.

Steven Kovacs is plagued by the relationships issues characteristic of the postmodern condition: the 'I need more space' slogan which his girlfriend puts forward when he proposes to her (read: moves too close and makes her feel uncomfortable), loneliness, fear of strangers, and the necessity to create and guard a clean, highly-strung outer image (or Jungian persona). This is a very fruitful field for the trickster. As Bauman writes in his assessment of the problems that arise from contemporary individualism, personal freedom does not always automatically lead to successful self-exploration (Jungian individuation):

> Though it carries many a trapping of personal autonomy and is conducted under the 'I need more space' slogan, the flight from the 'messiness of real intimacy' is more akin to a herd-like stampede than to an individually conceived and undertaken journey of self-exploration. The secession is hardly ever lonely – the escapees are keen to join the company with other escapees like them, and the standards of the escapee life tend to be as stiff and demanding as those which have been found oppressive in the life left behind; the facility of casual divorce spawns imperatives as inflexible and intractable (and potentially as displeasing) as the wedlock without the escape clause. The sole attraction of the self-chosen exile is the absence of commitments, and particularly long-term commitments of the kind that cramp freedom of movement in a community with its 'messy intimacy'. With commitments replaced by fleeting encounters, the 'until further notice' or 'one night' (or one day) stands, one can delete from calculation the effects which one's action might have on the lives of others.
>
> (Bauman, 2001: 52–53)

The Cable Guy, who exemplifies the 'symptoms' of the postmodern condition, attempts to heal the split by seeking 'connection' with Steven. He is also the organiser of 'liminal events' – such as family gatherings and dance parties which are perfect opportunities for him to demonstrate his entertaining, uniting and boundary-breaking qualities. Larry-Ricardo brings people together – but he also polarises them, challenges them, pushes them over the edge and into the liminal territory. In the karaoke scene party held in Steven's flat, the Cable Guy presides over a group of mismatched, unattractive, unlovable weirdos who gleefully dance, in the famous dreamy-psychedelic sequence, to his rendition of Jefferson Airplane's *Somebody to Love*. Rather fittingly for a shadowy trickster who parasites on metropolitan loneliness, urban disconnectedness and the non-existence of absolute truth, he is singing about the truth that is 'found to be lies', and asking his audience: 'don't you want somebody to love?'.

This musical allusion echoes the frustrated words of Lloyd Christmas in *Dumb and Dumber*: 'You know what I'm sick and tired of, Harry? I'm sick and tired of having to eke my way through life. I'm sick and tired of bein' a nobody. [pause] But most of all – I'm sick and tired of havin' nobody'. These bitter words are a reaction against Harry's diatribe in which he implores his friend not to take risks going to Aspen in pursuit of the beautiful stranger (played by Lauren Holly), but 'to stay here, hunt for jobs, keep saving our money for the wormstore!'. Lloyd pronounces his 'having a nobody' speech with a feeling that crosses the line between comedy and tragedy. For once in his life Lloyd is trying to be proactive, to be brave, to 'make a connection' with the woman he truly likes. The depth of the fool's tragedy, which implies the impotence of the common man against the cruel 'forces of nature', touches Harry, and he replies: 'OK, Lloyd. Aspen it is'. All Lloyd and Harry want is 'somebody to love'.

Listening to the reckless trickster impulse is not always a wise decision. Steven Kovacs's attempt to be open to new experiences and to outreach to others comes back with a vengeance. The karaoke scene becomes the moment when 'the clean' Steven crosses the boundary of 'appropriate' behaviour by sleeping with a prostitute. The urban professional's appeal for love, for understanding, for emotional connection, is refracted through his tricksterish shadow as the purchase of sexual services. His moral 'fall' is presented as a psychedelic sequence, in which close-ups, from a variety of different camera angles, of Carrey pulling faces and rolling on the floor, are interspersed (or rather juxtaposed) with shots of the prostitute massaging Steven's head and performing various other seduction rites. The next morning Larry-Ricardo is trying to assure the shaken Steven that 'she is clean': 'I tried her out last week' – he says – 'and I am as healthy as a horse'.

In yet another scene, Larry-Ricardo pushes the theme of love even further beyond the liminal boundary. He 'steals' Steven's parents. Having arrived at a party in his parents' house with his girlfriend, Steven is baffled to find his enemy there. The Cable Guy wears a bright blue cardigan, very inept in its cosiness, and obviously feels at home in Steven's parents' house. Instead of a nice family gathering, a traditional 'safe haven', the Cable Guy forces the participants (and especially the initiate, Steven) to overstep all kinds of limits. Larry-Ricardo's idea of 'having a good time' consists of taking off the protagonist's 'decent' mask. Thus, Steven's parents learn at the dinner table that their son enjoys watching men 'fight to death' and taking part in violent medieval dress-up shows. Moreover, Larry-Ricardo explains, when overwhelmed by aggression, Steven is capable of forgetting that 'it is just a show', and often recklessly starts chasing his rival wildly wielding an axe.

However, the most problematic boundaries for Steven are incest and open discussion of sex. Knowing this, the Cable Guy organises a game of 'porno password' which involves guessing 'dirty words' from word clues. Steven, who is in his mother's team, struggles to pronounce the words 'vagina' and 'nipple' out loud while no one else in the room seems to have the same trouble. Upon learning that the next password is 'foreskin', Steven cries: 'I can't say that to my mother!' to which his father's reply is: 'She's a grown woman, she can handle it!'. Steven jumps up and refuses to take part in the game, calling the Cable Guy a lunatic and a felon. 'He is projecting all of his anger onto me' – Larry-Ricardo pitifully complains to Robin. The ordeal culminates in Steven punching the Cable Guy in the face upon hearing from him (in whisper) that 'Robin showed me the birthmark on her left shoulder . . . very sexy'. This sudden release of aggression in a middle-class man is conceptually similar to the airplane brawl and the pub quarrel scenes in *Anger Management*.

Unlike Steven, the rest of the participants in the 'porno-password' game seem to view this as light entertainment and harmless fun. 'This is a safe place' – the Cable Guy explains to his victim – 'we are the people who love you'. From the height of Steven's middle-class cleanliness, even his own family, turned by his adversary into a hyper-edgy, porn-discussing madmen, is no longer a safe place. In the communitas created by Larry-Ricardo, Steven's pining for love tends to transmogrify into the desire for dirty fornication, sometimes projected onto the prostitute, sometimes onto his own parents. He is plunged into the atmosphere of Bahktinian carnivalesque, as medieval and indecent as the axe-wielding game. The Cable Guy's password-synecdoches (vagina, penis, foreskin, nipple), representing different sexual body parts, are grotesque images that 'preserve their peculiar nature' and are 'entirely different from ready-made, completed being' (Bakhtin, 1984: 25). Here Bakhtin writes about the emergence of the rational, cleansed, enlightened vision of the body and bodily processes. In contrast to these touched-up, completed, de-trickstered images, the 'originals' look too raw, too rude, too unfinished – not enough human. The ancient images are not 'sterilised' (or, indeed, aesthetically gothicised/romanticised in protest against this 'unnatural cleanliness'), but remain what they are, and crude as they are – sexual act, penis, vagina. These images

> remain ambivalent and contradictory; they are ugly, monstrous, hideous from the point of view of 'classic' aesthetics, that is, the aesthetics of the ready-made and the completed. The new historic sense that penetrates them gives these images a new meaning but keeps intact their traditional

contents: copulation, pregnancy, birth, growth, old age, disintegration, dismemberment. All these in their direct material aspect are the main element in the system of grotesque images. They are contrary to the classic images of the finished, completed man, cleansed, as it were, of all the scoriae of birth and development. [. . .]

Contrary to modern canons, the grotesque body is not separated from the rest of the world. It is not a closed, completed unit; it is unfinished, outgrows itself, transgresses its own limits. The stress is laid on those parts of the body that are open to the outside world, that is, the parts through which the world enters the body or emerges from it, or though which the body itself goes out to meet the world.

(Bakhtin, 1984: 25–26)

The game of porno-password threatens Steven's (non-existent) completeness; or rather – it foregrounds the fragmentedness of his postmodern psyche. Postmodernity did not kill the 'completeness', it only acknowledged modernity's failure to achieve it. It only disclosed the hidden trickster, with its grotesqueness, eternal growth, ambivalence, its 'scoriae of birth and development' and its disturbing fixation on those body parts that bring us into the world; connect us to this world. The trickster – the Cable Guy – does not destroy Steven's world; he merely points out to Steven that it is already in pieces. The loneliness, the absence of 'somebody to love' and the fear of 'dirty words' are somehow magically linked, and form the knot of ecopsychological issues which are prevalent in urban societies. In order to make a connection, one must go back to the basics of human existence and examine one's own place in this world. To make a connection, one must accept one's own incompleteness – one's own humanity. Steven does just that at the end of the film as he finally accepts the part that makes him human – his aggressive, unhappy tricksterish shadow.

Click (2006)

Adam Sandler's character in *Click* (2006), a successful architect Michael Newman (note the 'talking name'), also has problems with acknowledging the existence of emotional life. The scriptwriters Steve Koren and Marc O'Keefe outline Michael's ascent into professional bliss and simultaneous descent into personal hell in a Dickensian dream sequence: tired of his family constantly demanding attention and distracting him from work, he wanders into a department store in search of a 'universal remote control' which would simplify his relationship with numerous home appliances, and falls asleep on a display bed. In his dream, a god-like figure (Christopher Walken) offers him the device he has been searching for, free of charge. Little does Michael know that the helpful magus is Morty, the angel of death. Thus, Michael's obsession with success brings him closer to death instead of improving his life.

Instead of keeping the precious emotional connection with his loved ones, the protagonist opts for 'skipping' whole chapters of his life by pressing various buttons on his magical remote control. Michael skips any events he finds emotionally cumbersome, time-consuming or distracting from work duties – sex, emotional conversations, family gatherings, quality time with his children and parents. He switches his wife Donna (Kate Beckinsale) on and off whenever he wants her to stop arguing with him about his limited involvement in the family affairs. He switches off the noisy kids, speeds up the dog because he does not have time to wait until it finishes its business, and glides over any family rituals such as meals and family fun. Michael deliberately fragments and compartments his own life, making it one-sided, editing out whole chunks of human experience, thus turning himself into an incomplete person. However, he still enjoys his time at work and the rewards that come with professional success, such as contract signings, project pitches and parties. His ultimate aim is to become a partner in his company.

Douglas and Isherwood argue that 'industrialization has complicated life for the consumer. Regarding material goods there are, indeed, more of many things. But to keep up with the exchange of marking services necessary to happiness and necessary to a coherent, intelligible culture, he has to run harder to keep in the same place' (Douglas and Isherwood, 1996: 74). Michael's 'pick and choose' attitude reflects the fragmented character of modern life, but he is misguided in his thinking that he is firmly in control of his destiny. Eventually, the trickster slips out of the cracks and Michael learns that the remote control comes with a catch: after a number of 'skips', it memorises skipped sequences and creates an automatic programme which omits similar sequences in the future. Like any trickster in charge of a fragmented world, the remote control quickly wrestles the power out of the protagonist's hands and turns his life into a never-ending nightmare: whenever Michael wants to slow down and enjoy life, the cunning device flips onto the next chapter. Now his life resembles a truly weird sequence of disconnected experiences, and the remote control speeds on, omitting longer and longer passages of Michael's life, and concentrating primarily on big (ritual) achievements such as promotions. Even when Michael wants to 'remain' inside a moment – such as when he notices that his children have grown up and his daughter's hair is now longer – the device starts ticking like a bomb and whisks him out of the room.

The writers use easily decipherable metaphors for the description of Michael's workaholism: for instance, he cannot remember what happened during a 'skipped' event since his body was on 'autopilot' and he became 'a zombie' – a creature with a body but without a mind (cf. the 'possession by trickster' motif). During a family psychotherapy session, Donna complains to a bearded male therapist that 'Michael is making no effort to connect with me at all'. The therapy session is one of the few family moments which the device has not cut out of Michael's fabric of life. Meanwhile, Michael is very surprised to see 'this big mouth' (the therapist) in front of him. In his case, the therapist is the mediator who provides the substitute connection between him and his wife when the 'original' connection fails due to Michael existing in his 'zombified' state for most of the time. Eventually, Michael is dropped into a 'chapter' where Donna is happily settled with another man, and his teenage kids despise their father. Michael had 'somebody to love' – his family – but lost them to his heroic workaholism. Having failed to heal the split between the two parts of his life – home and work – he is now sent speeding towards his physical and moral demise.

The key to Michael's avoidance of all things emotional is similar to Steven Kovacs's fear of 'dirty metonymies': Michael is terrified of seeing his parents kissing, seeing them in bed or, indeed, expressing any feelings in front of them. His parents (played by Julie Kavner and Henry Winkler) belong to the freedom-loving sixties generation and have no problems with discussing either sex or feelings. Whenever Morty takes his protégé, with the help of the remote control, into 'the past', back into his childhood, Michael get embarrassed about his parents' antics, from kissing and hugging to his father's silly showmanship (he likes to perform simple 'magic' tricks). But the most cringeworthy chapter for Michael is the moment of his own birth – not least because (and quite in line with trickster's obsession with hyper-virile masculinity) Morty mentions that there is no visual difference between baby Michael and a baby girl. This theme (stubbornly recurrent in Sandler's films) provides the psychological base for Michael's workaholism: apparently, he feels so inadequate about the size of his penis that he feels the need to compensate for it with hard work and achievements outside the bedroom.

Similarly to *The Cable Guy*, the theme of incest in *Click* is closely linked to a cluster of ecopsychological issues: loneliness, social isolation, emotional alienation, the gap between personal and professional spheres of life. What Michael, in his heroic endeavour, is trying to deny is that he was born *out of an emotional connection* – the one between his mother and father. He also wants to deny the physical basis of this connection – sex. In repressing the whole issue, he rejects himself as a human being, as a man with feelings. He ought not to have been born. In the scene in which Michael finally appreciates his parents' attitude to life, he runs into their bedroom in the middle of the night and hugs his father. The bedroom is a symbolic place which is psychologically important for Michael precisely because he is trying to deny the trickster. He is trying to forget, to close his eyes on the fact that, to use Bakhtin's expression, the body is open to the world and the world is open to the body. Human beings are not closed (completed, perfect) entities – they are connected to other human beings.

By leaving out all things 'irrational' from his life, Michael speeds up his death. His body, fat and bloated from fast food, is rapidly crumbling; his heart is giving up. Contrary to his wish to control everything in his life, his body becomes grotesque, fat, shapeless, it 'outgrows itself, transgresses its own limits' (Bakhtin, 1984: 26). The ugly, grotesque trickster – the real master of Michael's body – is now bursting out of him. In the scene preceding his final 'wake up' on the display bed in the superstore, Michael dies from a heart attack, having disconnected himself from a life-supporting machine at the hospital. The metaphor of the heart (pitched in the film against the extended 'head' trope) comes to life the moment Michael dies surrounded by his family. The hero's death, trickster-style, is collated with his 'rebirth' when he finally rouses from his nightmare, this time intending to make his life more comprehensive; and include feelings and humanity into it.

The trickster, in the form of a technological device, is both the protagonist's destroyer and the healer of the split. The remote control drags the lifestyle problems of the protagonist to the surface of his life; it symbolises both his unstoppable ambition and his dysfunctional lifestyle. Initially, the device gives him choice – a lot of choice. The ability to choose, to build and rebuild one's identity from scratch from millions of lifestyle fragments and endless variants; the opportunity to pick and choose TV channels, clothes, furniture, holidays, houses, provides a sense of false safety, a false sense of being in control. The consumer culture creates a wonderful illusion that it is us, consumers, who build our own lives. In the godless postmodern world the ability to choose becomes godlike; consumers become their own gods. It is for this sacred choice, for the illusion of control that Michael Newman is working so hard. As he explains to his wife, he neglects his family *now* in order to be on top *later*. He is chasing this promotion because he wants to be top dog as soon as possible. He works in order to gain even more choice and pass it on to his children.

Michael Newman's god, however, turns out to be the angel of death, and instead of widening his range of life choices, he narrows it to the point when Michael has no time or space left in which to live. The remote control celebrates speed at the expense of emotional connection. The trickster, who personifies psychological fluidity and identity confusion, drags the protagonist through hell in order to show to him that the wholeness, and the sense of control he has been seeking all this time, are to be found in connecting with others, in keeping alive the precious emotional links, and not in the fast living and endless customisation of lifestyle.

New Ways of Connecting and Disconnecting

Family ties and communal hierarchy are not the only ways of making people feel 'needed' and 'attached'. In fact, they often tie people down and make them feel trapped. The natural community, Bauman reminds us in *Community: Seeking Safety in an Insecure World* (2001), is not always friendly. There is a big difference between the community of our dreams and 'the really existing community', 'a collectivity which pretends to be community incarnate, the dream fulfilled, and (in the name of all the goodness such community is assumed to offer) demands unconditional loyalty and treats everything short of such loyalty as an act of unforgivable treason' (Bauman, 2001: 4). The really existing community, Bauman continues using a series of expressive metaphors,

> were we to find ourselves in its grasp, would demand stern obedience in exchange for the services it renders or promises to render. Do you want security? Give up your freedom, or at least a good chunk of it. Do you want confidence? Do not trust anybody outside the community. Do you want mutual understanding? Don't speak to foreigners nor use foreign languages. Do you want this cosy home feeling? Fix alarms on your door and TV cameras on your drive [. . .]
> There is a price to be paid for the privilege of 'being in a community' – and it is inoffensive or even invisible only as long as the community stays in the dream. The price is paid in the currency of freedom, variously called 'autonomy', 'right to self-assertion', 'right to be yourself'. Whatever you choose, you gain some and lose some.
>
> (2001: 4)

Nowadays, Bauman reminds us, the distinction between 'us' and 'them', once based on geography and other natural bases of 'sameness', has become obsolete:

> Distance, once the most formidable among the communal defences, lost much of its significance. The mortal blow to 'naturalness' of communal understanding was delivered, however, with advent of informatics: the emancipation of the flow of information from the transport of the bodies. Once information could travel independently of its carriers, and with a speed far beyond the capacity of even the most advanced means of transportation (as in the kind of society we all nowadays inhabit), the boundary between 'inside' and 'outside' could no longer be drawn, let alone sustained.
>
> (2001: 14)

The absence of the boundary between the 'inside' and the 'outside' can be regarded as a positive or as a negative thing – depending on one's view of the trickster (and especially postmodernity as the fluid 'era of the trickster'). One view – the negative – is that media and technology, by uniting lonely urban individuals, is ever in danger of creating a terrifying collective shadow which will be ready to soak up any information and perform any tasks ordered by its hypnotisers. As media speeds up the spread of information, it also hastens the influence of this information on the minds of viewers and listeners. Instead of linking up separated individuals – putting them in touch with each other without impairing their independent thinking or interfering into their lives – the media merges them together, forces them to think identically, makes them purchase products they do not need, makes them believe in harmful ideologies, sells them policies such as military invasions. 'The bad' media trickster (the media shadow, in fact) also turns people into TV zombies and gluttonous victims of unabashed commercialism. Jack Nicholson's Joker in *Batman* (1989) and Carrey's mad scientist type Dr. Nygma in *Batman Forever* (1995) are examples of pernicious control-freaks – the first a hyperbolical, gothicised metaphor of capitalist greed, the second a parody of out-of-control, madcap scientific rationality.

Read this

The other view – positive – affirms the beneficial effects of technology as a connecting medium. It praises its ability to create and sustain made-to-measure communities, transcend geographical distances and – most importantly – its democratic nature. The trickster of technology transcends physical and virtual boundaries in order to make information accessible to anyone who wants it. This elation is counterbalanced with concerns about the moral, ethical, political and economic consequences of the freedom of information movement, as exemplified by the controversy surrounding trickster media projects such as WikiLeaks whose aim is to blow up conspiracies, and to unearth and reveal documents hidden from public view. Information – even classified – is still immaterial; in the hands of a skilful hacker it can escape the file (cf. 'the trapped trickster' motif) and spread itself throughout the world with potentially unpredictable effects. In either case, the 'connecting' abilities of the trickster principle are inseparable from its destructive qualities because it does not, and cannot, have a fixed moral stance beyond its love of freedom and hatred of restrictions.

Batman (1989), Batman Returns (1992) and Batman Forever (1995)

Batman narratives, as modern myths (narratively generalised yet psychologically viable and truthfully reflecting the state of society's psyche), mirror the core conflict of the capitalist economy, the economic 'trickster split': how does one maximise one's profits without exploiting human resources and causing environmental damage? During the course of Burton's film (and most Batman narratives), the Joker crosses the boundary between the world of crime and the world of politics, and 'goes legitimate' by taking over the city's businesses, thus gaining political power. The 'legitimised' trickster, the one who manages to cross the line between latency and consciousness, prohibition and influence, becomes the collective shadow. In transgressing this boundary, he loses his human face and human name (Jack Napier) and becomes the Joker.

The Joker's ascent to the surface of society is relatively straightforward. After killing his boss, Carl Grissom, he becomes the ruler of the city's chemical empire. Starting off as the outcast, he ends up controlling the minds of the inhabitants of Gotham city by employing various methods of persuasion, from fear to commercial advertising and free public entertainments. The Joker, whose face had been ripped open by a bullet, corroded by acid, and rebuilt by a back-street surgeon, is brokenness personified. His face is the perfect metaphor of the forcibly-smiling persona of the average Gothamite – putting on a brave face but, deep down, depressed and unhappy. The Joker even (badly) composes a quatrain for Vicki Vale (Kim Basinger) about this state of the urban psyche. He calls it 'laughing on the outside' while 'really crying' inside. The smile is terrifying; the smile is suicidal. This is the smile of loneliness.

The Joker represents the hidden brokenness of society which gradually seeps to the surface, dissolving any solid structures that impede its progress. The type of business he runs – the chemical industry – suits him as a trickster because it allows him to dissolve borders, alter bodies and create new objects from fragments and parts. His business reflects the fluidity of the trickster – and the instability of the psyche, artificially (and heroically) stabilised by consciousness with the help of science and rationality.

The Joker 'unpicks' the stitches that hold the social skin together and lets the demons run loose. Eventually, his mangled face starts to become visible through what used to be a civilisation. Metaphorically, the disintegration of society is shown in the screenplay via the idea of 'chemical disintegration' as the Joker alters chemical formulae of the cosmetic products his plant produces to make certain combinations of products mortally dangerous. When using them, people die 'laughing'. The 'laughing death' (read: the ultimate failure of the individual to keep his mask firmly in place and his persona intact) becomes a pandemic but, fortunately, Batman (Michael Keaton) arrives to save the city from the mortal combination of consumerism, exploitative capitalism and devastating loneliness.

Batman is the perfect hero for this task – he is both a business owner and a lonely introvert hiding in his dark tower from 'the messiness' of relationships and the complications that come with emotional connections. The 'dark castle on the hill' is Burton's favourite image for rendering the dark individualism of postmodernity. Batman consistently fails in his relationships with women – Vicki Vale in *Batman*, Selina Kyle (Michelle Pfeiffer) in *Batman Returns* (1992), even though they have identity problems similar to his own, and therefore are able to understand his convoluted, fragmented psyche.

Bruce Wayne is a thriving businessman during the day and the hero Batman fighting with the 'dark side of capitalism' (read: with his 'other' self) at night. During the day, Selina Kyle is a meek secretary but, when the night falls, she becomes a formidable female fighter – the Catwoman. Even the fact that, as Bruce Wayne puts it to Selina in the failed bedroom scene, they are the same – 'split right down the centre', their connection collapses after an intense and promising start. They fight the same enemies – the corrupted mayor and his pet monster the Penguin Man – yet fail to join forces and continue fighting on their own. Even their costumes, which, typically for Burton's visual aesthetics, are black and made from pieces (Selina's is roughly sewn together), emphasise the state of their disjointed psyche. Selina is also physically broken after being pushed by Max Schreck from the window of his company's building. Both Bruce and Selina are physically fragile and psychologically broken; both are 'incomplete' subjects, ridden with pain, and seeking completeness in each other.

However, being 'split down the centre' is not a durable relationships base as it places the emphasis on individual differences, and not on the unity. As Zygmunt Bauman writes, once we become concerned with our identities and the numerous guises they are capable of taking, we must give up the 'paradisiacal' psychological wholeness:

> people engaged in identity battles fear ultimate victory more than a string of defeats. The construction of identity is a never-ending and forever incomplete process, and must remain such to deliver on its promise (or, more precisely, to keep the promise of delivery credible). In the life politics wrapped around the struggle for identity, self-creation and self-assertion are the main stakes, and freedom to choose is simultaneously the principal weapon and the most coveted prize. To avoid this eventuality, identity must stay *flexible* and always amenable to further experimentation and change; it must be a truly 'until further notice' kind of identity.
>
> (Bauman, 2001: 64)

Batman's enemies tend to be metaphorical representations of the key aspects of modernity: economy and politics. The Joker, with his ability to erode bodies and souls, is meaningless consumption personified. While he is 'the other' face of the industry, the Penguin (Danny DeVito) is the hidden ugly face of politics. The bird-looking creature behind the Mayor of Gotham is aggressive, crude, ruthless, has an insatiable appetite for power and does not see anything beyond his own public achievements. His acute anger and ambition comes from a sense of abandonment and the hunger for love (he was left by his parents in the sewer, and adopted by an underground penguin colony). Crude as this metaphor is, it traces the moving force behind the politician's ambition back to personal issues, and not to some abstract and idealistic desire 'to do public good'. Modern politics is false, the Penguin narrative implies, because it is about filling your own psychological void, and about vanity, rather than improving the lives of 'the little people'. In fact, in *Batman Returns* the 'little people', far from benefiting from the political process, become the vehicle for the realisation of the Mayor's personal dreams of unlimited power.

Dr. Edward Nygma in *Batman Forever* (directed by Joel Schumacher; produced by Tim Burton) is the villain who represents scientific rationality, or rather its shadow – scientific irrationality. He works as a researcher in Bruce Wayne's business, 'Wayne Enterprises'. Typical for a trickster, in his shadowy guise Dr. Nygma adopts another name – the Riddler, because his stalking techniques include leaving scary riddles for their victims to solve. When his invention, a device which allows him to beam television directly into people's brains, steal their intelligence and control their minds, is rejected by his employer, he becomes a criminal associate of Two-Face, the evil *doppelganger* of the former district attorney, Harvey Dent.

Nygma/the Riddler is an archetypal 'mad scientist', a figure that has always been the Gothic 'flagman' of modernity promoting both the drawbacks and benefits of progress and science. The scientist has been the favoured subject of arts and literature since the beginning of the nineteenth century when the ecopsychological effects of the first wave of the Industrial Revolution became apparent.

Traditionally, mad scientist narratives, such as Mary Shelley's *Franken-stein* (1818), Nathaniel Hawthorne's *The Birthmark* (1846) and H. G. Wells's *The Island of Dr. Moreau* (1896), carry the Romantic/decadent message about the dangers of scientific hubris. Their message defies the Enlightenment faith in the invincibility of scientific rationality. The 'mad scientist' narrative disputes science's ability to replace God and govern the world in a logical way. Far from transforming the world in a positive manner, and making life better for everyone, doctors and scientists are depicted as madmen, sadists, vivisectionists, or simply people obsessed with 'conquering nature'. In their pursuit to rival God and replace the natural law with their scientific artifices they forget about the limitations of their own humanity, and, by way of retribution, go insane. Scientists in such narratives are traditionally lonely people as their frame of mind does not allow them to 'connect' with others. For instance, Victor Frankenstein abandons his family and beloved for the sake of his intellectual pursuits, and subsequently ends up losing them all to his evil creation – the Monster. In fact, he can be singled out as 'the first geek' of the Western culture who puts his ability to create virtual worlds and make virtual monsters above the community, physicality and 'the messiness of relationships'.

The most typical type of 'mad scientist' in contemporary cinematic and literary narratives is 'the geek'. The Oxford Dictionary defines the word 'geek' as 'a simpleton, a dupe; a person who is socially inept or boringly conventional or studious; *spec.* an assistant at a sideshow whose purpose is to appear as an object of disgust or derision' while 'geeky' means 'socially inept, boringly conventional or studious; strange, odd'. The word has its origin in the dialect word *geck*, meaning fool (*The Concise Oxford English Dictionary*, 1995, 9th Edition). The origin and contemporary connotation of the word taps into the idea of the scientist as a trickster – asocial and marginalised, but now also holding the key to the world's secrets in his hands. The 'geek' sits on the extreme end of Western individualism, being, in a way, its ultimate goal, its purest realisation. The geek is the one who does not accept the rules of the game and creates his own.

Dr. Nygma, the unlikeable and lonely geek who considers himself mis-understood and rejected, is longing for acceptance. His inability to connect in the 'natural' way (reflecting the individualisation and intellectualisation of the Western individual) gives birth to the monstrous idea of joining the minds of Gotham inhabitants via television (an apt but predictable metaphor for media addiction). Like the Joker, Nygma, with his multiple personalities, embodies psychological fragmentation. In the scene in which the embittered doctor transforms into a monster (the scientist-monster being the traditional dynamic of 'mad scientist' narratives), he is sitting in front of his computer changing his picture, trying out bodies, guises, clothes and names (Puzzler, Gamester, Captain Kill). His mercurial on-screen image represents both the 'consumerist' aspect of today's identity-shopping and the drama of psychological incompleteness. To reiterate Jameson's ideas, schizophrenia, which looked so tragically-fresh and gloomily-innovative in modernity, has now become the founding part of the culture.

Like the Joker and his 'chemical' advertising, the Riddler embodies the dark side of technology. Nygma's invention removes all physical boun-daries between himself and the audience, and, like the Jinni who has escaped from the bottle, his 'mad energy' is not easy to stop. Leaving the broken trickster in charge of 'the switch' puts in danger the entire Gotham community. The Riddler simply takes the idea of shared information to its extreme – mass mind control.

Retaining the trickster's fluid, playful, mercurial nature, the metropolitan shadows in the Batman trio gather their victims together to participate in mass-hypnotising projective-introjective exchanges. Speaking metaphori-cally, the media, with its transformative potential, ideological adjustability and political flexibility is a trickster who can lure and trap lost subjects seeking some 'wholesome meaning' in an increasingly fragmenting world. All they get from the Riddler and the Joker, however, is a promise of fake meaning, a set of riddles consisting of disjointed film quotes, sports reportage parodies, quiz show spoofs, creepy ads and soap lines. Whereas the trickster advocates a return to 'nature', the metropolitan shadow uses progress to keep individuals lost and isolated.

The World According to Geek

In his book *Jung and the Postmodern: The Interpretation of Realities*, Christopher Hauke argues that, relationship-wise, postmodernity is moving the individual in two contradictory directions: on the one hand, we are brought together by technology, television and advertising but, on the other, we are far from being a homogenous society:

> With the electronic shrinking of world space arises the paradox that, on the one hand, humanity suffers mass homogenisation (where the international ownership of PCs emerges as no different to the 'internationalism' of Coca Cola in every fridge), while, on the other hand, there open up opportunities for communications on a scale hitherto undreamed of. [. . .] There is a thrust in the opposite direction to that of homogenisation – the restoration of the individual subject, of difference and of plurality. (This is not a new position, or contradiction, either, as I believe we may detect parallel contradictory effects that arose from the technologies of earlier eras such as the railways and the telephone). It is in this sense that the postmodern is more a *phrase of the modern* that emerges from time to time, rather than a discrete 'stage' of some linear, developmental process.
>
> (Hauke, 2000: 73–74)

This statement supports our argument that the trickster principle is both the destroyer and creator of relationships. Yes, he thrives on disconnection – but he also provides new 'urban' ways of connecting. The 'geek' is in charge of the internet (which is the conceptual equivalent of the Cable Guy being in charge of television). As Sacha Baron-Cohen's character Brüno, a (rather impossible) gay fashion icon, explains in his fashion show *Funkyzeit*, autism is 'cool' because 'it is so funny'.

Recently there have been positive, even endearing, presentations of the geek type in Hollywood cinema, most notably in *Adam* (written and directed by Max Mayer, 2009) and in the biopic *The Social Network* (directed by David Fincher, 2010). The protagonist of *Adam* (played by Hugh Dancy) is a lonely young man with Asperger's Syndrome who works as an electronics engineer for a toy manufacturing company. *The Social Network*, rather bravely, places at the heart of the narrative Mark Zuckerberg, the founder and developer of Facebook.

The most widespread interpretation of the word 'geek' today is a computer addict – a person who shuns the society of fellow human beings and prefers instead to communicate with the heartless machine. The geek of today is an Asperger's Syndrome sufferer. He has difficulties relating to people emotionally, reading nonverbal signs, and recognising the listener's feelings and reactions. He is socially awkward and may appear as rude or uncaring. In other words, he fails to 'get' the accepted rules of social interaction – those 'objective' rules which everyone is supposed to know, which are implanted in the *habitus*, and into which human beings sharing the same culture are supposed to 'tap' automatically, subconsciously. It is normal to seek the company of your fellow human beings, and is not normal to reject the beautiful 'messiness of relationships' in favour of the psychological safety and stability of human–machine interaction. In not recognising the rules, in rejecting, albeit involuntarily, the 'norms' of social behaviour, the geek acts as a trickster refusing to accept the existence of some objective ('unbroken') social reality; an objective, prescribed inter-action scheme mapped out by some 'god' (who is dead).

Moreover, in his 'hacker' incarnation, and using the mercurial qualities of the internet, the geek also breaks into computers and computer net-works, thus failing to recognise, alongside the common sense of emotional interaction, the legislative and regulatory structure of society. In doing so, and in crossing virtual borders, they become criminals who should be punished like any other law-breakers. There is even now a new form of social protest – *hacktivism* – which presupposes using one's knowledge of technology for the purpose of obtaining and publicising information concealed from the general public by those 'in power' (businesses, govern-ment organisations).

The hacker is often depicted by those whose power he undermines as an evil trickster – or the evil shadow of the overall law-abiding community of internet users. He is an invisible, unnatural, elusive, unattractive, semi-transparent from lack of fresh air and exercise, people-hating creature (rather like Carrey's Dr. Nygma). For instance, the journalist and editor Tunku Varadarajan calls Julian Assange, the founder of WikiLeaks (the website that illegally publishes classified documents and videos, including U.S. Embassy cables and Iraq military videos), 'a nihilistic leaker-hacker dude, a rootless subverter of international public order':

> With his bloodless, sallow face, his lank hair drained of all color, his languorous, very un-Australian limbs, and his aura of blinding pallor that appears to admit no nuance, Assange looks every inch the amoral, uber-nerd villain, icily detached from the real world of moral choices in which the rest of us saps live. Call him the Unaleaker, with apologies to the victims of Ted Kaczynski.
>
> Assange is the founder and prime mover of WikiLeaks, a shadowy, show-offy little outfit that last week unloaded into the public domain vast quantities of classified American military intelligence stolen from the vaults of the war in Afghanistan. And in doing so, Assange, who expresses his credo in repeated, almost catechistic condemnations of American "war crimes" and in a naked disdain for capitalism, appointed himself to the role of anti-establishment truth-seeker. He is the

insurgent-in-chief, waging ascetic, selfless combat against warmonger-criminals in the White House and the Pentagon. [. . .]

But watching Assange wallow in the attention that has followed his voluminous data dump, one is struck by his strut, his hubris, his palpable vainglory. 'I enjoy crushing bastards,' he crowed to Der Spiegel, one of the publications favored with the right to publish his dubiously acquired material. 'The most dangerous men are those who are in charge of war,' he harrumphed. 'And they need to be stopped.'

('What Does Assange Want?', *The Daily Beast*, 28 July 2010)

'What Does Assange Want?' the journalist and former editor of *The Wall Street Journal* proceeds to ask in his geek-bashing article, and fails to come to a definitive conclusion. Little does he know that there is no point in asking the trickster about the rational foundations of his rebellion. His rebellion is against the system; against its rigidity and unfairness. It is not *for* – it is *against*.

Even Assange's sabotage activities are allegorised in the media in terms of cataclysmic trickster explosions, as unstoppable releases of underground contents. For instance, Robert Booth and Haroon Siddique write in *The Guardian* regarding the WikiLeaks disclosure of U.S. Embassy cables:

Shortly before 6.30pm on Sunday night, the first cracks appeared in the dam. The largest ever leak of US government classified documents streamed out online, revealing never publicly seen details about Iran, North Korea, Afghanistan and Russia.

Throughout the week the stream became a torrent of information about how US diplomats and foreign governments see the world. According to these classified cables, Saudi Arabia wanted Washington to bomb Iran, the UK harbours 'deep concerns about the safety and security of Pakistan's nuclear weapons', and Russia is considered a 'virtual mafia state' with its president, Vladimir Putin, accused of amassing 'illicit proceeds' from his time in office.

(*The Guardian*, 4 December 2010)

The geek is still a marginal creature in Western culture, but, as Steve Silberman writes in *Wired*, he (for they are primarily, but not exceptionally, male) is moving to the accepted side of the marginal because of the widespread nature of the phenomenon:

Nick is building a universe on his computer. He's already mapped out his first planet: an anvil-shaped world called Denthaim that is home to gnomes and gods, along with a three-gendered race known as *kiman*. As he tells me about his universe, Nick looks up at the ceiling, humming fragments of a melody over and over. 'I'm thinking of making magic a form of quantum physics, but I haven't decided yet, actually,' he explains. The music of his speech is pitched high, alternately poetic and pedantic – as if the soul of an Oxford don has been awkwardly reincarnated in the body of a chubby, rosy-cheeked boy from Silicon Valley. Nick is 11 years old.

Nick's father is a software engineer, and his mother is a computer programmer. They've known that Nick was an unusual child for a long time. He's infatuated with fantasy novels, but he has a hard time reading people. Clearly bright and imaginative, he has no friends his own age. His inability to pick up on hidden agendas makes him easy prey to certain cruelties, as when some kids paid him a few dollars to wear a ridiculous outfit to school. [. . .]

Even when very young, these children become obsessed with order, arranging their toys in a regimented fashion on the floor and flying into tantrums when their routines are disturbed. As teenagers, they're prone to getting into trouble with teachers and other figures of authority, partly because the subtle cues that define societal hierarchies are invisible to them.

(*Wired*, 9 December 2001)

On the one hand, Silberman accentuates the geek's resistance to authority, propensity towards civil disobedience and desire to create 'alternative worlds' which are different from the complex reality which is considered 'objective' by the majority. On the other, the author accentuates the majority's reaction to the unusual child: some kids see a source of entertainment in him, asking him to wear ridiculous outfits in public. One can even draw tentative parallels between the children's reaction to 'the fool' and medieval public entertainments. This parallel is probably archetypally correct since it describes the opposition between 'sameness' and 'otherness' which forms the basis of social interaction. The trickster principle is non-cooperative, and hence socially unacceptable and even dangerous. For the safety and stability of society it must be devalued – destroyed, ridiculed, dismantled, and repressed.

The Social Network (2010)

The Social Network is a brilliant example of the 'geek as a trickster' theme as it peddles all the perennial trickster issues: social rebellion, marginality and destructive behaviour towards any structures, rules and schemes. Aaron Sorkin's screenplay is adapted from Ben Mezrich's book *Accidental Billionaires: The Founding of Facebook, A Tale of Sex, Money, Genius, and Betrayal* (2009). The film, rather unusually, presents the geek as the winner in the social game, having collected a number of socially acclaimed prizes, from financial success to world-wide fame. The geek is the new hero, but his quest mostly happens in the privacy of his room, inside his head – and inside his computer.

Jesse Eisenberg, who portrays Zuckerberg, brilliantly conveys the protagonist's introverted traits: he rarely looks directly into the camera or at other characters, his reactions are crude, abrupt and unpredictable, and his statements are often insensitive or offensive. The film opens with a scene in which the protagonist gets dumped by his girlfriend Erica for being too arrogant and ambitious in the 'wrong way'. Mark wants to get access to the elite Harvard male clubs but his chances, as a non-pedigree nerd, are minuscule. The establishing scene characterises him as a difficult, socially inept, immature male.

The parallel sequence that follows the 'dumping scene' is significant from the narrative point of view as it shows the basic split between the two planes of the narrative (and two planes of Mark's life): the objective and the virtual. Mark goes to his student room, gets drunk and writes a nasty blog rant about Erica, including the claim that her breasts look like 34C while the actual size is 34B which she enhances with the help of 'her friends from Victoria's Secret'. Then he gets an inspiration to hack into the databases of student residence halls, and collect the information and pictures of the female student population of Harvard. The result is the FaceMash website which allows the users to rank the girls in terms of attractiveness. Mark and his friends are excited, crowding around the laptop and savouring the creative process. Their narrative line is interspersed with juxtaposing shots of elite males from the 'final clubs', drinking, gambling and ogling invited female students. The latter group is performing impromptu striptease on stage. In both the parallel storylines, everybody is having a good time according to their perception of a 'good time'. The extroverts and the confident ones are enjoying female company; the sulky introverts, who cannot 'get laid' due to their social deficiency, resort to entertaining themselves by humiliating women in the virtual world.

Sorkin's screenplay, however, does not concentrate on the narrow issue of social adjustment, or even Asperger's. It widens the message into the realm of social justice and civic engagement. The genius but penniless programmer who is being engaged by the Harvard elite, in the form of the uber-confident Winklewoss brothers (Armie Hammer and Josh Pence) and their friend Divya Narendra (Max Minghella), to build the HarvardConnection website, rebels and abandons their elitist project. Instead, he creates his own website aimed at the whole world – not just at the students of a particular university. Besides, he gets to work independently. No one tells him what to do, he works for himself. Nathan Heller, a Harvard insider, disproves the verity of Sorkin's narrative which he considers too hyperbolical and melodramatic:

Sorkin and Fincher's 2003 Harvard is a citadel of old money, regatta blazers, and (if I am not misreading the implication here) a Jewish underclass striving beneath the heel of a WASP-centric, socially draconian culture. Zuckerberg aspires to penetrate this world in order to make fancy friends and – well, do what, exactly? Wear madras? There were some kids at Harvard, in my era, with an interest in whatever gaunt remnants of old-style affluence remained, but the impulse was nostalgic and theatrical more than ambitious – people who arrive in the Ivy League these days do not come from black-tie dinners and wood-paneled rooms, nor do they enter such milieus after they leave. The kids entering Harvard in 2002 came largely from pressure-cooker public schools, dorm-room entrepreneurships, the cutthroat upper echelon of prep institutions, or, in my case, the all-weather-fleece-wearing wilds of San Francisco. Sorkin and Fincher's failure to discern the underlying culture of the place in the aughts may be why their portrait of today's Cambridge, Mass., strivers felt so tediously stock and two-dimensional to me: I recognized their Harvard, but only from *Love Story* and *The Paper Chase*, not my experience. To get the university this wrong in this movie is no small matter. In doing so, *The Social Network* misunderstands the cultural ambitions, and the nature of Zuckerberg's acumen, that made Facebook possible.

(*Slate*, 30 September 2010)

However, Heller's claim about the film's failure to depict the 'veritas' is wrong. *The Social Network* does not aim to portray the 'real' Mark Zuckerberg and his truthful conflict with the Harvard elite. As the scriptwriter told Mark Harris in *The New York Magazine*, 'I don't want my fidelity to be to the truth; I want it to be to storytelling. What is the big deal about accuracy purely for accuracy's sake, and can we not have the true be the enemy of the good?' (*The New York Magazine*, 17 September 2010). Sorkin and Fincher reshaped 'the reality' to get their point across: the film is more about the quest of the social trickster, on the one hand campaigning for justice, and on the other empowering ordinary members of society by giving them the opportunity to piece their own worlds together by combining fragments of reality and fiction. And even though the protagonist's initial aim is rather shallow (to get access to elite establishments instead of the inclusive events such as 'The Caribbean Party'), his final result is presented as almost revolutionary. In his quest to eliminate social (and racial) exclusion and the unfairness of the 'real' world, he builds and launches a website which allows its users to create and manage their own social realities; to choose their own circles of communication, to link up communities and engage in social activities of their choice.

The Zuckerberg of Sorkin's narrative becomes an existential hero fighting against both the monsters of social injustice *and* the monsters of inner emptiness by becoming 'the god' of his own universe and developing the tool for tailor-making ideal universes and worlds. The little introvert dares to defy 'reality' and replace it with the flexible tool for writing personalised narratives. Thus, he overcomes the two key postmodern issues – the 'doom of the gods' and the schizophrenic identity problem. In the absence of a 'central narrative' (or if the central narrative is unjust and needs to be challenged), all you have to do is create. One does not need a 'determining' narrative which comes 'from above' in order to hold one's life together. Life, the broken mirror consisting of a myriad of reflections, can be re-arranged according to your own standards and vision. One does not need a 'natural' community, a *habitus*, an identity-shaping culture or the artificial power of the state in order to feel connected and stay connected. Commitments, friendships, ties, even if they lose 'the messiness' aspect, become a matter of personal choice. And personal choice, the flagship idea of the capitalist society, both fragments and empowers the individual – very much like the trickster principle.

The protagonist's daredevil tricksterism in *The Social Network* does not remain unpunished. The one who dares to cross all possible virtual and legal boundaries by hacking into protected databases, and generally thinking that it is normal to be rude to people, gets sued for a number of transgressions (the litigation scenes are shown in the narrative prospectively). The protagonist has to deal with the existence of 'civilised' boundaries as well as with the reality of the litigation culture. He is punished with six months of academic probation after his FaceMash creation brings down parts of the Harvard Network, gets sued by the social success-obsessed Winklewoss brothers for failing to build the HarvardConnect website, and even prosecuted by his best friend Eduardo for dropping his percentage ownership share of Facebook, thus minimising his influence in the enterprise. Sorkin and Fincher endow Zuckerberg with real trickster qualities, presenting him as a man who has no regard for anything except his own decisions, his own personal choice; as a man who, ultimately, fails to 'connect' in real life while being the ultimate expert on virtual connectivity, either technical or human. He is both the fighter with the social stagnation and the destroyer of 'the true' communal spirit. In this, the protagonist of *The Social Network*, the quiet Asperger's boy who finds a way to influence the world, is the hero of our internet times.

Chapter 3

The Trickster and the Economic System

[handwritten: Frank]

Money: The Maker and Breaker of Boundaries

In his book *Andy Kaufman Revealed! Best Friend Tells All* (1999), the comedian's best friend, co-writer and sidekick Bob Zmuda states as one of Kaufman's biggest influences the lifestyle of a certain Mr. X (real name Norman Wexler), a hyper-eccentric Hollywood playwright and script doctor; the author of *Serpico* (1973) and *Saturday Night Fever* (1977). Every day Mr. X, who allegedly suffered from a mental health disorder, would get out and seek inspiration for his scripts in the outside world. For a few weeks, Zmuda worked for Mr. X as 'an inspiration assistant', helping him in any ventures he undertook, and getting paid $2000 per week in return for his services. Mr. X liked to set up situations involving real people being driven to the limit of their emotional and physical abilities. A sought-after script doctor, Mr. X was very rich but spent his money in an eccentric manner, paying his victims to behave in a certain way and manipulating their lives in 'real time'. He would then preserve their reactions with his tape recorder. Many of these ventures, despite their 'fictional' nature, were extremely risky – especially when Mr. X chose to taunt 'the wrong people'. Some of the scriptwriter's most harebrained stunts included gatecrashing the birthday party of a local mafioso's mother and insulting her; promising a young receptionist to buy all the pictures in the gallery if she performs fellatio on him; and purchasing an entire day's supply of bread and cakes from a patisserie, and then insisting that the bakers perform a naked dance for an additional sum of money.

Zmuda reminisces that Mr. X looked like a tramp, and rarely washed or changed his clothes (1999: 24–42). Physically repulsive, he relied, in a creative-experimental way, on the power of money, to facilitate any communication. As his inspiration assistant put it, 'Money does not talk, it screams' (1999: 37). Mr. X endowed money with the endless liminal power as it infallibly sped up the crossing of most boundaries. When people refused to obey his orders, he simply upped the stakes. On rare occasions when money did not work (for instance, when Mr. X committed a particularly outrageous

[handwritten margin notes: Relied on power of money; Money screams; Money allowed him to do anything]

public offence such as emptying his bowels, in protest against waiting in a long ticket queue, in the middle of the JFK airport lounge), he evoked the power of celebrity, announcing to the policeman, intending to arrest him, that he was a famous Hollywood script writer (1999: 41). After this eccentric scatological mutiny his assistant left him.

Not surprisingly, money is one of the key subjects of the trickster film. Or rather, the economic order often plays the pivotal role in trickster film narratives, with money being an important, and quite problematic, part of the trickster's life. Paradoxically, the trickster is both trampled by the economic order (like Charlie Chaplin's Tramp or Carrey's Lloyd Christmas) and attempts to deceive it (like Carrey's conmen Dick Harper in *Fun With Dick and Jane* and Steven Russell in *I Love You Phillip Morris*). The trickster serves as a metaphor for the central conflict of the capitalist system: he embodies the capitalist split between material gain and morality; between ambition and empathy; between ruthless exploitation and repressed guilt. It embodies the cocky, Ace-Venturian 'alpha male' aspect of capitalism: competitiveness, hunger for success, elimination of rivals, exploitation of subordinates. With this tricksterish split at its heart, capitalism is a perpetually unstable system, its smooth business-like surface always in danger of being overwhelmed by the very basic, and very dark, instinctuality that underpins it. The sociologist Zygmunt Bauman writes in *Community: Seeking Safety in an Insecure World* (2001):

> The modern – capitalist – arrangement of human cohabitation was Janus-Faced; one face was emancipatory, the other coercive, each being turned towards a different section of society. [. . .] To the 'lazy and passion-ridden masses' civilization meant, first and foremost, a curbing of the morbid predilections which they were assumed to harbour and which, if unloosed, would explode orderly cohabitation. To the two sections of modern society, the self-assertion offered and the discipline demanded were mixed in sharply different proportions.
>
> (Bauman, 2001: 26)

The capitalist individual is proactive, independent, separated from the mass – yet still expected, for the sake of earning a living, to conform to a certain framework, to confine himself to a certain lifestyle, to become a pliable part of the system. Again, this split is infected with trickster spirit and social protest, as shown in a number of trickster films: Lloyd Christmas and Truman Burbank (*The Truman Show*, 1998) struggle with economic inequality and corporate control; the lives of Adam Sandler's characters are dictated and shaped by corporate machines; and antagonists like the Joker in *Batman* (1989) represent the showy aspect of the industry, the one that turns *hoi polloi* into dumbed-down consumers susceptible to advertising and media control. The giant machine is both powerful and complex, and the individual is lost inside it. The two conflicting aspects of the capitalist system fight like the hands of the foolish Wakdjunkaga: paradoxically, it simultaneously allows one to choose one's destiny and takes it away. Before we discuss its dynamics in contemporary film, let us digress and trace the emergence and progression of this split in Western culture, and its reflection in the arts.

The Birth of the Picaro and the Rise of Human Agency

Rogue

From the Renaissance on, the trickster in the arts will be increasingly concerned with the problems of the individual, moving away from the collective escapist exercise in its carnivalesque forms, and utilising its explosive potential in personal rebellion. The problems referred to the trickster in literature (and later in cinema) have to do with individuation: existence, survival, personal independence, issues of social assimilation and creative freedom. Is the individual the product of society, and consequently the victim of his background, or the shaper of his own destiny? Is he an actor, a director or a silent, silenced member of the audience? Questions raised by Shakespeare in *Hamlet* are still acutely relevant for the Western society. Hamlet, with his militant brand of individualism and destructive-trickster habits, challenges the inertia of Rosencrantz and Guildenstern, two 'faithful lieges' who consider themselves ordinary people and have no desire to alter the world. In Act 2 second scene he mocks their lack of ambition:

HAMLET
   O God, I could be bounded in a nut shell and count
   myself a king of infinite space, were it not that I
     have bad dreams.

GUILDENSTERN
   Which dreams indeed are ambition, for the very
   substance of the ambitious is merely the shadow of a dream.

HAMLET
   A dream itself is but a shadow.

ROSENCRANTZ
   Truly, and I hold ambition of so airy and light a
   quality that it is but a shadow's shadow.

                        (Shakespeare, 2007: 1095)

In modernity, the question of 'the shaper of your own destiny' and whether the dream is, indeed, nothing but a shadow, inevitably tangles itself up with a number of economic issues: money, class and Bakhtin's 'egotistic lust and possession' (1984: 23). Picaro as a representative of the trickster principle in literature signalled the growing preoccupation with social mobility and personal wealth. A roguish social rebel is a version of the trickster; he is born the minute a social division emerges. As such, he invariably inhabits both economic arrangements and social transitions. Picaro uses his wit against people with significant economic and political power. The motif of the servant who is cleverer than his master is an ancient device, but picaresque novel as a distinct literary genre was born in sixteenth-century Spain as a heretical rebellion against the excessive power of the Catholic Church during the Spanish Inquisition. The genre's founding representative, *The Life of Lazarillo de Tormes and of His Fortunes and Adversities* (1554), an anonymous novel about the adventures of a cunning servant, was banned by the Spanish Crown for its representation of the clergy and the aristocracy.

Bakhtin, who was particularly interested in the literary-psychological transition from the medieval to modern, points out the 'beyond good and evil' quality of the new hero, who was destined to defy the classical-medieval rhetorical approach to the unity of human personality. The picaresque tradition negated the normative and static vision (and representation) of human beings:

> What is a 'picaro' — Lazarillo, Gil Blas and the others? A criminal or an honest man, evil or good, cowardly or brave? Can one even talk about services rendered, about crimes, about exploits that create and define his profile? He stands beyond defence and accusation, beyond glorification or exposure, he knows neither repentance nor self-justification, he is not implicated in any norm, requirement, ideal; he is not all of one piece and is not consistent; if measured against the rhetorical unities of personality that were available. A human being is, as it were, emancipated here from all the entanglements of such conventional unities, he is neither defined nor comprehended by them; in fact, he can even laugh at them.
>
> (Bakhtin, 1997: 407–408)

Bakhtin's description perfectly renders the essence of the trickster principle which was revived after the centuries of ideological rigidity and social slumber. From the inflexible characterisation, the hero has moved in the direction of ambivalent trickster psychology. There are numerous novelistic and comedic examples of trickster-picaros defying the rigid social structure and having a laugh at the expense of their much richer adversaries. The heroine of Defoe's *Moll Flanders* (1722) is a courtesan, thief and con woman who has extraordinary survival skills: she manages to stay afloat by sleeping with all kinds of men of means, both married and unmarried. The daughter of a jailbird, Moll's flirtation with 'a decent life' is shaky and uneven. Having spent most of her life robbing, thieving and conning honest people, she eventually ends up on a little farm in Maryland intent on living quietly and decently.

The protagonist of Pierre-Augustin Beaumarchais's *Figaro* trilogy (1773–1792) (which inspired Mozart's *Le Nozze di Figaro* (1786) and Rossini's *The Barber of Seville* (1816)) is a cunning servant with social aspirations. He easily outwits his master even when the latter summons his (rapidly diminishing) feudal rights (i.e., attempts to apply the 'right of the first night' (*droit de seigneur*) to Figaro's bride). A writer, civil rights activist and revolutionary, Beaumarchais infused the *Commedia dell'arte* structure of his picaresque comedies with a truly rebellious spirit. They became the literary satellites of the French Bourgeois Revolution. In the years before the revolution Louis XVI made an attempt to have the play banned. The picaresque hero, according to Bakhtin, 'is faithful to nothing, he betrays everything – but he is nevertheless true to himself, to his *own* orientation, which scorns pathos and is full of scepticism' (1997: 408).

The Trickster and the Middle Class

The trickster in the arts is traditionally presented as a low-life rogue, a tramp, servant, thief or conman, marginalised and sidelined by moneyed social strata. However, he has more in common with the middle class than it seems. For instance, the lowly picaro of the early modern period (1500–1800), ultimately, is concerned with upward social mobility and transition. The mercurial picaro is laughing at the dumb, stale, immobile aristocracy and, ideally, would like to leave the ranks of prostitutes and servants, and join the emerging professional class. The picaro is a by-product of modernity; he is a city dweller, born with the end of feudalism; he never misses the opportunity to climb out of the social pit into which he was born. He is the future bourgeois (and the future bourgeois revolutionary).

Indeed, the middle class shares a number of characteristics with the trickster principle. The two share the perpetual desire for personal achievement and transformation. Throughout modernity, the expanding new class embodied transition, movement, progress (personal and technological). The middle class, mobile and opportunistic, is 'betwixt and between', condemned to perpetual movement – always in fear of regressing, of becoming a 'loser', of falling back into the abyss. Under the smooth decency of its lifestyle lies the memory of the gap, the memory of the cracked past; there exists 'another layer' which is very much alive. The postmodern society, in which the middle classes constitute the predominant social force, is acutely aware of this cracked hidden layer which is the shadow of its smooth surface.

In his book *The Political Psyche* (1993) Andrew Samuels argues that, as a system, capitalism has a number of distinct tricksterish qualities.

He reminds us that one of the most prominent mythological trickster figures – Greek Hermes (Mercury in the Roman version) – apart from being the messenger of the gods and guide to the underworld, also acted as the patron of commerce. Samuels writes that Hermes

> articulates the relationship between the trickster and the market economy – that particular political phenomenon causing confusion, idealization and splitting across the twentieth-century world. [. . .] In the tale we hear of the deceit and lying of Hermes. This inspires associations to the ruthlessness of economic inequality, stock market fraud and insider trading. We also hear of the capacity of Hermes to bargain and negotiate in a compassionate and related style.
>
> (Samuels, 1993: 88)

Hermes is a suitable metaphor for the Janus-like duplicity of the capitalist economy; and the middle class bears the burden of the guilt for its comfortable lifestyle, knowing that someone else somewhere (the local working class in the classic industrial economy; developing countries in our service economy era) is working in tough conditions to guarantee it. Samuels argues that

> we made our commitment to this order of things a long time ago, and however much we may know intellectually that it does not work for us on the ethical level, however much we may know about the psychodynamics of greed and envy, we cannot seem to break our tie to our lover: economic inequality. It is a deep guilt over the undeniable fact of our love of economic inequality that takes us to the cheating heart of global capitalism, the partner we refuse to leave, having never really chose, remaining locked in an enigmatic relationship whose tensions drive us crazy.
>
> (1993: 89)

The trickster principle is 'beyond good and evil', and it is human beings who turn him into the shadow by applying their moral codes to his acts. The bourgeois guilt does not belong to Hermes – it belongs to people who experience it, unable either to get rid of the shadow or accept it. Exploitation equals repressed guilt. In fact, there exists a school of economics – the so-called evolutionary economics – which uses evolutionary methodology to describe economic processes. It argues that natural selection is inherent in the market economy, and that competitive process guarantees 'the survival of the fittest'. Meanwhile, millions of people pursue their own interests in the production of goods and services. Like in evolution, there is no overall plan. It is a spontaneous process with no specific goal, rational or otherwise (Skousen, 2008: 118).

Numerous literary tricksters have demonstrated the pitfalls of social division and the tricky nature of 'occupying the middle position'. E. T. A. Hoffman's *The Life and Opinions of the Tomcat Murr* (1819–1821) has as its protagonist a fat cat who, in the absence of his master (a composer and a tortured creative soul), usurps his table and assumes the role of an author. He writes an autobiography about his vain and vacuous bourgeois existence. The printer makes an error, and weaves the musician's sufferings and the cat's vacuous musings into one novel. From Dickens's little picaros dreaming of a better life to Mann's con man Felix Krull whose roots lie in a decomposed bourgeois family, the trickster principle has established its firm presence in the class wars of modernity. Cinema gave the trickster a new dimension and new powers to explore social conflicts: Buster Keaton's bank clerks and broken brokers, and Charlie Chaplin's tramps fight for survival against the backdrop of industrial estates, busy urban streets, and railway lines.

The Middle Class and the Body

Another aspect of the trickster's relationship with the middle class is the body. The grotesque body is hidden from the view of the middle class, turned into the shadow. The flesh, which had been 'rehabilitated' by Renaissance geniuses like Rabelais, was inevitably pushed by modernity back into its unconscious abode and left to brood and decay in the dark. As Bakhtin shows, in traditional folk culture, the grotesque-realist body (i.e., in its pure trickster form) is not horrible but accepted in its ugliness and beauty, and any exaggeration has a positive, assertive character:

> In grotesque realism the bodily element is deeply positive. It is presented not in a private, egotistic form, severed from the other spheres of life, but as something universal, representing all the people. [. . .] The material bodily principle is contained not in the biological individual, not in the bourgeois ego, but in the people, a people who are continually growing and renewed. This is why all that is bodily becomes grandiose, exaggerated, immeasurable. [. . .]
>
> The leading themes of this bodily life are fertility, growth, and a brimming over-abundance. Manifestations of this life refer not to the isolated biological individual, not to the private, 'egotistic' economic man, but to the collective ancestral body of all the people. Abundance and all-people's elements also determine the gay and festive character of all images of bodily life; they do not reflect the drabness of everyday existence. The material bodily principle is a triumphant, festive principle, it is a 'banquet for all the world' [a typical expression used in Russian fairytales to describe a great banquet which usually crowns the happy ending of a story].

(Bakhtin, 1984: 19)

The man of modernity, that lonely individual who, as Jung tirelessly wrote, is removed from the collective unconscious ('all the people', 'the collective ancestral body') distances himself aesthetically from any grotesque-realistic images. The enlightened individual, who has spent so much effort separating his unique mind from the muddled collective brain, no longer sees the trickster as a cheerful master of the banquet. For the 'private, egotistic' man, the collective equals vulgar. Everything pertaining to the body – excesses, food, defecation, sexual life, birth and death – become smoothed over or even totally covered up by the everyday aesthetics of modernity. Bakhtin argues that, because the essential principle of grotesque realism is degradation, 'that is, the lowering of all that is high, spiritual, ideal, abstract' (1984: 19), it is only logical that the bourgeois individual puts up numerous philosophical, aesthetic and scientific barriers between himself and anything that is 'natural'. However, certain art movements (the 'counter-rational' movements which argue for the supremacy of the unconscious and warn about the dangers of heroic rationality) drag the shadow-trickster back to the surface of social consciousness. This accounts for the abundance of shadows and doubles in the anti-bourgeois aesthetics of Romanticism, apocalyptic doppelgangers (especially in the form of vampire) of *fin-de-siècle*, and the stylistic and thematic *dance macabre* performed by modernist writers on the ruins of the Western individual (of which examples would be the scatological rebellion of James Joyce in *Ulysses* (1922) and T. S. Eliot's experiments in poetic disintegration in *The Waste Land* (1922)).

The trickster principle, therefore, has a very special relationship with the enlightened economic man. It resides in society's unconscious next to guilt, inequality, crime, body obsessions and secret longing for national/communal unity. He also occasionally brings issues to the surface or even causes them to explode. Modernity has banished him to the underworld (much like the notorious Loki), but in this underworld he is very much alive and constantly threatening to cause 'the doom of the gods'.

The Economic Trickster in Film: *Reductio ad Absurdum*

The trickster film portrays the capitalist system as unstable, undermined by constant 'stirrings' from 'within'; ready to crumble, ready to be reduced to chaos. It is has become a tradition in trickster film to evoke *reductio ad absurdum* to depict business structures and portray business ventures. Gotham City's chemical industries in *Batman* (1989) are governed by a raving mad maniac with a green face and unstoppable desire to poison everyone. Likewise, in *Batman Returns* (1992) Max Schreck, the mayor of Gotham and the owner of the city's power plant, is a villain who agrees to make another maniac – Penguin – the face of the city in exchange for non-disclosure of evidence about the plant's influence on ecology. In Charlie Chaplin's film *Modern Times* (1936), the idea of an efficient production process is amplified, for comical purposes, to the point when the quality of the product loses all relevance, and only speed, with which the labourers perform their tasks, remains important. In these films destructive or exploitative traits of the industry are grotesquely exaggerated. Cinematic tricksters imply that capitalism, despite being built on rational premises, is constantly in danger of going mad. The *reductio ad absurdum* method is used in the films to show that, however stable a business looks on the outside, or even on the inside, it is never really far from failure.

Another path the trickster takes in relation to capitalism, and especially the market economy, is implying that acquisition of property is equal to theft (such a comparison is the pinnacle of comic absurdity, but there are strands of political thought that famously proclaim exactly the same idea!). This type of *reductio* is evident, for instance, in the two Jim Carrey films, *Fun With Dick and Jane* (2005) and *I Love You Phillip Morris* (2009), in which a typical middle class, 'decent' family guy and successful career man gradually transforms into a con man. His entrepreneurial skills transmogrify into thieving abilities, and he gets into conflict with the law. Carrey's protagonist in *Fun With Dick and Jane* does not acquire any additional 'skills' in order to become a robber – he just extends his survival abilities from the times when he was a middle manager in a company called *Globodyne*. Likewise, Steven Russell in *I Love You Phillip Morris* is transformed from a con man into a CEO overnight because, on the surface of it, nobody can see the difference between the two occupations!

Failure to Perform a Determinable Function

Joblessness and accompanying misery are key ingredients in the explosive mixture that launches the conflict in trickster film narratives. Trickster protagonists often fail to fulfil what the father of the science of sociology Emile Durkheim (1858–1917) calls 'a determinable function' – that is, your own unique role in the capitalist society (Durkheim, 1964: 43). Durkheim outlines the anthropological and social differences between pre-industrial and developed/capitalist communities in his seminal work *The Division of Labour in Society* (1893). He argues that the pre-industrial society is marked by a 'positive', 'mechanical' solidarity in that all members of the group resemble each other, are replaceable, and their individual differences are played down. None of them is supposed to have a sphere of action that is peculiar to him. In other words, members of a group held together by a positive solidarity are not in any way unique; but neither do they aspire to become 'personalities' (Durkheim, 1964: 131). If we graft Turner's liminality onto this picture of undisturbed collectivity, we will get a society in which the tricksterish and potentially explosive liminal is controlled, pre-programmed and then released in carefully shaped batches. Any change must be recorded and accounted for.

By contrast, each member of the 'organic' society is a recognisable personality. In the Durkheimian universe, there is no place for losers. Organic communities, Durkheim postulates, are primarily characterised by the division of labour, and that is what holding the different pieces of the system together – despite the undeniably fragmented character of the system. To be a successful member of this society everyone must acquire a profession, a role, and subsequently perfect themselves in this role whilst making their way up the professional ladder. 'The determinable function' becomes a mantra, or, as Durkheim himself put it, 'the categorical imperative of the moral conscience' of the industrial Western consciousness (Durkheim, 1964: 43).

Capitalist society is, metaphorically speaking, a body consisting of various organs, each of them assigned its own unique function. They are all completely different yet they cannot help but stay together because their survival depends on the health and effective functioning of the entire system. Their narrow specialisation is due to the principal rule of capitalist productivity: the division of labour. Industries do not need workers who can perform every step of the production process – but do it very slowly; they need rows of people, each knowing his or her little operation to perfection. Durkheim postulates that the capitalist individual's 'natural milieu is no longer the natal milieu, but the occupational milieu. It is no longer real or fictitious consanguinity which marks the place of each one, but the function which he fills' (1964: 182). Compared to the stifling collectivity of the mechanical society, the capitalist individual is free and responsible for his personality and his decisions. To be a person, Durkheim proclaims, is 'to be an autonomous source of action' and not 'a simple incarnation of the genetic type of his race and his group' (1964: 403).

But here Durkheim seems to have met face to face with the trickster king of the modern society; with the paradox which he ultimately fails to explain – the paradox of individual freedom versus the numerous restraints of the new social order. The trouble with the professional, narrow-specialised society is that it is highly fragmented and, at the same time, very difficult to enter. This happens because the existing 'organs' mutually complement each other, and 'new elements cannot be grafted upon the old without upsetting the equilibrium, without altering the relationships, and, accordingly, the organism resists intrusions which cannot produce anything but disturbance' (1964: 151). Moreover, even if (or when) one eventually gets 'in' and becomes a fully-functioning segment, he surrenders a large portion of his freedom to the system. Durkheim admits that by entering into such a society the individual, in effect, agrees to be 'tied down' and accept the duties which he has not 'expressly desired' (1964: 228–229). But then again, he counter-argues, an 'organic' society based on capitalist economy always leaves a large space for personal initiative. Besides, the 'great many obligations and duties' imposed on the individual by the system and family 'have their origin in a choice of the will' (1964: 228–229). In other words, it is individual subjects themselves (consumers, employees, taxpayers) who consciously enter the contractual 'cage'.

Also, the social and economic division of labour is beneficial for the individual because, in pre-industrial societies, Durkheim reminds his readers, 'any ill-formed organism is doomed to perish', whereas with the division of labour in place, 'a puny individual can find within the complex cadres of our social organisation a niche in which he can render a service' (Roberts and Hite, 2000: 51). The individual needs society, and society needs the individual because 'a function can only become specialised if that specialisation corresponds to some need in society' (2000: 51). The individual, it appears, fulfils his very important role and occupies his very important place for the social and economic benefit of society. At the same time, every new specialisation results in increase and improvement of the production process. There are more products available for people to consume. But how, Durkheim inquires, are the industries going to make consumers 'feel the need for more abundant or better-quality products'? (2000: 51). Where, indeed, might new demands come? His answer is that the demands will spring from the same cause that determines the progress of the division of labour: 'in order for life to continue, the reward must always be proportionate to the effort' (2000: 51).

Without directly criticising it, and sometimes even without openly discussing the issue, the trickster film manages, in its unique comical way, to scrutinize the inevitable tension between individuals and their assigned positions in the workplace and the social structure. Trickster protagonists not only fight (or attempt to fight) for their social position, but also make sure that their reward 'is proportionate to their effort'. Carrey's characters are never far from the nightmare of being fired, made redundant, demoted or losing out on promotion opportunities. Meanwhile, their jobs are repetitive and uncreative. What is looming ahead of them is a professional dead-end. The jobs of Stanley Ipkiss (*The Mask*), Truman Burbank (*The Truman Show*), Dick Harper, Carl Allen (*Yes Man*) control their lives; not much is left beyond the scope of the protagonists' professional duties. The characters are attached to corporate giants, their day is pre-organised and pre-planned, and they build their private lives against this everyday backbone of masked professionalism. When the mask is taken off, they are helpless (Stanley Ipkiss, Carl Allen), lost without a meaning (Truman Burbank, Dick Harper, Joel Barish (*Eternal Sunshine of the Spotless Mind*, 2004)), or altogether incapable of establishing stable relationships (Lloyd Christmas, Fletcher Reede, Joel Barish).

Chaplin's Tramp

Charlie Chaplin's criticism of modernity is concentrated in the figure of the Tramp – a little man, predictably nameless, trapped in the hostile urban environment, looking for jobs, grabbing opportunities. He is a by-product of the city, just as the metropolis is a by-product of the industrial revolution. He is juxtaposed to politicians, millionaires and industrialists (the 'legislative' part of the system) and the police (the system's 'executive' part) who push him around like a marionette. The Tramp's world is reduced to absurdity when he dutifully attempts to accomplish everything these giants ask of him because their demands are nonsensically high and greedy.

Modern Times (1936) opens with an Eisenstein-style montage comprising an overhead shot of a flock of sheep, fading into a similar overhead shot of a multitude of workers flocking to a factory in the morning. These are followed by a number of short establishing shots – the streets of the city, the inside of the factory. This sequence serves both as a social commentary and to establish a context. Chaplin's protagonist is one of the cogs in the machine called 'Electro Steel Corporation', where he works on a conveyor belt. The Tramp's task is to tighten nuts on the never-ending stream of steel plates. His actions are closely monitored by several people: the manager, the factory owner who can watch live footage of everything that is happening in the different parts of his empire thanks to a 'futuristic' video security system, and a big-brother-type supervisor housed in a special 'controller' room, who can speed up or slow down the production line. Surrounded by cameras and machines, the Tramp ceases to exist as an individual and becomes a piece of equipment. He is a mass man, working on a mass production line, surrounded by similarly dehumanised individuals.

Two powerful extended metaphors make up the base of the film's visual iconography: the machine and the eating process. Chaplin rhythmically uses the motives of 'eating' and 'swallowing' throughout *Modern Times* to emphasise the 'dog eat dog' character of industrial capitalism. In the famous sequence, a new time-saving invention – a 'feeding machine' – is tested on him. The machine, as their inventors advertise it, would eliminate the need for a lunch break, and the workers would continue doing their job while being fed. The Tramp is squeezed into the seat, his head is fixed, and the robotic hand starts pushing food into his mouth. But, as its timings are very specific and it is programmed to spend only so many minutes per dish, the 'feeding hand' is not concerned with the fact that the Tramp has not finished chewing the previous piece of food. In the classical *reductio* sequence, the machine breaks down, goes completely mad, starts shoving the corn down the Tramp's mouth uncontrollably, and ends up consuming more time than it could have saved. Its disintegration foreshadows the Tramp's mental breakdown caused by overwork.

Chaplin employs Eisenstein-esque social density (in fact, the two were friends), amplified by apt mise-en-scenic symbolism and crisp, tight editing. In yet another scene, the Tramp gets trapped in a complex contraption which looks like a giant clock mechanism. This visual metaphor means: time is money, money is time, and production is a carefully measured, rational process. The Tramp becomes the prisoner of speed and efficiency. The idea of 'eating' is a perfect rhythmic trope for a trickster film as it suits the carnivalesque roots of the trickster principle and emphasises the trickster's close ties with all things bodily and low. In *Modern Times* (very much like in Fritz Lang's *Metropolis*, 1927), the hungriest creatures are the personified machines, which, in a shadowy re-enactment of Bakhtin's carnivalesque celebration, crush and chew the little men. Their unstoppable gluttony gives away the dark underside of modernity, rationality's inevitable *reductio ad absurdum*.

When the Tramp's section of the conveyor belt is ordered to speed up, he does his best to complete his bolt-tightening task, but fails to keep up with the stream, and ends up suffering from a mental breakdown. The machines have metaphorically swallowed him up. From now on his place of residence will be the underbelly of society, with all the other criminals and madmen. The Tramp's 'madness' metamorphoses into an (involuntary) revolt when he starts disobeying commands and chasing people with his giant nut tighteners. Logical organisation of the workplace has reduced itself to nonsense as all the time-saving, planning, measuring and organising (presented in the film in a series of visual metaphors – clocks, mechanisms, video surveillance, the conveyor belt) is shattered during a destructive rampage when an exhausted human cog explodes all over the money-making kingdom of instrumental rationality. The system's hidden layer erupts, splashing its poisonous contents over the shiny outer surface. The Tramp is eventually captured and carted off to a mental hospital.

In *Modern Times* Chaplin's Tramp does not become a conscious rebel (like he does in *The Great Dictator*) but rather lets his inner trickster escape and wreak havoc on the dehumanising, oppressive system. After being released from the psychiatric institution, the Tramp accidentally gets himself into another scrape: he picks up a red 'danger' flag that had fallen from the end of a truck, and frantically waves it in an attempt to attract the driver's attention. Instead, he attracts the attention of a mob of left-wing demonstrators, who accept him as their leader and start chanting the *L'Internationale*. He is arrested as a communist instigator and sent to jail. Chaplin externalises the trickster principle, carefully splitting it off from the protagonist's persona, thus relieving him of responsibility for social dissidence. The Tramp, a naïve common man, law-abiding citizen and likeable fool, simply could not have staged anything as spectacularly rebellious as a factory pogrom or an industrial action.

As Enid Welsford, William Willeford, Conrad Hyers, Gerald Mast and many others have observed, Chaplin's comedy, apart from being very modern, is also deeply tragic. His presentation of inescapability, of the plight of the individual and the inevitable tricksterish revolt is approaching Shakespeare's 'tragic fool' images. Chaplin, Conrad Hyers writes, 'was an archetypal hero, grappling with universal human problems – not just cream pies and sight gags. The range of emotions to which he appealed also gave universality to a figure that so deftly interlaced pathos and humour' (Hyers, 1996: 5).

Chaplin, who, at the age of seven, ended up in the Lambeth workhouse together with his mother and brother, understandably refused to glorify modernity as a linear development with a brilliant futuristic vision shining ahead. The Chaplin brothers' life at the workhouse involved separation from their mother, compulsory uniforms, shameful poverty and physical abuse (Kohn, 2005: 18). In *Modern Times*, the trickster trapped in the body of the small, powerless, insignificant individual ends up on the streets, then in prison, then in a badly-paid job, then on the streets again. Meanwhile, his perceived foolishness is merely a projection; a reflection of society's imperfections concealed behind the façade of decency, humanity and rationality. Chaplin's social message is that the shadow of the metropolitan society is the underworld of crime, poverty and illegality. The Tramp is the trickster principle personified; his inadvertent dissent, eruption and subsequent assent into the underworld is caused by the flaws in society's structure. In the course of the film the Tramp crosses the border and transfers from one group of binary opposites – employment, sanity, obedience, lawfulness – to another – insanity, civil disobedience, political protest, vagabondage and theft.

Tim Burton's Industrial Horrors

Tim Burton may be regarded as an anachronistic director as in his films he likes the idea of going back to high modernity, to the time when the West still had its working class, still retained its industrial might, and still suffered from the social and political problems that come with a sizeable working class presence. His industrial *reductio*, however, is Romantic rather than realistic as he prefers not to discuss social issues openly. Instead, he foregrounds, in symbols, their psycho-anthropological consequences. The director's version of the trickster in *Batman* and *Batman Returns* is a powerful madman, the *doppelganger* of the factory owner.

Burton's retro-postmodernist aesthetics was partially influenced by German Expressionism. Charlie Chaplin was making his films in the midst of the modernist havoc, when technological urbanism was in equal measure churning out ethereal futuristic visions and dismal doomsday scenarios. Chaplin saw the tragic-comic potential of the modern experience. Meanwhile, his deeply concerned German Expressionist colleagues – Fritz Lang (*Metropolis*, 1927), Friedrich Murnau (*Nosferatu*, 1922), Robert Wiene (*The Cabinet of Dr Caligari*, 1920) – were more inclined to see its abstract-symbolic side. Their atmospheric lighting, avant-garde mise-en-scène and harsh contrasts replicated the architectural angularity of the modern metropolis, and conveyed to the audience the psychological fragmentedness and emotional insecurity of the urban experience. For instance, in *Metropolis*, Freder, the pampered son of the city's owner Joh Fredersen, hallucinates that the giant M-Machine ('capitalist Moloch') devours columns and columns of workers marching into its fiery, giant open mouth. Upon waking he realises that a horrible industrial accident has happened, which his cloudy consciousness transformed into the symbolic vision of human sacrifice.

Batman is an old comic (initially created in 1939), rooted in late modernity with all its social and industrial conflicts: the metropolis is still a relatively fresh phenomenon, fragmented psyche is still a tragic thing, the production process, and with it the working class, still resides with the West, and the service economy is a thing of the future. Burton draws inspiration from the Expressionist aesthetics, selectively borrowing its visual elements for his own projects. In *Batman* and *Batman Returns*, Expressionist shadows and angles perfectly suit Burton's narrative material: the industrial horror theme, the subjects of urban criminality and urban alienation, the idea of 'mass' everything – mass man, mass media, mass hysteria, mass hypnosis. Burton defends his version of Gotham City:

> So few great cities have been built. *Metropolis* and *Blade Runner* seem to be on the accepted spectrum. We (Burton and the production designer Anton Furst) tried to do something different although people tend to lump things in categories. We conceptualized Gotham City as the reverse of New York in its early days. Zoning and construction was thought of in terms of letting light in. So we decided to take that in the opposite direction and darken everything by building up vertically and cramming architecture together. Gotham City is basically New York caricatured with a mix of style squashed together – an island of big, tall cartoon buildings textured with extreme designs.
>
> (Fraga, 2005: 23)

Burton's mise-en-scenic decision is psychologically correct. The citizens of Gotham are isolated from each other both physically and emotionally; the streets are busy with hurrying and scurrying individuals, all preoccupied with their own problems. However, with the arrival of the Joker (Jack Nicholson), the tricksterish shadow of urban modernity, all of them suddenly lose their autonomy and become prone to mass hypnosis. With his disintegrating face, criminal background and leadership talents, the Joker personifies the hidden layer of modernity. He does not just 'erupt' (like Chaplin's characters), spluttering the social surface with dirty contents – he rises to the surface in all his might, devouring any pockets of resistance and remnants of independent thinking. Batman, who, metaphorically, represents the modern individual, has to fight off this gigantic, fast-spreading collective shadow.

Bruce Wayne's identity throughout *Batman* and *Batman Returns* remains truly fluid and ranges from a madcap superhero to a presentable entrepreneur. His 'businessman' guise is very important as it points to the mytho-economic origins of his conflict with the Joker – and his conflict with himself. Put simply, the Joker is a bad capitalist whose roots go deep into the criminal world, while Bruce is a good capitalist – and an aristocrat too. Out of this split the trickster is born who, in the best tradition of the collective shadow with a postmodern twist, usurps TV channels, poisons beauty-addicted consumers with his unsafe products and performs botched cosmetic surgery on his victims. He turns the achievements of technology and culture upside down and inside out, showing the culture's broken, unstitched lining. His own physical fragmentedness coincides with the disintegration of the urban individual's psyche. He makes incisions, cuts and slices, and then stitches up, creating monstrous creatures with multiple identities and ugly masks. The culmination of his shadow-creating efforts is the enormous crowd at the Gotham City's 200th Anniversary Parade, at which the Joker emerges sat upon a throne, dressed in a clashing combination of purple and turquoise, and surrounded by his cronies. He then announces to the crowd before puncturing the giant balloons filled with poisonous gas (gas, chemicals, being boundary-transgressing and body-dissolving substances, are the bad trickster's favourite weapons): 'Now comes the part where I relieve you, the little people, of the burden of your failed and useless lives. But, as my plastic surgeon always said: if you gotta go, go with a smile.'

In one of the scenes, Batman finds himself in the TV operator's room surrounded by many screens, all showing Joker's face. To escape from this conditioning, consumer grooming, fragmentation, multiplicity, as well as to save his fellow citizens from these ills, Bruce Wayne must kill the 'bad capitalist' – the capitalist who has risen from the underworld of crime, and whose 'investment capital' comes from unclean sources, from below, and not from 'above', from the treasure chests of aristocracy (the wealth that has been 'clean' for centuries). Analysed in terms of social class, the Batman narrative is blindly idealistic. The ruthless, proactive entrepreneur is the hateful enemy of aristocratic Batman. The unstoppable *nouveau riche* threatens to take away the non-existent paradisiacal order of things. The despicable middle-class man blocks the aristocrat's connection with his 'people'. Therefore, he must be eliminated, and the world returned to its primeval state.

Tricksters, however, are notoriously difficult to kill. When pushed down from Gotham Cathedral by Batman, the Joker dies – but his 'laughing device', which has been hidden in his pocket all this time, keeps making giggling noises. The 'bad' capitalism, this visual metaphor predicts, will have the last laugh. Bruce Wayne has not healed the split, and has not eliminated his shadow – he just postponed the final battle. Capitalist democracy, with its emphasis on individualism, brings in its train – contra its own convictions – the dark shadow of collectivity because it still needs the mass man *to produce* the goods, and then *to consume* them. The mass man is indispensable.

Jim Carrey's CEOs and Con Men

Carrey's films of the last decade or so portray the individual (and his trickster) as fighting off the monsters of the so-called New Economy – the type of economy in which economic activity is dominated by the service sector, and manufacturing jobs have been outsourced overseas. Carrey's protagonists (as well as their doppelgangers) strive to survive in the new globalised world. They reflect the new 'office rat' problem: junior white-collar workers trying to make it all the way to the top. In fact, Carrey only played two blue-collar tricksters: the triple-named Chip-Larry-Ricardo in *The Cable Guy* and Lloyd Christmas in *Dumb and Dumber*. Neither of them is involved in manufacturing or production – Larry-Ricardo is a self-employed plumber and Lloyd drives a limo. The rest are clerks, lawyers and lower managers; one is a policeman (Charlie in *Me, Myself and Irene*, 2000).

Carrey's protagonists' white-collar jobs are never safe because the world in which they live and operate is fast-moving and unpredictable – almost magically so. It is grossly material and scaringly immaterial at the same time. Companies come and go. Money is invisible, and everyone is paranoid. Even when everything is going well, people know that there is a trickster at work underneath all this complex but smoothly-working structure, and that a collapse is imminent. One minute Dick Harper, a hard-working middle-manager for the aptly-named Globodyne corporation, is promised a super-promotion, the next he loses his job, the company goes bust, the value of his house goes down. The TV journalist Bruce Nolan in *Bruce Almighty* (2003) hopes to get a promotion but is overlooked in favour of his colleague. This seemingly minor incident serves as the trickster trigger in the narrative as it sends Bruce on a journey to 'seek truth' in this unfair world. Meanwhile, the professional conman Steven Russell in *I Love You Phillip Morris* destabilises a big company by infiltrating it and secretly re-directing the money to his bank accounts.

The fact that some of Carrey's middle-class tricksters come from real life serves as proof of the trickster film's faithful reflection of the outside world. At least two of his films are based on real stories; namely the so-called *Enron* scandal (*Fun With Dick and Jane*) and the life and adventures of a con artist Steven Jay Russell (*I Love You Phillip Morris*). Both films have 'decent-looking' protagonists who end up being criminals; and both foreground the idea that the line separating middle-class lifestyle from the abyss of poverty and criminality is very thin indeed.

Fun With Dick and Jane (2005)

The narrative base of *Fun With Dick and Jane* is the fictionalised story of the American energy giant Enron (renamed Globodyne in the film) based in Houston, Texas. The company infamously declared itself bankrupt in October 2001. Outwardly successful, in reality it was poorly managed, reliant on 'convoluted business deals to maintain its growth objectives' and 'encouraging so much unbridled creativity that one result was creative fraud' (Fox, 2003: iv–v). The charges against Andrew Fastow, the company's chief financial officer, included, for instance, creating false partnerships which allowed him to conduct sham transactions, inflate the company's profits and 'manipulate its balance sheet by moving debt off the company's books when it was illegal to do so' (2003: v). All in all, Fastow was indicted on 78 counts of fraud, conspiracy and money-laundering (2003: vi).

The story received much public resonance not just because of the grandiose scale of the scandal which involved thousands of deceived shareholders, lost pensions and ruined livelihoods. What the sad story of Enron brought to light was the hyper-flexible, all-permeating nature of the new globalised capitalism, and the lack of legislative or, indeed, geographical boundaries to control it effectively. As Scott Klinger and Holly Sklar argued in *The Nation* not long after the scandal:

> The pivotal lessons from the Enron debacle do not stem from any criminal wrongdoing. Most of the maneuvers leading to Enron's meltdown are not only legal, they are widely practiced. Many of the problems dramatically revealed by the Enron scandal are woven tightly into the fabric of American business. Outside the spotlight on Enron's rise and fall, government policies and accounting practices continue to reward and shelter many firms with harmful habits just like those of Enron.
>
> (*The Nation*, 18 July 2002)

Enron, the most prominent example of the New Economy company, had a number of harmful but perfectly legal and wide-spread habits (which eventually led to its downfall): excessively compensating executives for risky and dubious practices, tying employee retirement funds to company stock (thus letting them take the blow when the bad news arrived), stacking the board with insiders and friends, and using clever tax loopholes (*The Nation*, 18 July 2002). The political journalist and author John Nichols discusses the hyper-mercurial nature of the New Economy in terms of boundaries. The freer-than-ever trickster of global economy refuses to act within the frame. Nichols argues that Enron was a business model which did not respect limits – geographical, moral (greed, fraud), or indeed the limits of common sense:

Its global reach, powered by as much as $2.4 billion in loans backed by US taxpayers and aided by barrier-breaking 'reforms' pushed by the World Trade Organization, made the Houston-based corporation not merely the seventh-largest in the United States but the sixteenth-largest in the world. Before its empire began to unravel last fall, Enron was regularly featured on *Global Finance* magazine's annual list of the 'world's best global companies.' Enron was a globalizer on a grand scale, its grubby big hands stretching from Houston to London to Bombay to Maputo to La Paz. Forget about trying to chart the maze of Enron's 874 'offshore partnerships'; the corporation bragged quite openly about 'business units' (Enron Americas, Enron Europe, Enron Australia, Enron South America, Enron Japan, to name but a few) that traded in the world's natural gas, crude oil, metals, plastics, fertilizers, forest products, lumber, steel and, ominously, the weather. The short-hand description of Enron in most US media reports continues to refer to the corporation as a 'Texas energy giant'. But that does not begin to describe the conglomerate that, in addition to being the planet's largest energy trader, had a hand in virtually every economic sector – in every country – that a corporate jet could reach.

(*The Nation*, 14 February 2002)

Carrey's protagonists operating inside these colossal yet mercurial systems, business heavyweights that exist everywhere and nowhere and possess extraordinary evaporating skills, have no other choice but match their own survival abilities to the tricksterish nature of their workplace. The system, giant as it is, can be undone at any moment. Dick Harper is used in the role of the 'fool' by Globodyne's top management when he is invited to the head office and offered a promotion as the Vice-President of Communications. The bosses immediately entrust Dick with a live appearance on the show *Money Life* where he would announce the company's quarterly projections. Little does he know that he has been set up, that the company's stock is about to go into free fall, and that on the show he would be grilled by the journalistic heavyweight Sam Samuels and independent presidential candidate Ralph Nader. Having failed to explain why the company's CEO, Jack McCallister, has just sold a considerable share of his stocks, Dick is reduced to a bumbling, babbling human punch bag. Meanwhile, Jack McCallister is about to take off from the roof of Globodyne's headquarters in his helicopter.

The 'reversal of fortunes' is a motif that is deeply, painfully human. Dick believes he is going to be the King of the World as he is ascending to the fifty-first floor of the company's headquarters to hear the good news about his appointment. His less fortunate rival, who leaves the elevator a couple of dozen floors earlier, shouts from behind the closing doors 'You son of a bitch!' A bird's eye view camera is showing Dick dancing in the empty elevator, singing along to R. Kelly's *I Believe I Can Fly*. The viewer knows instinctively that, when the protagonist is singing that he is going to 'fly through that open door' and 'achieve miracles in life', the premise is about to end and the explosive trigger of the principal conflict is about to happen. Dick's foolishly heroic ambition is about to be tested by the cruel trickster-Fate.

And the cruel, unpredictable, volatile fate ruining the plans of small men in Dick's case is the new brand of capitalism. Dick, an ordinary human being, cannot counter its daredevil might and its agility. He failed to 'fly' but Jack McCallister still escapes in his helicopter. The city, with its over-powering angularity, is defined in the film by movement in two directions – down and up. Lifts, rooftops, staircases and helicopters symbolise the opportunities for ascent and the tragic consequences of descent. In the scene in which Dick attends the only managerial interview in town, he pushes a stack of empty plastic bottles down the spiral staircase in the hope of slowing the progress of his rivals. As he is running to the top, the bottles are tumbling down the staircase, filling the clean, uncluttered 3-D office space with a terrible rattle noise. The trick does not help, however – although he might have deterred the progress of some of interviewees, there are plenty more of them in the corridor next to the interview room. Faced with a never-ending stream of people, Dick gives up.

Dick is pushed down by Fate's hand, and before he can face the giant, he has to go through all the circles of social hell (unemployment, poverty, illegality, repossession threat, theft, robbery, forgery). With his new 'expertise' and skills, he can now out-trickster Jack McCallister by obtaining a sample of McCallister's signature, forging it and establishing a trust fund to reimburse all of the employees of Globodyne. The message of the film is rather controversial: Dick's trickster abilities, obtained in the criminal underworld, now match the skills necessary to survive in the fluid, unpredictable and intrinsically unfair world of the New Economy. The protagonist is pushed into becoming a criminal; moreover, he is rewarded for it.

'Luhu-zeher!'

This is the title (pronounced with a unique camp drawl) which Ace Ventura, Carrey's inimitable pet detective, awards to a rival male he wishes to humiliate. Ace Ventura is mock-masculine, hyper-virile and idiotically cocky. He is the ultimate universal trickster, but his emphasis on 'not being a loser' is specifically tailored for the modern society. Winners are individuals who are ahead and above of the mass; they are the ones who make the rules and the ones who then monitor the implementation of these rules. Losers, on the other hand, have to watch, listen, imitate, and be obedient. The loser is the ordinary man.

Loser, fool, clown, everyman are all words that lie within the trickster's semantic range. In the trickster film, however, the gap between losers and winners is ever narrowing, so that the best and the luckiest of the professionals are never far from failure. Dick might be the employee of a hyper-innovative corporation in the twenty-first century, but he is turned by his bosses into the 'eternal' figure of the fool. When Carl Allen (*Yes Man*) starts giving out loans to every one of his customers as part of his 'yes' programme, the audience is waiting for a disaster to happen. The viewer expects him to get discovered and sacked because his behaviour is irrational, and instead of calculating the risks he takes chances. Chance-taking has no place in the bank. Or has it? His risky strategy proves to be successful, and he earns a promotion, to the audience's surprise and relief. In one of Carrey's early comedies, the career of the successful lawyer and compulsive liar Fletcher Reede (*Liar Liar*, 1997) takes a turn for the worse when a spell is put on him which makes him unable to tell a lie. Like this, his superhuman powers are taken away and he has to win the case by telling the truth.

William Willeford mentions the sacred connection and interchangeability (ritualistic, anthropological, literary) between the figures of the fool and the king. 'The Fool' – Willeford argues – 'stands beside the king, in a sense reflecting him but also suggesting a long-lost element of the king that, we may imagine, had to be sacrificed at the founding of the kingdom, an element without which neither the king nor the kingdom is complete' (Willeford, 1969: 156). The king and the fool (in our case the winner and the loser) assume complementary roles (1969: 159). The winner's position, his power are not enduring because he is still a human being; he is 'mortal in relation to the eternal model that he embodies' (1969: 159). In the world of New Economy, in which those on top are at the mercy of unpredictable stock market conditions and hierarchical shifts, and in which business egos mercilessly clash and compete for top leadership positions, there are bound to be casualties. There are bound to be losers and fools.

Shakespeare's 'wise fools' certainly provide good examples of this hypothesis: In Act 5 of *Hamlet* the Prince famously tells Horatio that 'the noble dust of Alexander' may find new use as a stopper for a beer-barrel, and 'imperious Caesar' might also be stopping a hole somewhere to keep away the draught (Hamlet's comment is not only irreverent but also scatological). In fact, Hamlet draws the parallel between the great and mighty rulers and 'poor Yorick', 'a fellow of infinite jest, of most excellent fancy', because death is the great equaliser. In *King Lear*, the king brings ruin upon himself due to his foolish pride, and ends up roaming a heath during a thunderstorm, accompanied by his Fool and by Kent. The king is reduced in stature and equated with his Fool. Luck, fame, money, power are all things tricky (and tricksterish) in their transience.

Failure for the urban professional means loss of the determined place in the Durkheimian society. It means inability to retain the status of 'useful' in the metaphorical body of organs in which each body part strives to become narrow-specialised, and, consequently, unique and difficult to replace. In Carrey's films, various tricksterish chances, incidents and accidents dissolve this narrow specialisation of the protagonists and take away their work-place, which also happens to host their professional and personal identity. Many of Carrey's protagonists – Stanley Ipkiss, Fletcher Reede, Bruce Nolan, Carl Allen, Dick Harper – define themselves through their jobs while an 'open' trickster like Steven Russell has the ability to morph into men of different professions and even imitate professional slang. Some of Carrey's fools, try as they might, cannot altogether see what their 'deter-minable function' is. After failing at a number of jobs, a pair of chronic losers, Lloyd and Harry from *Dumb and Dumber*, come to the conclusion that their ideal narrow specialism would be cultivating worms – and even establishing a 'worm business'.

The 'worms' is an allegorical source of social commentary on Lloyd and Harry's unwanted lives. Their inability to find their place in the sun makes them invisible, marginalised nobodies. Like many other Carrey protago-nists, they are not organs at all but replaceable cells and have very little say in the way the system is organised. They are everymen, struggling and failing to become 'heroes', and ultimately displaying headless, heroic idiocy.

The Mask (1994)

The job of Stanley Ipkiss, the protagonist of *The Mask*, is certainly not 'proportionate to his effort'. He is a bank clerk, 'a puny individual' bullied by his manager (the boss's son) and living in constant danger of being fired. His social status (as well as his 'alpha maleness rank') in Edge City is pretty low: he does not have a flashy car, does not own a house and has to rent a stupid flat with a stupid landlady attached, female colleagues ignore his advances and he is not allowed into the city's hottest nightclub. Even his talismanic 'power tie', which is supposed 'to make you feel powerful', cannot help him compete with stronger males – either at work or in the night club. He is invisible.

In the words of his colleague Peggy (Any Yasbeck), on whom he has a hopeless crush, Stanley is a 'nice guy'. This quality, however, is as extraneous in the world of banking as it is in the mafia-controlled nightlife of Edge City. The city has an edge. Deep beneath its civilised exterior lies what Stanley's friend Charlie (Richard Jeni) calls 'the darkest heart of the urban jungle' where the males fight for power, influence, and beautiful females. One must be aggressive in order to survive. One should not display any signs of 'weakness' in the jungle: when the car mechanics perceive the obvious absence of obligatory toughness in Stanley, they rip him off by claiming that his old car needs 'more repairs'.

When Stanley attempts to join the alpha-male club and get through the Coco Bongo security, he is immediately shown his place, which is beyond the velvet rope: because he is a nobody, he is thrown out of the club; because he is a nobody, a passing car splashes him all over; and the porter who brings him his rotten Studebaker also makes sure that Stanley understands the fact that he is a nobody. But the worst is yet to come – just when Stanley is humiliated, soaked, snubbed, assaulted and verbally abused by virtually every male in town, when he is in the lowest of spirits and looking worse for wear – he chances to meet Tina Carlyle (Cameron Diaz's breakthrough role), his bank client.

Meeting with Tina Carlyle is the last straw in the pile of disasters that make Stanley face the abyss of his own 'loserness'. Crushed, he drives home but his car falls apart on the bridge. Upon coming out, he catches a glimpse of something unusual in the dark water. Thinking that it might be a person drowning, the nice man Stanley dives in and rescues a green mask. He takes it home unaware that it contains the supernatural powers of Loki, the Norse god of mischief.

The discovery of the mask is narratively linked to Stanley's infatuation with Tina. The woman becomes the 'trickster trigger' in the comedy's plot. Falling in love with an expensive woman makes Stanley rethink the uncomfortable issues of money and male status. Plus, she belongs to the city's 'underworld': she has a mafioso boyfriend who sends her to banks on reconnaissance missions. By falling in love with a dangerous female (dressed in red), Stanley metaphorically reconnects with his inner 'underworld', as well as automatically 'connects' to all the underworlds of the urban jungle.

When Stanley becomes the Mask, he releases his inner trickster, and with it all the powers of chaos and anarchy. His old loser self is swept away by the wave of carnivalesque disorder. The task of winning over an expensive woman drives the formerly meek guy to rob banks, assault the police and confront the local mafia. Predictably, the turmoil he causes in town is as carnivalesque as it is deathly. The Mask is still the trickster rather than the shadow, especially in comparison to Nicholson's Joker, but some of his tricks cross the boundary of cheerful insanity and acquire darker shades; for instance, he guns down local hooligans and shoves exhaust pipes up the car mechanics' rectums.

To match the tricksterish power and ruthlessness of the urban jungle, Stanley has to shed his natural niceness and become a shadow of himself (Dick Harper chooses a similar path when he starts breaking the rules, ignoring the law and behaving in a generally antisocial way). The loser becomes the winner when he stops being a good citizen and an obedient 'organ' of the corporate machine. He wins by applying the law of natural selection to human life. In the end, however, Stanley comes back to his humanity and substitutes the very efficient 'survival of the fittest' technique with a set of normal human relationships. The human being is back, but only after going through the hell of animal existence with its ruthless competition and fragile liminal balance between life and death.

The Invisible Middle-Class Anger

Many hard-working trickster protagonists become angry for no apparent reason. Carrey seems to be especially keen to explore this issue; but other trickster films, among them *Drop Dead Fred*, *Click*, and *Anger Management*, also have as their protagonists people whose job clashes with their personal life. Sometimes the trapped anger is released – or even triggered by therapists or pseudo-therapists who themselves act as tricksters in protagonists' lives. Once it is released, the effect is calamitous. In the scene in which Warren Schmidt (*About Schmidt*) is left alone with Vicky Rusk (Connie Ray) while her husband John (Harry Groener) is gone in search of canned beer, Vicky (who is an occupational therapist by profession) tells Warren that she sees in him 'a sad, sad man'. When he responds that, of course, he is sad because he has just suffered a terrible loss, Vicky comes up with the idea that Warren's main hidden problem is not sadness, but anger. It is anger that makes him leave his house and travel in his van across the middle of the United States. When the therapist mentions anger, the trickster in Warren escapes and crosses the boundary between the therapeutic and the personal relationship. Having mistaken her genuine 'motherly' concern for him for sexual attraction, he makes sexual advances which are aggressively rebuked. Realising that he has mistakenly crossed into enemy territory, Warren jumps up and runs to his van which he sees as a kind of safe and reliable 'womb'. The repressed trickster has escaped, and wrecked his newly-acquired friendship with the Rusks.

That anger transforms into trickster is not an accident. In the sterile post-industrial society, where all the corners are smoothed up and all the grotesqueness is carefully camouflaged, there is no place for strong and raw emotions. In fact, strong emotions are a taboo. The trickster, so oversized and explosive, poses a danger for the hyper-polite, super-nice, largely well-bred urban population. Overall suppressed, the urban trickster is relegated to the criminal underworld and the land of slums and ghettoes. Trickster rebellion is for outlaws, rappers, the homeless, and disaffected youths. Your normal non-liminal middle-class man (or woman) is expected to comply with the rules of urban behaviour.

The tension between the tough demands of the workplace on the one hand, and the requirements and formalities of post-industrial lifestyle on the other, provides a very fertile soil for the trickster. In this sense, capitalist democracy is deeply oxymoronic as it demands externally civilized behaviour while promoting competitiveness and foregrounding survival skills.

Urban environments – overcrowded underground stations, packed trains, busy subways, streets in peak hour, queues, coffee houses, traffic jams – build up stress because, deep down, they appeal to our most basic, animal reactions – fight or flight response, fear and panic, self-preservation, greed, competitiveness, domination and subjugation. They promote impulsivity. They trigger acute reactions and natural responses that we, as civilized human beings, are not supposed to show in public. In his book *The Metropolis and Mental Life* (1903), the German sociologist Georg Simmel explores the change in human reactions prompted by the peculiarities of the urban environment:

> The psychological basis of the metropolitan type of individuality consists in the *intensification of nervous stimulation* which results from the swift and uninterrupted change of outer and inner stimuli. [. . .] Lasting impressions, impressions which differ only slightly from one another, impressions which take a regular and habitual course and show regular and habitual contrasts – all these use up, so to speak, less consciousness than does the rapid crowding of changing images, the sharp discontinuity in the grasp of a single glance, and the unexpectedness of onrushing impressions. These are the psychological conditions which the metropolis creates. With each crossing of the street, with the tempo and multiplicity of economic, occupational and social life, the city sets up a deep contrast with small town and rural life with reference to the sensory foundations of psychic life. The metropolis exacts from man as a discriminating creature a different amount of consciousness than does rural life. Here the rhythm of life and sensory mental imagery flows more slowly, more habitually, and more evenly. Precisely in this connection the sophisticated character of metropolitan psychic life becomes understandable – as over against small town life which rests more upon deeply felt and emotional relationships.
>
> (Schwartz and Przyblyski, 2004: 51–52)

Simmel proposes that, as a result of this incessant bombardment of the senses, the metropolitan type of man 'develops an organ protecting him against the threatening currents and discrepancies of his external environment which would uproot him. He reacts with his head instead of his heart' (Schwartz and Przyblyski, 2004: 52). Strong as this 'organ' is, the repressed animal-trickster beneath the shield gains energy as our basic instincts are denied an outlet for their activity.

Besides, in order to achieve professional, material and personal success (because of the cultural emphasis on progress and achievement) human beings have to negotiate their way through life. This includes constant, and often tense and uncomfortable interaction with fellow citizens. In the process of this interaction we have to continuously define and redefine what it means to be human because the instinctual, the competitive, keeps seeping onto the surface against our will. The problem of keeping the trickster in its place lies at the heart of the division of labour. People have to compete for the limited number of good jobs available, and therefore be ambitious, ruthless, unkind to each other. The reality of the division of labour does not go well with the superficial niceties of the rules of urban behaviour.

As the American psychotherapist Sheldon Kopp writes regarding the role of instincts in human interaction:

> The presence of human beings offers a continuous challenge to the face we would present to the world. Each of us has been taught to maintain some measure of constraint of our primitive appetites, to present at least the appearance of sociability and self-control. The virtues of good character (however they may vary from group to group) are supposed to be in evidence. Some element of respect for the other, of cooperation, of candour, and of modesty are expected. A certain modicum of civilized demeanour is demanded, as we play out the masked dance of social accommodation. We act as though we are not driven by powerful biological urges, not haunted by dark primitive images, as though our social identities represent who we really are. In order to maintain this acceptable sense of theatre, social interaction is replete with ceremonies, conventions and ritual dialogues which preserve the gloss of civilization.
>
> (Kopp, 1974: 32)

All the while, 'the urban type' is forced to maintain what Jung calls 'the persona' which is, in fact, analogous to Simmel's 'organ' which protects the inner contents of the psyche from the harsh conditions of the fast-changing external environment. The persona is, according to Jung, a 'functional complex which has come into existence for reasons of adaptation and or necessary convenience, but by no means is identical with the individuality. [. . .] [It is] a compromise between the demands of the environment and the inner structural necessity of the individual' (Jacobi, 1973: 27–28). In a well-adjusted individual, the persona is a 'subtle protective coating that makes for easy, natural relations with the outside world' (1973: 28). This 'official' mask has two aspects: 'the ego-ideal', or wish image on which the individual 'would like his nature and behaviour to be modelled', and the traits approved by the external collectivity (1973: 28). There is always tension building up beneath the mask between the personal and the collective, one's personal vision of oneself and the officially approved, unified, collective norms of behaviour. Human instincts make this conflict even more complex as they bring about another, 'uncontrollable', unknown dimension into the equation. It spurs the conflict on and stirs up the tension.

Trickster protagonists suffering from repressed anger often realise that there is something 'weird' going on in their head but cannot pinpoint the source of psychological discomfort. They split off the anger until it becomes personified in a shadowy trickster – a friend, enemy, stalker or even a psychotherapist. The trickster – and the trickster in narratives – is born with the release of stored-up tension, the frustration, the anger, but it also helps protagonists to understand where 'it all went wrong'.

Anger Management (2003)

In *Anger Management* Nicholson's character is the antagonist – a devilish 'anger therapist' who opens the plug holding Dave Buznik's (Adam Sandler) strong emotions. Therapy is presented in the film as a way of releasing the demons which, when free, ruin the artificial façade of Dave's life. On the surface of it, he has a 'perfect' life – a girlfriend he loves and a silly but creative job (he designs pet clothes). Dave is extremely nice to everyone and avoids confrontation and potentially explosive situations.

One day, however, a very different side of him comes to the surface. While on board a plane, he supposedly has 'an anger attack' for the first time in his life. There are numerous reasons for his sudden revolt: someone else has occupied his seat, and he has to sit next to a seedy man with a weird smile. The air conditioning diffuser is broken. The new neighbour has the habit of laughing loudly and stupidly while Dave is trying to sleep. Like any public expression of raw emotion, this laugh makes Dave very uncomfortable. Even worse – the seedy guy asks Dave, pointing at a big-breasted actress on his screen, what his 'position' on breast implants is. His voice is so loud and he sounds so excited that female passengers in neighbouring seats become alarmed. In order to get rid of the annoying passenger, Dave requests a pair of headphones, but has to wait a long time before the air stewards, who keep chatting and giggling between themselves, remember about his existence.

After reminding the staff about the headphones several times, Dave becomes more desperate and grabs one of the stewardesses by the hand. Amazed at this sudden physical contact with a stranger, the hostess tells him not to raise his voice. She reminds him that 'our country is going through a very difficult time right now, and if you are not going to cooperate . . .'. Like this, and much against his 'civilised' and refined will, Dave becomes embroiled into a very public exchange of unpleasantries which is clearly getting out of control. Eventually a big guard arrives and incapacitates the argumentative passenger, who refuses to 'calm down' at the 'difficult time for the country', with an electroshock weapon. The camera then cuts from the shot of Dave shaking from the shock to the horrified women in the middle aisle. Dave's humiliation is complete and, worse, is unashamedly public – something he has feared since childhood when a bully pulled off his pants in front of his prospective 'girlfriend'. The next syntagma of the film begins with a shot of Dave in court where he is found guilty of assault and consequently 'prescribed' 20 hours of anger management therapy. He learns, with horror and disbelief, that his new therapist is the very guy who caused his spectacular downfall during the flight.

The location for Dave's first anger attack is not surprising. Symbolically, the plane in the twenty-first century is what the train used to be in the nineteenth – a space where the body feels at its most vulnerable; a place where people feel anxious, and now – in the era of terrorism – become easily suspicious of each other. Whereas railways were the servants of capitalist modernity, airlines serve post-industrial capitalism because they link distant financial centres, factories and consumers (Headrick, 1988: 12). The effect of a train journey is psychologically uprooting – but it still leaves the passenger with a limited sense of control over the environment because the wheels still 'touch the earth'.

By contrast, on board the plane passengers feel 'in mid air', displaced. The enclosed, stifling space of the airplane is where people feel 'on edge', at the mercy of some external forces. Ideally, if they cannot control these forces, they would at least like to trust the science which has built this plane and made it possible to safely cross such vast distances. They would like to trust the accuracy of rationality; they would like to believe in its infallibility and invincibility – after all, their lives depend on it. Passengers are constantly on alert because, deep down, they do not trust this technology and suspect that flying inside a 'metal bird' is somehow unnatural.

Besides, airports and planes are spaces where large numbers of people are 'processed' every day. Following a number of contemporary cultural theorists (Georges Benko, Mark Augé, Zygmunt Bauman) we can call transitional spaces like airports 'non-places'. As George Benko argues in his analysis of the relationship between mobility and space in postmodernity, 'non-places combine the characteristics of those spaces which people simply move through, and of imposing a form of behaviour on their users that can be described as machine-like, reducing individuals to the status of operators' (Benko and Strohmayer, 1997: 23). It is a space

> devoid of the symbolic expressions of identity, relations and history: examples include airports, motorways, anonymous hotels rooms, public transport . . . Never before in the history of the world have non-spaces occupied so much space. But we are not dealing with a contrast between a good place, human, and a bad place, dehumanized. Living in a small village, where everyone is watching you, is not always a pleasant experience. A place can have too much 'soul'. This 'soul' shapes the milieu, and the results can be oppressive. Conversely, a

non-place is not necessarily unpleasant. Waiting in an airport lounge
for one's flight can be an occasion for calm reflection.

(1997: 23)

And, most importantly, 'the frequenting of non-places today provides a
historically unprecedented experience of solitary individuality and non-
human mediation between the individual and the collectivity' (1997: 26).
Non-places embody the split, so characteristic of modernity, between the
public and the private realms. Crowds of strangers are brought together;
squashed in relatively small spaces, subjected to stressful situations and
asked to 'remain calm'. The airport crowd – just like any urban crowd – is
prone to all kinds of barely hidden 'shadow activities', from restrained mass
anxiety to open hostility. The plane syntagma of *Anger Management* also
shows what happens when, in the culture which values privacy above
openness, two or more strangers are forced into a potentially intimate
situation. The psychical distance between people on the plane is very small.
Being a trickster, Dr. Buddy Rydell explores and exploits this tension by
crossing certain boundaries which are normally supposed to be observed in
official interpersonal communication. He laughs, he snores, he makes
cheeky comments. His hand rests too close to Dave's (a special metonymic
cut-in shot is devoted to this issue). Modernity separated people yet it
occasionally brings them together – a situation which is potentially fraught
with all kinds of 'trickster inflammations' and outbursts.

Another leading sphere of urban life, with its paradoxical connotations of
speed, convenience and stress, is the road. This is why Dr. Rydell chooses a
traffic jam as a platform for one of his 'anger control' exercises. The car is an
enclosed space; a space which can potentially kill or trap the driver and the
passengers. Even when it is physically safe, psychologically it is not. Heavily
congested urban traffic is fraught with negative trickster potential.

In the traffic jam scene, Nicholson's character makes Dave stop the car in
the middle of a bridge, thus blocking the flow. Dave's therapeutic task is to
sing, in a perfectly calm voice, *I Feel Pretty* from Leonard Bernstein's *West
Side Story* (1957) disregarding the swearing, hooting, alarm screeching and
suchlike insults aimed at him. The hidden aim of the exercise is not to keep at
bay the 'anger monkey' (in Dr. Rydell's therapy talk), but to expose the
'unmanly', weak, effeminate elements in Dave's character – the ones that do
not go well with the tough corporate culture in which he has to survive every
day. In order to match his behaviour to the male ideal of his culture, he has
to release his hidden anger, acknowledge it, and then own up to it. Dave has
to resolve the paradox of Western culture – how to be a powerful man
without being a ruthless brute. Keeping up appearances is all that matters.

Dave's lack of confidence and hidden anger are tied in the film to the
perennial trickster issue of the penis size. Penis size is the traditional
metaphor for masculinity and masculine behaviour. It is a mercurial trope

as it has a miraculous ability to extend into many spheres of life and penetrate the smallest aspects of male existence. Ironically, the small penis also becomes a scapegoat. Dave lacks confidence and cannot stand up to his bullying boss – and he blames it onto his penis size. In the toilet he stands next to Linda's ex-boyfriend Andrew (who is still in love with her and hopes to win her back) and becomes very stressed about the unfavourable difference between their genitals. Whenever he compares himself to other males – his boss, Andrew the 'reliable' rival, Dr. Rydell – he feels like a loser. What is repressed in him, however, is the rough, aggressive 'top male' whom he usually associates with 'low classes'.

Dave, the nice and decent middle-class professional, is forced to take group therapy sessions with predominantly low class men – drunkards, drug-addicts, failures, prostitutes who, to Dave's civilised disgust, express their feelings openly and vigorously. He is reluctant to join the group (and even sits separately) until he is introduced to them as 'the guy who has assaulted the flight attendant' which is immediately translated by the working-class guys as 'the woman beater'. Most people in the anger class are non-white-males; they are either female or belong to various ethnic minorities. Dave is also assigned an 'anger buddy' whose name is Chuck (John Turturro) and with whom Dave is supposed to engage in mutual therapy.

In fact, Chuck is yet another shadow who is capable of bringing out Dave's worst qualities. Eventually, Chuck manages to 'drag him down to his level' when he involves him into a pub brawl during which Dave incidentally hits a waitress with a cane. Now, Dave is a real woman-beater and aggressor. And although his 'beating', 'fighting' and 'assaulting' are all accidental – metaphorically speaking, they are escaped fragments of tricksterish masculinity which in real life is repressed in him, they still define him and influence his life in a feasible way.

The issue of the hidden anger and its expression is closely connected with the problem of social class; the problem of good breeding; exemplary behaviour; the problem of emotional self-expression. Dave is terrified to 'release' the trickster because, for him, anger and aggression belong to the realm of the underdogs, underclasses, scum, underpaid people. He regards anger as 'primitive', and so the narrative presents powerful emotions as if they just 'happen' to him, they are split off and realised in several shadow figures. They exist separately. In the end of the film Dr. Rydell manages to 'elevate' Dave to the appropriate level of masculinity by pretending to take away his girlfriend thus forcing the protagonist to fight for her.

The climax of this trickster narrative takes places in a suitably masculine setting – at the stadium – during a New York Yankees match. Dave runs through security, usurps the microphone and proposes to Linda in front of the whole audience. His 'initiation' is a ludic event; it happens in a public place; a place where crowds gather to watch 'rough' and manly games.

Symbolically, this is equal to the birth of a hero. After this climax all the trickster has to do is dissolve, and he does – but not before leaving a congratulatory note on the stadium score board.

The Cable Guy (1996)

Ben Stiller's dark comedy *The Cable Guy* (1996) also discusses the social aspect of suppressed anger. The three-named Chip-Larry-Ricardo is a blue-collar worker and the shadow of a 'clean' and successful town-planning consultant Steven Kovacs (Matthew Broderick). Like Dave Buznik in *Anger Management*, Steven is a professional who is somewhat 'impotent' in his niceness and good breeding. As in Dave's case, his malleable and fragile character does not go well with the system for which he is working. Also, like Dave, he has a phobia of working-class people.

The traditional double (and shadowy trickster), Larry-Ricardo takes the protagonist with him 'to the underworld'. Metaphorically speaking, he drags him 'down' until Steven reaches his social level. The aggression and roughness, personified in the Cable Guy, gradually merge into Steven's character (or rather, emerge out of his character). Not surprisingly, Steven's tough masculinity becomes visible during ludic events – collective games (basketball with colleagues after work), role plays (medieval knight fights), even family gatherings ('the sexual puns game' which Larry-Ricardo insists on playing with Steven's parents, rather to the poor architect's incestuous horror).

That Steve's trickster ('the anger monkey') escapes during public events is not surprising. In the words of Sharon Rowe, sports are important liminal events because they are both ludic and controlled – they are rituals promoting collective identification, collective projection and collective transformation. Sports, Rowe argues, like the tribal rituals Turner describes, 'are occasions for public reflexivity and metacommunication' (St. John, 2008: 136). They do so because of their projective-introjective dynamic, because 'athletes serve as symbolic representations of ourselves. Through their efforts we witness ourselves in defeat and in sublime transcendence' (2008: 136). Like any other postmodern play phenomenon, Graham St. John adds, sports is a consumer product because 'commodification of free play is central to life under capital' (St. John, 2008: 152). However, even in this commercialised form it has ludic power and communal importance because it brings together the fragmented, alienated urban individuals; and because it provides new, collective meaning for what Zygmunt Bauman calls 'restless, fickle and irresolute identities' (Bauman, 1996: 32, quoted in St. John, 2008: 152).

In fact, sports games can be considered liminal happenings even though they are commercialised, relatively safe and limit the public's participation in performances. The projective-introjective flow between the viewers and the sportsmen, although non-physical, is nevertheless psychologically vital.

This exchange makes the audience feel 'as one', united, having a collective goal, a collective meaning. Far from being deliberately 'excluded' from the stage, the spectators participate in the game via this emotional exchange, gaining power and joy from their unique liminal experience. Controversially, they also provide a vent for bottled-up energy and aggression.

In the scene in which Steven takes his new friend along to play basketball with the colleagues from work, the 'two aggressions' – those of Steven and Larry-Ricardo – are still separate. Steven is watching his friend with disgust and disbelief: the Cable Guy turns into an unstoppable wild beast, breaks the rules of the game ('we're playing prison rules, ha?!'), deliberately collides with other players, pushes people to the floor and pulls terrible faces (given Carrey's 6'2 frame, the brawl looks impressive and physically powerful indeed). The game sequence is shot in slow motion, as if to emphasise the dreamy nature of this uncontrollable, violent process. The culmination of the Cable Guy's alpha-male efforts is the 'scoring moment', when he jumps onto the back of Steven's best friend Rick (Jack Black) and pushes the ball through the net, breaking in the process the glass backboard, while the other players are helplessly looking on. The bird's eye camera shows him lying on the floor, sweaty and covered in glass fragments. 'I love this game' he gushes.

This uncontrollable explosion of masculine, competition-driven rage and power terrifies Steven. After all, is not sports supposed to be a controlled release of the trickster, akin to a metaphorical wrestling cage in which men can have their testosterone surge without going 'over the top' thanks to a set of rational rules and regulations? However, rules and regulations, as team sports often demonstrate, are not always easy to follow when you have two groups of supercharged males aiming for victory. Basic reactions are often far more powerful than rules and any other fragile constructions of the civilised brain. That is why the meek Steven is looking at the sweaty giant in awe, and is quick to renounce the image he sees in the mirror: 'You ruined the game. [. . .] We are not even friends, I don't even know you.'

The scene at the 'Medieval Times' club further clarifies Steven's relationship with his well-hidden masculinity. The club is supposed to be a liminoid space – kitsch and commercialised, with established rules, cheap decorations and medieval-punk waitresses offering cola and fried chicken to 'the lords'. This kind of role play is safe in its liminoidness because the precapitalist, medieval bestiality is held in check by the god of commerce, and the instruction-creating and barrier-raising rationality. Nothing is real in postmodernity, and this all-permeating fakeness is in itself a guarantor of safety. But the god of commerce is himself a trickster, and therefore no space where he reigns is safe. Steven and Larry-Ricardo are munching on their chicken, watching armoured 'knights' wielding various swords and axes, when 'the king' announces that 'now two noblemen from our audience will fight to death to resolve a grievance'. This is when Steven realises that, even with all the signs of commercialisation and consumerism – the cola, the drinks bar, the table service, the fried chicken legs – the place is not secure. It is not capitalist-liminoid, but in fact pre-capitalist-liminal. It is a medieval ludic place where rough men let off their steam while the mad crowd is wildly cheering. Health and safety is gone out of the window, rules are non-existent and all possible boundaries are crossed. Worst of all, it is 'a fight to death' which means that the very last boundary – the entrance into the underworld – can be easily crossed as well.

While preparing for the fight, Steven is trying to discern the line between 'fantasy' and 'reality', between safety and danger in a place like this. Is it all for real? Is this hatred, with which Larry-Ricardo is brimming, real as well? 'Is it safe?' – he asks Larry-Ricardo, concerned about the armour and the absence of any instructions. His friend's reply is: 'You are my sworn enemy and are about to meet your demise!'. And indeed, Larry-Ricardo is 'fighting to death' with all the seriousness of an actor – roaring, charging like a mad bull and wielding his axe with no apparent concern for either safety or health. He knocks Steven off his feet several times, each time nearly seriously hurting him. Steven stubbornly refuses to 'fight back' because he thinks that the battle is a set-up and one of Larry-Ricardo's silly tricks. Meanwhile, the Star Wars music keeps dragging the fight back onto the liminoid level while the aggression the Cable Guy displays is truly liminal.

The culmination of the contest is jousting. Finally, the meek Steven's fight or flight response switches onto the 'fight' mode – which, in fact, means that the trickster has done his job well. Spurned on, and amazed at his own brutality, Steven knocks the Cable Guy off his 'steed' with such a forceful blow that it makes his 'sworn enemy' plummet onto the floor. When Steven runs up to his enemy-friend and takes off his helmet, the stunned but satisfied-looking Larry-Ricardo announces to him: 'Well done, good sir. You're the victor. But we will meet again.'

Participation in a ludic event is a form of initiation, and the event triggers a transformation in Steven. From now on, the architect's demise is sealed. He used to know his boundaries – but he no longer does so. Even though the trickster is fully 'separated' from the protagonist, the rough, working-class, testosterone-driven lover of low entertainment manages to 'drag' the clean middle-class guy down to his level and taint him with his shady activities. The first instance of 'crossing the line' is the installation of illegal channels in Steven's new flat. Then come the 'present' of a very expensive entertainment system (including a karaoke machine) and a prostitute whom the Cable Guy hires for Steven 'as a token of friendship' (however failing to tell him that she is 'a working girl', and is not genuinely interested in him as a man). The karaoke party, with its weird participants, the undercover prostitute, blackmail photography (Chip takes pictures of Steven and Heather (Misa Koprova) having sex) and stolen goods, is the 'culmination' of tricksterish illegality and edginess.

The karaoke mini-climax results in Steven rejecting Chip's friendship and excluding him from his life. In return, the Cable Guy completely ruins Steven's life by driving his 'tricksterisation' to its logical (or illogical) conclusion. The video of Steven slagging off his boss magically appears in all the computers in the office. Steven gets fired; he also gets arrested for possession of stolen property. Meanwhile, 'the sworn enemy' worms his way into the hearts of Steven's parents and his girlfriend, Robin. One by one, he takes away all of Steven's people who begin to think that Steven has recently become too angry, irrational and impulsive (at one point, Steven punches Chip in the face in front of Robin and the parents). By the time the final battle between the urban individual and his shadow takes place, Steven's career, personal reputation and love life are reduced to ashes.

On the one hand, Steven's demise perfectly fits into the 'changing fortunes' theme of traditional trickster narratives. Fate is a tricky customer and can turn the highly successful man into a loser any minute. Put this way, 'fate' does not promote complacency and keeps everyone in fear of failure. But on the other hand, Steven's story is era-specific as it documents the changing fortunes of a middle-class male professional, a 'clean' but somewhat directionless urbanite. It shows the very thin line between winners and losers, success and failure, legality and illegality, 'the real thing' and blatant commercialism in the complex post-industrial world.

Chapter 4

The Trickster and Contemporary Powers

Contemporary trickster film shows the individual as unfree, as trapped within existential boundaries. The ubiquitous 'system' in the life of trickster protagonists takes a number of forms: the state, the workplace, consumer culture, family demands. Ranging from 'silly movies' (*Ace Ventura*, *Dumb and Dumber*, *Beetlejuice* or *Drop Dead Fred*) to existentialist masterpieces which raise the problem of the individual's control over his or her life – for instance, *The Truman Show* (1998) or *Eternal Sunshine of the Spotless Mind* (2004), trickster films raise the problems of human agency and creative spontaneity in contemporary world. Whereas many of the boring protagonist's problems are of personal character – oppressive parents and failed relationships – these issues are inscribed into the constrictive and over-regulated framework of urban culture. His individuation takes place in the atmosphere of metropolitan disconnectedness, in the world of corporate hierarchies and all-pervasive consumerism.

The Powers

When the dictatorship of custom, tradition and religion is lifted (the ritual, Turner argues, is specifically created to induce people 'to want to do what they must do' (Turner, 1975: 56)), and the freedom of personal choice is introduced, human beings do not automatically become wonderfully, and boundlessly, emancipated. The Marxist theorist Terry Eagleton is sceptical about the ability of contemporary society to make people free. Not only they are not free, he argues; far from that – they remain faithful servants of the capitalist system, forced to keep it afloat by taking an active part in the never-ending cycle of consumption and production:

> One of the most moving narratives of modern theory is the story of how men and women languishing under various forms of oppression came to acquire, often at great personal cost, the sort of technical knowledge necessary for them to understand their own condition more deeply, and so to acquire some of the theoretical armoury essential to

change it. It is an insult to inform these men and women that, in the economic metaphor for intellectual life now prevalent in the USA, they are simply 'buying into' the conceptual closures of their masters, or colluding with phallocentrism.

(Eagleton, 1996: 5)

The postmodern multiplication of identities, which is sketched out so well in the lives of trickster film protagonists, is, in fact, a consequence of lifestyle changes which became perceivable for the first time in Western societies as early as the mid-nineteenth century. Elimination of the so-called natural community does not necessarily mean unrestrained freedom. Instead of the tyranny of communal rules, the hegemony of the *habitus*, citizens of the modern metropolis are faced with the Durkheimian 'organ network' or the Weberian 'iron cage'. Marshall Berman writes in *All That is Solid Melts into Air*:

> To be modern is to live a life of paradox and contradiction. It is to be overpowered by immense bureaucratic organisations that have the power to control and often to destroy all communities, values, lives; and yet to be undeterred in our determination to face these forces, to fight to change their world and to make it our own. [. . .]
>
> To be modern is to find ourselves in an environment that promises us adventure, power, joy, growth, transformation of ourselves and the world – and, at the same time, that threatens to destroy everything we have, everything we know, everything we are. Modern environments and experiences cut across all boundaries of geography and ethnicity, of class and nationality, of religion and ideology: in this sense, modernity can be said to unite all mankind. But it is a paradoxical unity, a unity of disunity; it pours us all into a maelstrom of perpetual disintegration and renewal, of struggle and contradiction, of ambiguity and anguish. To be modern is to be part of a universe in which, as Marx said, 'all that is solid melts into air'.
>
> (Berman, 1983: 13–15)

Long before Berman, Jung too criticised the 'bureaucratic' structure of modern society. As a psychologist, Jung was concerned with the hidden dangers of state control in the West. Industrialisation indeed dissolved natural communities with their 'mechanical solidarity' and cohesion based on common roots of identity (Durkheim, 1964: 105), and replaced them with urban crowds consisting of individuals who have very little to do with each other. Jung warned that these fragmented, porous societies, despite their democratic veneer, instrumental rationality and atomistic individualism, have a tendency to solidify (with the help of media) into shadowy monsters with one mind, one soul and one dangerous ideology (often national-socialist). The banishment of old demons does not automatically make a society more 'modern' or less irrational for, Jung argued, 'mankind is not just an accumulation of individuals utterly different from one another, but possesses such a high degree of psychological collectivity that in comparison the individual appears merely as a slight variant' (CW18: para. 313).

The State, Jung postulated, has been transformed in the minds of its subjects into a kind of king: it is invoked, made responsible, grumbled at, and perceived as 'the inexhaustible giver of all good' (CW10: para. 554). Meanwhile, society is elevated to the rank of a supreme ethical principle (CW10: para. 554); it establishes and dictates lifestyles, often as effectively as the Durkheimian 'mechanical society'. Both of them, society and the state, limit the freedom of the individual at the micro, macro and any other imaginable level.

Not many good citizens, however rational, would be able to resist the 'engulfing force of attraction, when each man clings to the next and each drags the other with him' (CW10: para. 326f). The individual has to develop (or *individuate*, to use Jung's term) in an environment in which his mind is constantly in danger of being infiltrated, and infected, by the 'spirits' in the form of state-endorsed ideologies, social witch-hunts and political rituals. Jung writes in *Two Essays on Analytical Psychology* (1928):

> The old religions with their sublime and ridiculous, their friendly and fiendish symbols did not drop from the blue, but were born of this human soul that dwells within us at this moment. All those things, their primal forms, live on in us and may at any time burst in upon us with annihilating force, in the guise of mass-suggestions against which the individual is defenceless. Our fearsome gods have only changed their names: they now rhyme with *ism*.
>
> (CW7: para. 326)

And now, as Christopher Hauke rightly points out, we also have to worry about 'the effects of the global economy, mass media representation, and the homogenisation of styles and values – governed by those of North America and Europe – which comprise equal, and to some extent, more hidden, threats to the potential for subjects to become individual men and women' (Hauke, 2000: 169). As well as the scary state octopus, operating via bureaucracy and delivering its message through the media, there exist other individual-crushing giants; the new goliaths of the modern world. Zygmunt Bauman adds the media to the list of today's manipulators of the individual:

> Thanks to the immense capacities of electronic technology, spectacles can be created which offer a chance of participation and a shared focus

of attention to an indefinite multitude of psychically remote spectators. Due to the very massiveness of the audience and the intensity of focused attention, the individual finds himself or herself fully and truly 'in the presence of a force which is superior to him and before which he bows', the condition is thereby met which Emile Durkheim set for the reassuring power of moral guidance designed and enforced by society. The guidance is these days aesthetically, rather than ethically, operated. Its principal vehicle is no longer the ethical authority of leaders with their visions, or moral preachers with their homilies, but the example of 'celebrities in view' (celebrities *because* of being in view); neither the sanctions attached nor their scattered yet rough power of enforcement is its principal weapon.

(Bauman, 2001: 66)

Whereas mythological tricksters fight with personified representatives of the deterministic principle – Zeus, Thor, Odin – cinematic tricksters attempt to cause socio-political Ragnarök by insisting that the decrees and rules imposed by the gods of politics and economy are invalid because their inventors have long been dead. The rebels' reckless bravery leads to mixed results, often culminating in the death of the instigator, but it always manages to achieve its main goal – to rattle the cage, to shake the system – even if not to bring it down.

The Tramp Against Political Monsters

The use of socio-political tricksters in cinema goes back to Charlie Chaplin's nameless 'little men' swayed by the vast forces of modernity: industrial giants, political ideologies, social change. The Tramp is the tragic-comic mass man without the voice – the fact which the cinema of the silent era was expressing perfectly. Chaplin was reluctant to switch from 'the silents' to the talkies' for a number of reasons, including the cost of the new technology and its impact on his comedic style, which was physical and improvisational. His techniques were 'too far varied to limit his movements to the vicinity of a hidden microphone' (Flom, 1997: 52–53).

Chaplin's mass men are as ordinary as they are tragic. A typical Chaplin protagonist lacks a name (although in his autobiography Chaplin calls him 'Charlot'). He is the Tramp (*A Dog's Life*, 1918; *The Pilgrim*, 1923; *The Gold Rush*, 1925; *City Lights*, 1931; *Modern Times*, 1936) or the Jewish Barber (*The Great Dictator*, 1940). The absence of the name in trickster narratives symbolises the state of 'not being born', not being regarded a human being. In Chaplin's films it means being dismissed as a mere nuisance by the 'higher powers'. Under the given circumstances, Chaplin's invisible citizen has two choices: to comply and to swallow the bitter pill, which would put him in danger of joining in the collective shadow; or to rebel and take the risk of being overrun by the giant system. He loses in either case but he attempts to change his fate anyway.

The 'divine powers' of modernity are grand, influential and well-organised. The individual with a number instead of a name is nothing more than a plaything of the Shakespearean 'wanton gods'. Instead of joining the crowd and complying with the rules of the system, the little Tramp stages his own one-man revolt which, in different films, leads to different results. For instance, he wins in *A Dog's Life* but loses in *Modern Times*. This also depends on the genre: the earlier *Dog's Life* is pure slapstick – schematic and stereotypical, while *Modern Times*, Chaplin's first (reluctant) talkie, is equally melodramatic and comedic.

A Dog's Life (1918)

A Dog's Life opens with an establishing shot of a gloomy morning city, followed by the shot of the Tramp sleeping in his fenced enclave which he shares with his clever mongrel, Scraps (a real canine acting talent, later upgraded to 'pet status' by Chaplin). The fact that the fence is thoroughly holed makes it convenient for the Tramp to steal sausages when itinerant vendors unknowingly put down their steaming tin buckets next to his 'house'. A policeman passing by notices the transgression, and attempts to drag the Tramp out of his enclosure. Needless to say, all his attempts are unsuccessful as Charlie's character is cunning and agile. He repeatedly manages to escape the representative of law and order by rolling in and out of the enclave through a large gap under the wooden fence. When the policeman runs into the 'room', the Tramp rolls out; when the policeman runs out, the criminal rolls back in.

From this initial scene the motif of crossing and re-crossing the boundary seeps onto other planes of the narrative. The motif establishes the Tramp as a marginal creature, unwanted by society, and therefore relegated to exist inside his wooden cage. Having lost the fight for a job at the employment office, his only options are to scavenge from waste bins and to keep stealing food. The latter he does brilliantly and to a great comic effect – like in the scene with the hot food street stall, from which the protagonist successfully pinches cakes and sausages. Eventually fortune smiles on the Tramp when, assisted by his ingenious dog, he steals a wallet from a pair of pickpockets, and uses the money to set up a farm and start a happy married life with his girlfriend.

The Pilgrim (1923)

In *The Pilgrim* the symbol of the border has a political significance. The film opens with the Tramp, an escaped convict, changing into a minister's dress and taking a train to a small Texan town near the Mexican border.

The plot then unravels as a 'mistaken identity' case: in the small town where he gets off, the Tramp is taken for the reverend Mr. Pim (who was expected to arrive), and asked to perform his duties. Despite doing his best and even turning his sermons into improvisational comedy pieces, the fugitive is eventually discovered, taken by the sheriff to the Mexican border and kicked onto 'the other side'. After witnessing a shooting match between local outlaws, the Tramp realises that Mexico is probably not the safest place in the world. The final scene shows him, still in his ministerial guise, walking along the Mexican-American border in the perfect metaphor for the Turnerian 'betwixt and between'. He is neither here nor there, neither wild nor civilised. He is a criminal, an unwanted element of society, and has to be kept away from its mainstream cleanliness. He had illegally infiltrated society, and therefore needs to be returned to his usual place of abode – the margin.

The Great Dictator (1940)

The saddest of Chaplin's tricksters is the little Jewish Barber from *The Great Dictator*. Chaplin (who both wrote and directed the film) resorts to allegory to portray the fascist regime. Germany is renamed Tomania, Austria becomes Osterlich, Benito Mussolini is parodied as Benzino Napaloni, the dictator of Bacteria, and Hitler is Adenoid Hynkel. During the making of the film, the Chaplin Studios and the director personally received numerous threats from pro-Nazi sympathisers. For instance, in 1938 a German film magazine *Film-Kurier*, published in the United States, printed the following reaction to Chaplin's decision to make a film about the 'great leader': 'So, the Jewish minority in the USA is not disturbed in making game of the leader of a great foreign nation. Some day ago a regulation was laid down that prohibited despising foreign heads of state. When will America stick to this fundamental social convention in international relations in order to prevent such effronteries as the Jew Charlie Chaplin has up his sleeve?' (quoted in Flom, 1997: 144).

In spite of all these difficulties, the film was a tremendous success, both as a powerful humanitarian message and a long-overdue debut in talking pictures (1997: 145). However, Chaplin wrote in his biography in 1964: 'Had I known the actual horrors of the German concentration camps, I could not have made *The Great Dictator*, I could not have made fun of the homicidal insanity of the Nazis' (quoted in Flom, 1997: 129).

The film's protagonist is a Jewish Barber. Having lost his memory after a plane crash during the First World War, he is released from hospital years later, and finds himself in a changed country – 'a nation of blue-eyed blondes' presided over by a 'brunette dictator'. The Barber returns to his shop in the ghetto, only to discover a group of stormtroopers painting the word 'Jew' on his windows. He confronts them and a comic scuffle ensues, during which he is saved several times by a beautiful girl named Hannah (Paulette Goddard). Hannah uses a frying pan to inoculate his offenders. Eventually, the soldiers get hold of the rebel and are about to hang him when Commander Schultz, a high official in the Nazi Government, intervenes. Although the Barber cannot remember this, he had actually saved Schultz's life during the First World War (this is shown in the opening scene with the burning plane). The commander orders the troopers to leave the Barber and Hannah alone.

Meanwhile, Hynkel is planning to invade the neighbouring country of Osterlich, and needs money for the project. He is planning to get financial help from a Jewish financier, and therefore relaxes the prosecution of Tomanian Jews. The financier refuses, and Hynkel reinstates the prosecution. When Schultz voices his concerns about this decision, Hynkel condemns him as a traitor and dispatches him to a concentration camp. After a series of tragic-comic twists and turns, Schultz and the Barber escape from the camp wearing military uniforms. Because the Barber looks like Hynkel, he is mistaken by the border guards for 'der Phooey', and escorted to the capital to make an address to the newly-conquered people of Osterlich. At the same time, the real 'Phooey' is mistaken for the Barber, and arrested by his stormtroopers. The little Barber pronounces a speech in which he advocates peace and makes a point that fascism is the monstrous offspring of the desire to organise the world in a rational way. He famously says: 'We think too much and we feel too little.'

Chaplin's understanding of human beings as oxymoronic creatures, being capable of meanest horrors and as well as kindest gestures, fits very well into the trickster tradition. In his famous autobiography Chaplin outlines his theory of humour as a tension between the tragic and the comic. He writes that humour is hidden in

> the subtle discrepancy we discern in what appears to be normal behaviour. In other words, through humour we see in what seems rational, the irrational; in what seems important, the unimportant. It also heightens our sense of survival and preserves our sanity. Because of humour we are less overwhelmed by the vicissitudes of life. It activates our sense of proportion and reveals to us that in an over-statement of seriousness lurks the absurd.
>
> (Chaplin, 2003: 210)

Chaplin also argues that his own method of creating comedic narratives is based on subtle balance between the tragic and the comic:

> In the creation of comedy, it is paradoxical that tragedy stimulates the spirit of ridicule, because ridicule, I suppose, is an attitude of defiance: we must laugh in the face of helplessness against the forces of nature –

or go insane. I read a book about the Donner Party, who, on the way to California, missed the route and were snowbound in the Sierra Nevada mountains. Out of 160 pioneers, only 18 survived, most of them dying of hunger and cold. Some resorted to cannibalism, eating their dead, others roasted their moccasins to relieve their hunger. Out of this harrowing tragedy, I conceived one of our funniest scenes. In dire hunger, I boil my shoe and eat it . . .

(Chaplin, 2003: 299)

The director has always been able to use comic effects to describe tragic things – and to attract attention to these tragic events. For instance, the Barber's role is mostly silent, and, as Eric Flom shrewdly notes, 'nicely contrasted with the vocal and physical characteristics of Hynkel' (Flom, 1997: 132). His lack of voice and amnesia are expressive metaphors for the Holocaust, referring to the silencing and stripping of identity of the large ethnic group. The Barber is only given a significant speech when he is mistaken for Hynkel, not as himself. Without a mask (the uniform, the Tomanian identity), he is reduced to the role of the Tramp – pushed deep into the margins of society (and the margins of existence), forgotten, repressed, exterminated. He is forced to live in an enclave just as the Tramp is shut inside his wooden cage which he is forbidden to leave. By contrast, Hynkel and the Minister of Interior, Garbitsch (a parody of Joseph Goebbels), are given lengthy speeches.

'Der Phooey' pronounces his first speech in the film in German gibberish with English commentaries on the background. Chaplin turns Hynkel's performance into a comic masterpiece: 'der Phooey' is wildly gesticulating, pacing up and down the platform, demonstrating how the people of the country must 'tighten their belts' (the Minister of War, Herring, tightens his, but it immediately bursts unable to hold his fat belly), and using his mesmerising stare to bend microphone stands. The scene is a brilliant example of the Chaplian pantomime in which the sound is used primarily to enhance the message conveyed by movement. Hynkel's presence and manic physicality are far more expressive than his speech (which does not make sense anyway). Twice throughout the speech, Hynkel stops the audience's wild applause with a hand gesture, and a dead silence ensues. Like this, Chaplin uses the tricks of the sound era to show the power of gesture – and the power of the visual.

The classical 'mistaken identity' motif is used in the film in a bitter-ironic way to express the idea of the shadow. Due to the fact that their appearance is almost identical, Hynkel is mistaken for the Barber, and Barber for Hynkel. The little Jew as Hynkel's shadow extends in the narrative into the idea of a monstrous and tragic projection which turns Jewish people into the shadow of the whole of Tomania. This menacing and profoundly archetypal parallel is made clear in the narrative against the background theme of modernity and its discontents. Collective shadows are created by governments using the power of technology, which can be effectively employed to turn independently thinking individuals into mere agents of the state machine. Preceding the Barber-as-Hynkel's final address is the speech given by Garbitsch in which he declares that 'in the future, each man will serve the interest of the State with absolute obedience':

> Today, democracy, liberty, and equality are words to fool the people. No nation can progress with such ideas. They stand in the way of action. Therefore, we frankly abolish them. In the future, each man will serve the interest of the State with absolute obedience. Let him who refuses beware! The rights of citizenship will be taken away from all Jews and other non-Aryans. They are inferior and therefore enemies of the state. It is the duty of all true Aryans to hate and despise them. Henceforth this nation is annexed to the Tomanian Empire, and the people of this nation will obey the laws bestowed upon us by our great leader, the Dictator of Tomania, the conqueror of Osterlich, the future Emperor of the World!
> (THE GREAT DICTATOR Copyright © Roy Export S.A.S.
> All rights reserved.)

This diatribe is followed by the little Barber's impromptu and naïve address to the people of Osterlich. In this scene, the protagonist becomes Chaplin's mouthpiece and implores the nation in the grip of the collective shadow, which is shaped, propelled and empowered by the media, to pause and think about the consequences of their actions. In a wider context, he denounces modernity as a failed project and humanitarian disaster: instead of ensuring abundance, machinery has caused want; speed is discouraging people from establishing contact with each other; the airplane and the radio have brought human beings together but are now at the service of mon-strous ideologies; knowledge has turned humans into cynics; rationality has drained them of emotion and made them unkind. All that has been neglected has transmogrified into the terrifying collective monster of enor-mous proportions. Blind fascist violence is both the consequence and the pinnacle of the project that is modernity:

> I'm sorry, but I don't want to be an emperor. That's not my business. I don't want to rule or conquer anyone. I should like to help everyone if possible; Jew, Gentile, black man, white. We all want to help one another. Human beings are like that. We want to live by each other's happiness, not by each other's misery. We don't want to hate and despise one another. In this world there is room for everyone, and the good earth is rich and can provide for everyone. The way of life can be free and beautiful, but we have lost the way. Greed has poisoned men's

souls, has barricaded the world with hate, has goose-stepped us into misery and bloodshed. We have developed speed, but we have shut ourselves in. Machinery that gives abundance has left us in want. Our knowledge has made us cynical; our cleverness, hard and unkind. We think too much and feel too little. More than machinery, we need humanity. More than cleverness, we need kindness and gentleness. Without these qualities, life will be violent and all will be lost. The airplane and the radio have brought us closer together. The very nature of these inventions cries out for the goodness in men; cries out for universal brotherhood; for the unity of us all. Even now my voice is reaching millions throughout the world, millions of despairing men, women, and little children, victims of a system that makes men torture and imprison innocent people. [. . .]

This speech, made in English, is a response to Hynkel's gibberish pantomime at the start of the film. Chaplin, who takes over his character and almost appears 'as himself', finally utilises spoken word as it is meant to be used – to deliver a message. Chaplin's speech is a powerful trickster feat as it escapes the frame of the film, overcomes the restrictions of intradiegesis, and reaches out to audiences across the world. And although the (intradiegetic) audience appears to be cheering, the ending of the film is open and the Barber's fate is yet to be decided. Once again, the trickster is left between the states, in mid air, awaiting a resolution to his ordeal. This tricksterish 'open state', the rejection of the final solution plays a trick on the audience's desire to see all loose ends neatly tied up. There is no neat decision for a terrible political conflict. There are bound to be loose ends because 'the system' is an artificial, self-delusory invention which, when driven to its extreme, becomes ever more ruthless than 'the black tide of mud' it has long been disowning.

One Flew Over the Cuckoo's Nest (1975)

Perhaps the most famous trickster film about the horrors of institutional oppression is Milos Forman's One Flew Over the Cuckoo's Nest (1975) in which Jack Nicholson's character, Randall Patrick McMurphy, a criminal, rebel and rogue rolled into one, stages an open revolt in a mental institution to which he is sent after feigning insanity to avoid a prison sentence.

The screenplay is based on Ken Kesey's famous book of the same name published 13 years earlier. The troubled McMurphy joins the group of meek and scared patients suffering from a variety of mental health problems: the fragile and stuttering Billy Bibbit (Brad Dourif), the wimpy and outspoken (but deep down very indecisive) Charlie Cheswick (Sydney

Lassick), the highly intelligent but frightened Dale Harding (William Redfield), and 'Chief' Bromden (Will Sampson), an enormous but silent Native American who spends most of his day pushing a broom. The ward is governed by Nurse Ratched (Louise Fletcher) – a pale-faced, puffy, deeply unattractive, coldly sadistic matriarch. She ruthlessly imposes discipline and keeps her patients in awe. Her manipulation of the male patients amounts to symbolic emasculation. All members of the ward show signs of institutionalisation and, as most of them suffer from a lack of confidence, are unable to voice their concerns or defend their rights.

The finality of Nurse Ratched's word is challenged with McMurphy's arrival. Dissatisfied with the overall passivity, meekness and institutionalisation, he starts crossing boundaries of 'prescribed' behaviour, getting bolder and bolder with each move. He challenges the patients to vote for the World Series baseball game to be shown on the television on the ward; escapes over the wired fence, hijacks a bus and takes the patients deep sea-fishing; bribes the guard and smuggles women and alcohol into the ward; instigates Billy to have sex with Candy; and arranges a night of drinking and generally disorderly behaviour. His rebellion ends tragically: he is lobotomised. In the final scene of the film the 'mute' (but in reality selectively silent) Chief lifts up a hydrotherapy console, breaks the window with it, and escapes into the wilderness. The film famously ends with a long shot of Chief fading into the distance, applauded and cheered by the rest of the ward, all against the extra-diegetic background of the uncanny, heavily thereminned central musical theme.

Kesey wrote *One Flew Over the Cuckoo's Nest* in the 1960s, at the time of rapid social change and explosion of nonconformity; during the emergence of reactive postmodernity. It was also the time when the theoretical background of postmodernity was being formed. By placing the amoral rebel at the centre of the narrative, Kesey was expressing the spirit of his decade. Although *One Flew Over the Cuckoo's Nest* is not a postmodernist novel, it truly reflects the idea of the (illusory) 'end of authority', the powerful rebellion against the 'failed god', for the representatives of rationality in the book and in the film (there are narrative differences between the two) are pitiless to the point of inhumanity.

Nicholson's character in the film is the 'social' type of the trickster – the one who shakes the walls of a bureaucratic system in the hope to bring them down. McMurphy arrives into the narrative already 'repressed' and 'captured' as he is transferred from prison into the hospital. To emphasise the theme of captivity, Forman constantly visually foregrounds barriers, fences, partitions, sliding windows and other symbolic 'separators'. Thomas J. Slater analyses camera movement in the scene of McMurphy's arrival:

> For the second shot of the film, Forman pans from a window inside the hospital ward across the bed of one of the patients and on through

the room. The shot is from the viewpoint of a patient who could have been watching the car coming and then turned back to look across the room. [. . .]

Forman's starting the shot from the barrier formed between the two worlds by the wall and the opposite movement of the camera from the opening shot further support his quick division of the world in the film between the outside and the inside.

(Bloom, 2008: 126)

In fact, Forman makes full and creative use of the ward's 'natural geography': sometimes the camera shows the world as it is seen from the nurses' station (the focaliser observing the patients); sometimes the camera is outside and looking inside into the nurses' station through the sliding window; there is also the aforementioned window-ward pan and the shot in which the camera is positioned next to the hydrotherapy console (McMurphy as a focaliser). In this shot the camera is looking at the patients but its view is restricted by the partition inside the room.

The trickster, quite predictably, is very keen to transcend the boundaries while the nurses are militantly defending them using the discourse of 'cleanliness' and 'contamination' (which also taps into the larger metaphor of the contamination of consciousness by the unconscious contents). When McMurphy runs into the nurses' station in order to switch off the annoying bland music and startles an unsuspecting junior nurse, he is warned that 'patients are not allowed into the nurses' station' and that 'that music is for everyone'. It is even prohibited to touch the boundary: 'Your hand is staining my window' – Nurse Ratched remarks to McMurphy who has inadvertently touched the glass. In this symbolic context, the rebel's escape through the barbed fence (with the help of the tall Chief Bromden), and subsequent hijacking of the bus, can be seen as a minor triumph of transgressive forces over the deadly, sterile and sterilising, unwieldy power of oppressive consciousness.

McMurphy, the 'unclean' one, in reality reflects the concealed absurdity of the system. Superficially, everything is white and unpolluted. Deep down, the boundary between madness and 'normality' is not clear at all. McMurphy's reduction of the system to absurdity, to chaos, reveals its true face. There is no such thing as a system. It is local, subjective, and created by flawed human beings. Thinking that 'the system', the local *habitus*, is the truth, which has to be protected by boundaries from the 'black tide of mud', is pure self-deception. Kesey and Forman successfully use *reductio ad absurdum* to show the insane undercurrent of the seemingly sterile, perfectly working mechanism.

Nicholson's impish face and on-screen charisma are perfect for the role, for which he won an Oscar. McMurphy is loud, boisterous, jumpy. He shouts and runs around. Like the rest of the 'fools', he is dishevelled, shabby, unattractive. His disorderly behaviour and untidy appearance are juxtaposed to the neatness and black-and-whiteness of the nurses' and wardens' uniforms. In the opening scene, Nurse Ratched arrives at work wearing white plimsolls which contrast with her prim black cape and hat. Her thinking, as this colour combination metaphorically implies, is black and white. The cape bears allusions to monastic dress (cf. Jung's idea of the state replacing the church as the new form of *habitus*). These allusions are suitable because McMurphy's intention is to threaten the very idea of 'rational organisation', the very idea of 'the order'. The one who is compared by a hospital consultant to a 'rolling stone to which the moss does not stick' intends to fight against the very existence of such a thing as stagnation.

Martyr-like as he sounds, McMurphy is no angel. True to the postulates of the trickster principle, he has no morals and, as he explains during his first interview at the clinic, 'fights and fucks too much'. In his prison documents, which are passed on to the mental health authorities, he is described as 'belligerent' and talking 'when unauthorised'. It is abnormal and crazy to 'speak when not spoken to' when the safest option is to remain silent and swallow any bitter pills shoved into your mouth by those in power. McMurphy's 'too-muchness' extends to everything he does, from gambling and basketball to his attitude towards officialdom, be it law enforcers or 'the thought police'. He enjoys driving the conflict to its extreme, escalating the tension. In fact, he sees his own criminal propensities as a proof of being alive: 'At least' – he announces to Dr. Spivey – 'I am not sitting here like a goddam vegetable', hinting at the dumb, bland 'normality' of most American citizens who do not question the existing laws.

In a way, McMurphy takes on the role of the trickster-therapist (or rather, tries to wrestle the role of the therapist from Nurse Ratched) by giving the patients voice, involving them in sports games and making them enjoy fresh air. The therapist is one of the many guises of the trickster (and Nicholson would play another 'trickster-therapist' in *Anger Management*). His idea of therapy is giving the patients freedom, which is psychologically correct: the goals of psychotherapy are release, liberation, a (hopefully) controlled explosion. Release promotes healing. By contrast, the head Nurse's strained group therapy clearly does not achieve any 'liberation' of the repressed contents. The patients fight, they are reluctant to speak up and they lack confidence. They are too scared to benefit from the Nurse's therapy sessions which are less of a coherent dialogue than a Gestapo-like questioning.

As a 'therapist', McMurphy is not concerned with making his 'explosions' controlled, for he grants freedom to his friends (sex, alcohol, gambling) without thinking about the consequences. Billy's suicide, for instance, is down to the rebel's encouragement to stop listening to the two matriarchs – Billy's mother and the Nurse (who befriended her in order to maintain a higher degree of control over the patient). And although his approach is deeply flawed in that he ends up hurting his 'patients' by overflowing them with freedom which they are not capable of handling, his initial instincts are right. Voting to watch baseball, using hydrotherapy in a 'creative way' (pouring water over everyone), organising the 'fishing' outing are all meant to stir up the spirit of rebelliousness, to resurrect human agency in the group of institutionalised and silenced people. He would not have been the amoral trickster without the prostitutes and alcohol. His heroism is as wonderfully reckless as it is thoughtlessly amoral.

Although he is the carrier of the anarchic and unconquerable trickster principle, McMurphy himself is human, and therefore vulnerable. He is not strong enough to lift the hydrotherapy console ('but at least I tried', he says). Throughout the film, the short McMurphy transcends the limits of his physicality by using Chief Bromden as a physical extension of himself – climbing onto his shoulders in order to jump though the wired fence, teaching him how to play the game for which he himself is not tall enough. The human body has its limitations, especially when assaulted by the powerful scientific machine. But when the rebel is dead, the Chief keeps his mini-revolution alive by lifting the console which McMurphy himself failed to lift. The foolish rebel has transcended the limits of his human body by infecting the ward with his spirit, and therefore he has not failed – he won.

Chinatown (1974)

The key (psychological, anthropological) element in trickster narratives is always that of the effort, of trying, of overcoming the fear of failure. However, sometimes failure is inevitable no matter how hard the trickster probes and violates the surface. J. J. Gittes, Jack Nicholson's protagonist in Roman Polanski's *Chinatown* (1974), is a private detective specialising in divorce investigations whose curiosity leads him into trouble with the Los Angeles authorities and police. Gittes penetrates the surface of the narrative like a worm, burying himself in mysteries, tying loose ends and unravelling threads, but eventually loses the game to those who hold the real power in town: the local owners of real estate, property and land.

Chinatown belongs to the neo-noir genre and has a convoluted, psychologically tense story (the screenplay by Robert Towne won an Oscar). It is set in Los Angeles in 1937 and has as its narrative background the so-called 'California water wars' – the dispute between the city of Los Angeles and the inhabitants of Owens Valley over water rights. In the film, Gittes uncovers a ploy to fake the draught in the San Fernando valley by dumping fresh water from the dam into the sea, thus forcing the farmers to sell their land cheaply. The land would then be re-sold by the local magnate Noah Cross (John Huston) and his accomplices at a much higher price.

Nicholson's cheeky detective first enters the world of 'big players' without realising what political and personal horrors his nosy probing might uncover. Hired by Evelyn Mulvray (Faye Dunaway) to investigate her husband's suspected infidelity, he ends up discovering a tale of murder, incest and political corruption. The man behind it all, the inscrutable Noah Cross, organises the murder of his son-in law and business opponent, Hollis Mulvray, ruthlessly disposes of the San Fernando valley farmers and bribes the LA police. The detective also uncovers the fact that Cross had sexual contact with his daughter Evelyn when she was a teenager, and that they have a daughter together. Cross's inscrutable mask of an important public official hides a rotten face for which the agile but vulnerable trickster-detective aims.

With his curiosity and reckless bravery, Gittes acts in the narrative as the trickster principle, and is consequently punished by overstepping various lines and 'being a nosy kitty cat'. His creative detective work often takes him into uncharted territories: he sleeps with a woman above his station, challenges men who have serious political and economic power in their hands, wanders uninvited into private premises and obtains classified information. However, like most tricksters, the detective is not careful what methods he uses to get to the elusive 'truth'. Just as McMurphy ends causing a patient's suicide, Gittes's brash curiosity and probing leads to tragic events. The storm he causes – incest revelation, fraud discovery, Evelyn and Katherine's escape to Mexico – climaxes in the scene in which the police open fire on Evelyn's car as she and her daughter are attempting to flee from Noah.

The detective's body, the body of the trickster, is constantly violated, cut, bruised and kicked. When he jumps over the fence at the Oak Pass Reservoir to find out what kind of foul play is going there, and discovers that water is being dumped into the sea, he is caught by the ex-sheriff Claude Mulvihill and accused of trespassing. His nostril is sliced open with a knife by Mulvihill's henchman (a cameo from Roman Polanski). Apart from the nose wound, which requires wearing unsightly white plaster and symbolically links him to the clown/fool figure, Gittes is severely beaten up by the farmers when he crosses into their territory for investigative purposes. He also nearly drowns in the reservoir when, upon hearing two gunshots (the signal for opening the sluice gates), he jumps into the empty channel seconds before water starts gushing onto him. As Gittes is the one who 'speaks when not spoken to', his body must suffer for his misdeeds. However, every time his physical integrity is violated, the detective miraculously manages to pull himself together, literally and metaphorically, and continues his journey for the truth.

During the interview in Cross's magnificent garden preceding the climax with the car chase and Evelyn's subsequent murder, Gittes keeps throwing bits of truth at Noah. The detective shows documents which he discovered about the dam fraud, and accuses Cross of assassinating Hollis Mulvray for political purposes. On the subject of money, the private investigator says: 'Why are you doing it? How much better can you eat? What could you buy that you can't already afford?' The trickster's persistent needle-sticking produces the desired effect: the magnate's mask finally comes off and he says: 'You see, Mr. Gittes, most people never have to face the fact that at the right time and the right place, they're capable of *anything*'.

Cross's 'anything' means the world without obstructions, the world without impediments. Money is a trickster that is capable of seeping under the toughest walls and helping their owners overcome all kinds of limitations, physical as well as psychological. It is Noah who has no boundaries, not Gittes. All the trickster is doing is digging for the truth, and the truth is ugly. His final aim is to drag the dirt onto the surface. The agility of his mind, however, cannot match the wondrously mercurial qualities of Noah's money. Gittes fails to save Evelyn, and he fails to bring Noah to trial for any of the crimes he had committed. The film ends with Lieutenant Escobar, who is no doubt paid by the magnate for his services, ordering Gittes to go home and warning him that he is doing him 'a favour'. The cunning detective has been outtrickstered by the unstoppable penetrability of money.

Work, Home, Community

Apart from the grand limiters of personal freedom such as political regimes and corrupt governments, protagonists of the trickster film suffer from minor, local forms of oppression: the influence of family, community, workplace. To the best of their limited abilities, and with varying results, they attempt to wrestle control over their lives from these local 'deities'. They challenge and, ultimately, reject the 'order of things' imposed onto them by those who know 'how things should be'. Protagonists in this type of trickster film try to escape a certain lifestyle framework which makes them feel trapped and unable to move ahead.

Drop Dead Fred (1991)

Ate de Jong's *Drop Dead Fred*, starring Rik Mayall, is a perfect example of this type of film. Its plotline is a model trickster narrative: A young woman called Lizzie Cronin (Phoebe Cates) loses her job, her husband, car and money within the same lunch hour. Everything seems to crumble at once, and Lizzie herself seems to be the cause of all these troubles. Having left her cheating husband, she moves in with her mother, a matriarch and control freak obsessed with cleanliness. Lizzie remembers that, as a child, she had an effective psychological response to her mother's constant manipulation: an imaginary friend called Drop Dead Fred – a rebellious and impudent creature who always found new and inventive ways of spoiling and messing up Mrs Cronin's perfect order. Fred is suitably mad-looking: he wears bright yellow pants paired with fluorescent green jacket. His hair is red and spiky (in fact, his manic appearance could have inspired the makers of *The Mask*). Eventually, the matriarch gets fed up, locks the trickster inside a music box and secures it with sticky tape so that Fred cannot escape.

On the first night in her mother's house Lizzie opens the locked box, the green spirit jumps out and immediately renews the partisan war against the oppressive and controlling parent. Under Fred's influence, Lizzie's behaviour gradually becomes uncontrollable: for instance, she sinks her friend's ship and claims that it was 'Drop Dead Fred' who made her do it and throws platefuls of spaghetti at fellow-diners when she is out with her prospective new boyfriend, Mickey (Ron Eldard).

Goaded by her mother, Lizzie attempts to revive her marriage. However, this project ends in disaster when she overhears her husband Charles (Tim Matheson) speak on the phone with his girlfriend, explaining to her that their current arrangements are perfect as Lizzie is naïve and meek, and therefore could be easily manipulated. Lizzie makes the decision to leave both the husband and the mother, and starts a relationship with Mickey who has adored her for her creative quirkiness since they were childhood friends. At the end of the film, Lizzie is able to detach herself from the people controlling her life thanks to Drop Dead Fred who 'transfers' her to her childhood home and asks her to challenge the scary matriarch with the magic phrase 'I am not afraid of you'. After this 'therapy session' he disappears. In the final scene Lizzie meets Mickey's little daughter, Natalie, and the girl explains to her that she made a terrible mess in the kitchen because 'Drop Dead Fred' made her do it.

The trickster serves a traditional therapeutic role in the narrative: he appears at the crucial moment in the protagonist's life, makes her cross the liminal threshold (van Gennep's 'separation'), takes possession of her body and mind, drags her through the period of uncertainty and transition, drives the situation to the climactic point when her whole life is completely ruined, makes her realise what is wrong with her, exorcises the problem (releases the repressed psychic contents), returns her to 'normality' (incorporation), and finally disappears. He does not disappear forever, however, because tricksters never die. He just changes 'the carrier' and continues his therapeutic-rebellious activity in someone else's life.

About Schmidt (2002)

The trickster principle stands on the side of freedom, but this does not mean that freedom is always a blessed and easy thing to possess. In *About Schmidt* (directed by Alexander Payne; based on a novel by Louis Begley) freedom does more trouble than good for the protagonist, a 66-year-old man named Warren Schmidt (Jack Nicholson). The trickster principle in the life of this actuary working for an insurance company arrives in the form of retirement. Warren is prudent to the point of being boring. His main interests before retirement had largely consisted of calculating other people's risks, and he is unable to deal with the sudden onset of freedom. Looking for some meaningful occupation during his retirement, Schmidt decides to 'adopt' an African orphan.

When Warren's wife Helen (June Squibb) suddenly dies of a stroke, he goes on a road trip from Omaha, Nebraska, to Denver, Colorado in his wife's retirement present, a Winnebago motor home. The trip plays a dual purpose: it is both a way of fighting depression and an attempt to prevent his daughter Jeannie's marriage to a weirdo loser named Randall (Dermot Mulroney). Warren's plan fails, he endures the wedding, and comes back home in time to receive a letter from a nun in Tanzania who informs him that his adopted orphan Ndugu appreciates his financial help and wishes him well. A picture is enclosed drawn by the boy, depicting two stick figures, a father and son, holding hands and smiling. The final shot shows Warren looking and the picture and silently weeping.

About Schmidt lacks an obvious trickster figure, which does not diminish the power of the trickster principle at work at the heart of the film's narrative. Schmidt needs to fill the void in his life left by the job; freedom makes him think about his life and search 'for himself', for some meaning. His spirit, which had been entrapped in the risk-calculating job for many years, is suddenly released and starts playing havoc with Warren's formerly neat and organised life. After retirement, he starts noticing the gaps and holes in his existence – such as the fact that his daughter Jeannie (Hope Davis) is not very fond of her father. His workplace had dictated his lifestyle; his wife had looked after his physical wellbeing and maintained the house. Everything had been decided for him. In fact, after Helen's death, Warren's house is reduced to hellish disarray, with supermarket bags and dirty clothes covering the floor, and flies residing in cupboards. Warren stops changing clothes and, when he needs to pop out, (mainly to buy frozen pizzas in the supermarket), just throws a coat over his pyjamas.

Nicholson's character rarely speaks intradiegetically, and his thoughts are voiced over by an extradiegetic narrator – himself. It is as though he can finally see his own life from a different point of view, and comment on it. Another form of extradiegetic narration are his letters to Ndugu the orphan, in which the former actuary pours out his soul about Helen, Jeannie, old age and existential emptiness. Shots of Warren at his table writing the letter are intercut with shots depicting his 'thoughts' – such as Helen's annoying habit of collecting little figurines or Randall's waterbed-selling job.

When Warren travels in his Winnebago to Jeannie's wedding and endures several days in the house of the groom's mother, the flamboyant and oversexed Circe of the suburbs, Roberta Hertzel (Kathy Bates), he is pushed out of his comfort zone. During his Odyssey (and Odysseus was a trickster too), the former clerk is poked and challenged at every turn: he nearly seduces the wife of a camper at a trailer campground and has to flee in embarrassment; visits his childhood home and finds that it has been replaced by a tyre shop; gets a stiff neck on the eve of the wedding and is given mind-altering drugs by Roberta as a cure; and is aggressively propositioned by Roberta in her outdoor jacuzzi (and, once again, has to seek safety in his trailer). Finally, he fails in his main mission: to prevent the wedding. The event takes place, complete with drunken guests, embarrassing best friends and ugly fat brothers. To the best of his abilities, Warren pronounces a positive and hopeful 'father of the bride' speech, in which he manages to find kindly words for the groom and his relatives. The 'bad father', who had neglected his daughter's emotional life for years, has no right to tell her who to marry. However, with this clumsy speech he finally 'makes a connection'.

Although Warren thinks that he failed in his quest, in reality he did not. In one aspect his adventure was very successful – it has set him moving. As 'rolling stone gathers no moss', Warren's life is now changed forever. So much so that he now has a meaning and a continuity – in the form of the little orphan Ndugu from Tanzania. As Warren says before the start of his journey, 'life is short and I can't afford to waste another minute'. His life has not been wasted.

Jim Carrey's Tricksters

Jim Carrey's gradual shift from the relatively 'pure' trickster characters (Ace Ventura, the Mask) to the more 'human' roles (Truman Burbank, Bruce Nolan in *Bruce Almighty*) deserves special attention.

It is possible to distinguish an 'earlier' and a 'later' stage in Carrey's acting career. His earlier characters, as a rule, seem to exist in a state of non-awareness and confusion typical for a creature that is both 'subhuman and superhuman, a bestial and divine being whose chief and most alarming characteristic is his unconsciousness' (Jung, 1951, CW9/I: para. 472). But it is also this unconsciousness that gives the trickster his (mock-heroic) super-powers. One of Carrey's earliest creations, Ace Ventura, does amazingly idiotic things – like gate-crashing a posh party and flooding their toilet, or locking himself inside a plastic rhino, and then squeezing himself out through a hole in the backside – but these mishaps do not deflate his faith in his superpowers.

Carrey's 'pure' trickster is a loser who occasionally wins – by sheer luck – and who cannot admit his 'loserness'. His crazed, daredevil behaviour and total defiance in the face of adversity is a parody on both the classical tragic hero and the contemporary brainless superhero. Ace Ventura, for example, is an unpredictable creature wearing impossible clothes (an equivalent of the traditional jester's motley dress) and sporting his trademark oversized quiff. He is cool and nonchalant in his own cocky fashion, with amazing (physical and psychological) regenerative powers which manifest themselves in quick restoration of confidence after such mishaps as falling into a shark tank (*Ace Ventura: Pet Detective*, 1994) or being humiliated by the angry Wachootoo tribe (*Ace Ventura: When Nature Calls*, 1995). Even though Ace outtricksters members of the tribe in a series of trials, he nevertheless gets a beating in a sequence reminiscent of Wakdjunkaga's silly adventures.

Carrey's jesters are 'linked' to their 'natural' abode – the world of the instincts – via animals. Ace is always surrounded by pets and wild animals (in fact, his profession is 'animal detective') and Stanley Ipkiss/the Mask has a helpful mutt named Milo. Lloyd and his friend Harry from *Dumb and Dumber* are the proud owners of a worm farm and a headless parrot Petey. Harry works as a dog groomer, and he and Lloyd are planning to open a pet store called 'I Got Worms!'. The basic, toilet humour of Carrey's early films, from peeing in a bottle on the motorway (*Dumb and Dumber*) to the (unbelievably gross) rhino birth of *Ace Ventura: Pet Detective*, refers to the trickster's pre-conscious, innocent nature, and his lack of awareness of shame, which the 'civilised', conscious mind associates with personal hygiene. And, of course, Carrey's 'pure' tricksters, in line with the mythological tradition, are seriously oversexed. The grotesque characters Ace and the Mask are very virile and macho-seductive. The more realistic and 'human' Lloyd, however, can only attract a woman in his dreams, in which the seduction ritual is conducted in a typically rough trickster fashion, complete with the brutal annihilation of a rival (Lloyd rips his heart out) and 'romantic' fart jokes.

After trying his hand at 'shadowy' roles (The Cable Guy, Dr. Nygma), Carrey changed the direction of his career by switching to more realistic characters – Truman Burbank (*The Truman Show*), Andy Kaufman (*Man on the Moon*, 1999), Peter Appleton (*The Majestic*, 2001), Joel Barish (*Eternal Sunshine of the Spotless Mind*), Dick Harper (*Fun With Dick and Jane*), Steven Russell (*I Love You Phillip Morris*). The protagonists of Carrey's mature period (starting with Truman Burbank) have their doppelgangers integrated rather than split off into green-masked maniacs or media-controlling freaks. The trickster, with his disorganised, anarchic stance, gives way to a hero desperately, and consciously, trying to assert his free will against various deterministic factors: political (God-like governing figures), social (society's normalising prescriptions – such as the traditional family), economic (jobs – or their absence; corporations and corporate culture) and personal (friendship, love, sex, emotions). The transformation of Carrey's protagonist from a pure clown to a comic-dramatic actor resembles the 'trickster maturation' path described by Joseph Henderson:

'At the end of his rogue's progress he is beginning to take on the physical likeness of a grown man' (Jung and von Franz, 1964: 104). In the Winnebago hero myth this stage is called Hare, or the Transformer. It shows the mischievous child as 'becoming a socialised being, correcting the instinctual and infantile found in the Trickster cycle' (1964: 165).

The stories of Stanley Ipkiss (*The Mask*), Bruce Nolan (*Bruce Almighty*), Carl Allen (*Yes Man*) and Steven Russell (*I Love You Phillip Morris*) are characterised by an enormous gap between the protagonists' professional and personal lives. The issues of finding a partner, choosing between having children and being free, dealing with parents and parents-in-law, selecting and joining a community (property, house, area) become truly weighty and urgent in the world of urban disconnectedness. As a result of all these quarrelling domestic and social voices, Carrey's characters (in their pre-mised, default positions) are left 'hanging in mid-air', groundless, baseless, split into numerous identities, broken into a myriad of pieces. The personal freedom they are supposed to enjoy feels like yet another type of trap. This dramatic gap, emptiness and tension, however, are a good source of comedy as they produce endless misunderstandings, misinterpretations, *faux pas*, farcical transformations and possibilities for renewal. In trickster film, the perceptually dramatic, and even tragic, modern/postmodern split becomes comic. The gap gives birth to the trickster.

The Truman Show (1998)

Truman Burbank epitomises the 'lonely heroism' characteristic of Carrey's mature comedy-drama; the kind of reckless desperation that comes out of rebellious rejection of helplessness, powerlessness and group-think.

An everyman whose artificial life is watched by millions of other common people, Truman is owned by a media giant. He was legally adopted by a media corporation, which generates revenue by displaying advertisements and selling the show's spin-offs and merchandise. Truman is the star of his own reality show yet is completely unaware of his 'stardom'. The director of this reality soap opera, Christof (note the 'talking name'), is a madly controlling but inspired artist – conceptually reminiscent of the Author in Tom Stoppard's *Rosencrantz and Guildenstern Are Dead*. Truman (true man, everyman, real man, new man, free man) has a dream of escaping the little island named Seahaven which, in the true Hamletian fashion, has become his 'prison'. His dreamland is Fiji, and he fantasises going there and joining his beloved.

Meanwhile, the people in charge of the show make sure that their star is aware of his limitations. Moreover, they deliberately create these limitations. In order to prevent Truman from escaping the island, they instill in him a fear of drowning. The sea is the main boundary that separates Truman from his freedom. He is also given a number of responsibilities: a job, a wife, a mortgage. His wife insists on 'having a baby'. The show's script supplied him with a kind mother (Holland Taylor) and a loyal friend Marlon (Noah Emmerich). Marlon, rather like the friends of the biblical Job, keeps reminding Truman that it would be wiser to submit himself to the existing order of things rather than venture to find one's way in life, meaning, of course, that the *habitus* that is Seahaven is pre-scripted and unalterable.

Truman, the tragic trickster, is trapped within this pre-planned, out-of-control web of familial, communal and professional relationships orchestrated by the god-like Christof and his team. All Truman's attempts to leave the island are nipped in the bud: the bus, in which he hoped to 'reach Fiji', breaks down; the ferry leaves without him; and his reckless escape in a car with Meryl ends up with him being captured and returned to the set.

But, as Truman has already rattled his box, it starts to fall apart. He eventually escapes the house unnoticed, crosses the sea on a yacht and breaks free. His freedom does not come cheap. He has to survive a deadly storm conjured up by Christof and his crew, and is subsequently 'resurrected' as a man who is in charge of his own destiny. His release, the release of the trickster, finally happens when the bow of his yacht rips through the dome protecting his former small world – the prison which he has outgrown. The moment of breaking out of the film set symbolically unites the seemingly random trickster principle with the idea of the 'hatching' of the new personality. Truman is reborn as an individual, heroic in his ability to make an effort, brave in his defiance of failure, impertinent in his decision to challenge collective opinion, localised norms of behaviour, political prescriptions and prudent financial considerations. He re-emerges as someone who can teach his massive audience, consisting of common people like himself, to place his or her free will above the interests, and actions, of the 'determining factors'.

Chapter 5

Gonzo Trickster and the Art of Comic Insurrection

In his book *Andy Kaufman Revealed!*, Bob Zmuda, the best friend and co-writer of the controversial and inimitable prankster, explains his own decision to become a practical comedian by the aggressive and conservative politics of the U.S. government in the 1960s. After witnessing the Chicago police violently breaking up a peaceful hippie 'love-in' in Lincoln Park, the former law-abiding, conservative kid started joining leftist political societies and socialist theatre groups. He felt that the State wanted to foster passivity and dependency in its subjects, and that developing a critical perspective, however guerrilla and antisocial, was the only way out for a responsible citizen:

> I was p**sed. Mayor Daley [Richard Joseph Daley, the longest serving mayor of Chicago] had created not a 'programmed' good kid in a short-sleeved white shirt with a pocket protector and a slide rule, ready to become a 'productive' citizen, but rather a warrior, a radical commando, prepared to topple the system that had become irreparably corrupt. But in my case, instead of a gun or a bomb, my weapon was between my ears: my wits and a rapidly developing sense of humour. And I was ready for war.
>
> (Zmuda, 1999: 13)

As Andrew Samuels shows in his books (1993, 2001), depth psychology and politics are profoundly connected. The prerequisite for a man – a comedian, a writer, an actor – lending his services to the trickster principle, and becoming the mouthpiece for a chaotic and socially disruptive rebellion, is a certain degree of discontent amplified by a feeling that 'something is rotten in the state of Denmark'. Zmuda is not alone in his desire to use shock therapy for the purpose of waking the placid 'little men' from their political slumber. In the rare 'out of character' interview with Neil Strauss for *Rolling Stone* magazine, the notorious prankster Sacha Baron-Cohen explained his motivation to enter the dangerous vocation of gonzo trickster, or a professional prankster whose jokes essentially eliminate the border between fantasy and reality, by the desire to drag people out of their apathy:

> I remember, when I was in university I studied history, and there was this one major historian of the Third Reich, Ian Kershaw. And his quote was, 'The path to Auschwitz was paved with indifference'. I know it's not very funny being a comedian talking about the Holocaust, but I think it's an interesting idea that not everyone in Germany had to be a raving anti-Semite. They just had to be apathetic.
>
> (*Rolling Stone*, 15 November 2006)

Gonzo tricksterism (like gonzo journalism whose founding father was Hunter S. Thompson) is a dangerous business. Occasionally it implies risking your life, endangering your health, and generally looking like an idiot. It also involves psychological dangers: in gonzo tricksterism, the line separating fantasy and reality, the mask and the life, is very subtle and, as a consequence, is incessantly crossed and uncrossed. It is not always possible to tell the joke from cruelty and gross rudeness in Allen Funt's *Candid Camera* series, Andy Kaufman's erratic and badly planned performances, notorious projects of Sacha Baron-Cohen or Russell Brand's tactless remarks about other people's personal lives. Sometimes the boundary does not exist *a priori*.

'Gonzo' and the Notion of Truth

Drawing on Martin Hirst's etymological research, Sonja Maier concludes that the origin of the word 'gonzo' is still unclear:

> According to Hirst, the closest French expression he could find was 'gonze' meaning 'guy' or 'bloke' (see 6ff). The word's earliest appearance in a dictionary dates to the Random House dictionary of 1987, which refers to HST's journalism and states its origin to be either Italian or Spanish (see Hirst 6). The Italian and French root words 'gonzo' (meaning 'fool' and 'dolt') and 'ganso' (meaning 'idiot' and 'bumpkin') do not correspond to the adjective's meaning in Thompson's case since Thompson's gonzo style 'is neither dull nor foolish' (Hirst 7). Due to the various different and often contradicting explanations it is not possible to pin its meaning down to either a single origin or a single meaning. Hirst summarises correctly, when he states that 'excitement and seriousness of HST's contribution to journalism hands on one small word, but we don't know where it came from'.
>
> (Maier, 2010: 27)

According to Bob Franklin, gonzo journalism, contra the conventions of standard ('objective') journalism practice, 'features a bold, exaggerated, irreverent, hyperbolic and extremely subjective style of writing, which positions the author at the centre of the narrative' (Franklin, 2005: 95). The distinguishing requirement for a gonzo journalist is 'to write in the first person and to become the dominant participant in the narrative' (2005: 96). Gonzo reporting methods presuppose subjectification of reality, stream of consciousness writing techniques, personal involvement, participation in the event being reported, and other suchlike activities aimed at preventing the reader from getting to the core of the objective 'truth' and from seeing reality 'clearly'. Thus, the very notion of 'truth' becomes obsolete, irrelevant, extraneous. In this sense, gonzo journalism is inherently postmodern.

Gonzo tricksterism is based on similar principles. It involves reality jokes (often rude, humiliating and rough), personal domination of the comedic narrative, and, in some cases, the erosion of the boundary between the comedian's private life and his on-stage characters. In fact, gonzo tricksters significantly differ in the degree of personal involvement with the 'mask'; for instance, Andy Kaufman deliberately created 'performances' out of his private life, while Sacha Baron-Cohen, on the contrary, strictly guards his privacy.

One of the most common gonzo trickster activities is playing pre-planned jokes on unsuspecting members of the public or audience. The resultant event, which is often quite gross and/or politically incorrect, constitutes a comic 'happening'. The comedian takes a very active role in the event, which, of course, is not risk-free due to the understandable fact that reactions of the angry, scared or embarrassed accidental performers are not always predictable. In addition to financial and physical risks, the gonzo trickster is putting his career and reputation in jeopardy because the authorities and the public are likely to misunderstand and misinterpret his intentions or – which is even worse – interpret them correctly. The aims of the gonzo comedian are to challenge and shock the public, to push them out of their comfort zone, to defamiliarise their 'normal' surroundings and vapid perception of reality. This can only be done by dissolving the boundary between fact and fabrication, when the viewer suddenly finds himself in a peceptional limbo, unable to come up with definitions of anything happening on stage. The gonzo comedian is deliberately unsafe in that he risks his life in order to ruin the reputation of other people. His jokes are not funny; they're openly maladroit and tasteless.

This de-sanitised, seemingly uncaring attitude towards the viewing audience characterises both postmodernity and the trickster principle. Or postmodernity, with its schizophrenic brokenness, *as* the trickster principle. Theoreticians (and critics) of postmodern art have long and variously discussed its ability to turn perceivably 'serious' and 'tragic' pieces of information into objects of meaningless consumption and trivial entertainment.

Jean Baudrillard, in the already mentioned article on the volatile nature of the First Gulf War, claimed that the war, with its heavy civilian and military casualties, and its well-documented and very realistic human suffering, did not take place altogether. It was, he argues, a work of fiction. This brave and seemingly insensitive hyperbole is meant to draw the readers' attention to the fact that any 'unadorned' information about a 'real' event presented by the media (Western or otherwise) was constructed and reconstructed by inevitably biased people, and, as such, is more of a man-made story than a truthful report. The very action of reconstituting an event renders it meaningless. Television, Baudrillard argues, should not be trusted with the task of presenting the audience with a 'truth' simply because 'the truth' is not a complete, eternal, irreducible entity. Contrary to the biblical story, the truth is not an apple that grows on a tree and can be picked up and immediately consumed:

> just as everything psychical becomes the object of interminable specu-lation, so everything which is turned into information becomes the object of endless speculation, the site of total uncertainty. We are left with the symptomatic reading on our screens of the effects of the war, or the effects of discourse about the war, or completely speculative strategic evaluations which are analogous to those evaluations of opinion provided by polls. [. . .] Whom to believe? There is nothing to believe. We must learn to read symptoms as symptoms, and television as the hysterical symptom of a war which has nothing to do with its critical mass.
>
> (2000: 64)

Television, in its empty, multiple and fragmentary tricksterism, is not really preoccupied with attaching moral values to its products. Moral values represent the long-gone epoch of the reign of the 'bourgeois subject'. These days, in the epoch of the trickster, anything fixed is out of fashion. The long-standing critic of postmodernity, Terry Eagleton, gleefully writes in his book *The Illusions of Postmodernism* that, for contemporary anti-rationalists, phrases like 'how things stand' smack of objectivism, scientism, phallocentrism, transcendentally disinterested subjects and a number of other creepy affairs (1996: 12). Some radicals, Eagleton continues, would even see utterances like 'Lord John Russell then became Prime Minister' as insidious instances of positivism (1996: 12). Eagleton's comrade-in-arms Fredric Jameson asserts that the society of multinational capitalism is the society of the spectacle, the society that has lost the linguistic norm; the kind of society that transforms reality into images and is therefore charac-terised by the fragmentation of time into a series of perpetual presents (Malpas, 2001: 23–36). It can no longer concern itself with the moral backbone or with the didactic 'sense' of entertainment.

Gonzo journalism was a consequence of the postmodern erosion of boundaries between styles, genres and writing traditions. Gonzo tricksterism shares certain traits with its older brother; for instance, as in subjective journalism, the author-ego in reality comedy 'is in the centre of the self-dramatization' (Bleichner, 2004: 147, quoted in Maier, 2010: 25). At the same time, both are forms of the genre called Performance Art, which has its roots in medieval performance traditions (minstrels, troubadours, jesters, etc.). Performance art (which is more 'liminoid' than 'liminal', to use Turner's terminology) was revived during the explosion of postmodern creativity in the 1960s and 1970s when there was a proliferation of creative provocateurs such as Andy Warhol, Carolee Schneemann and Christ Burden. These artists were delivering performances and creating works of art after two bloody World Wars, the horrific global events which have numbed the audiences, and significantly complicated the modernist task of shocking the viewers and scaring them out of their small, grey, petit-bourgeois lives.

Gonzo Trickster and His Audience

As we have seen from previous chapters, the trickster principle is very much about making an effort, feeling mediocre and little, and being afraid of failure. It is about personal, political and social apathy. It is also about breaking the shell of socially accepted 'normality', and acquiring a 'face' and 'voice'. The trickster principle's gonzo incarnation is not an exception. Andy Kaufman's characters, including the character of 'himself', are all failures – whingeing, crying, mumbling and shouting; disturbing and challenging the viewer. By contrast, Baron-Cohen's bullish 'foreigners' – Ali G, Borat, Brüno – are confident failures, classical fools, who, for most of the time, do not realise that they are regarded as 'weird' by the mainstream culture. By being different from the average viewer, by being so indecently 'in-your-face', they disturb what they see as the listless surface of social water.

By doing all these highly unsettling activities, Kaufman and Baron-Cohen hold the mirror up to the audience, making them doubt their own sanity and the 'reality' of the event happening on stage. The event becomes internalised, introjected, ingested. The show leaves the stage and invades the audience. Even more – the audience, their collective shadow, their collective presence *creates* the show. The event that is taking place on stage is not real precisely because it is happening *in people's minds*, confirming their fears, stirring up their innermost thoughts. Like the Player in Tom Stoppard's *Rosencrantz and Guildenstern Are Dead*, the gonzo trickster makes the audience defenceless by exposing his own – invented or real – vulnerabilities. In Act 1 of the play, the Player is complaining to the 'little powerless people', Rosencrantz and Guildenstern, that showbusiness is a difficult trade because viewers are often ungrateful. All they really want is cheap entertainment. A skilled actor, however, can tap into the collective brain of the audience and successfully manipulate it:

> There we were – demented children mincing about in clothes that no one ever wore, speaking as no man ever spoke, swearing love in wigs and rhymed couplets, killing each other with wooden swords, hollow protestations of faith hurled after empty promises of vengeance – and every gesture, every pose, vanishing into the thin unpopulated air. We ransomed our dignity to the clouds, and the uncomprehending birds listened. Don't you see?! We're *actors* – we're the opposite of people! Think, in your head, *now*, think of the most . . . *private* . . . *secret* . . . *intimate* . . . thing you have ever done secure in the knowledge of its privacy. . . . Are you thinking of it? *Well, I saw you do it!*
>
> (Stoppard, 1991: 25)

Andy Kaufman was the kind of entertainer who seemed to guess his viewers' thoughts and 'saw them do it'. He fed his viewers with as much cheap entertainment as they could swallow. The same can be said of Baron-Cohen's style. The two are highly comparable because both have had 'foreign men' as their anchor characters, both have used wrestling as a form of titillating and annoying the spectator (voyeur), and both have pushed participating audiences to the breaking point.

The concept of 'foreignness' – which is central to both Kaufman's and Baron-Cohen's work – is a significant part of the postmodern landscape. With society being so diverse – culturally, ethnically, socially – we are all foreigners now. 'The foreigner' is an extended metaphor covering both the plurality of discourses and the inevitable discord between them. When the split becomes truly visible, people instinctively attempt to regain the lost paradise that is 'sameness' – cultural or racial homogeneity, and other 'god-like' ideas. And here, of course, lies the danger. In an attempt to 'heal' the split, proponents of 'sameness' usually end up making it wider and more painful. As they see it, 'the foreigner' sits in the centre of the wound like a wooden splinter. What Christopher Hauke says about racism can be extended to other self-definition issues: 'Racism is part of the sustained splitting of the human psyche that constitutes modernity and everyday life' (Hauke, 2005: 106). The trickster often takes the form of the foreigner because he embodies the split. He also embodies, mimics and predicts, the possible consequences of the easy way of closing the wound, which is by evoking the collective shadow.

Most importantly, both Kaufman and Baron-Cohen have placed the (profoundly tricksterish) concept of failure at the centre of their edgy art. As Zmuda explains, 'failure and perceived mediocrity were concepts Andy toyed with his entire career. [. . .] [Tony] Clifton's style was not to entertain but to provoke, and his goal was not to be applauded off the stage but physically removed. Andy was getting into deeper waters by pushing the audiences to reject him, but in some ways it was almost a compulsion' (Zmuda, 1999: 137). Like many conceptual artists of his time (including his fellow provocateur and friend Andy Warhol), Kaufman was interested in the tricksterish activity of elevating the ordinary to the level of art (1999: 45). His performances included dozing onstage in a sleeping bag and slowly eating ice-cream while the bemused audience was watching on. In other words, he (with the help of his accomplice Bob Zmuda) was keen to recast the everyday as the liminal. Or liminoid. In fact, Turner's division between the liminoid and the liminal is not valid here because the gonzo trickster, in his human guise, channels the onstage 'action' back to the people. He disowns his own act. His performance is not a personal but a collective, public, ludic happening.

In the best traditions of jester art and other kinds of performative tricksterism, Kaufman and Baron-Cohen are keen observers relying both on scripted material and improvisation. Dan Mazer, the executive producer on *Borat*, admits that the film was made using guerrilla and gonzo practices: 'There was no script. The movie is an experiment – a new form of filmmaking for an age in which reality and entertainment have become increasingly intertwined. Real events and real people push the film's fictional story, [especially] when scenes played out in unexpected ways' (McCreadie, 2008: 167).

Hating or loving artists like Kaufman and Baron-Cohen, the audiences are nevertheless pleased to be entertained in a rough way. In the age of postmodern fakeness, only real anger and genuine frustration will do. In his heyday Andy Kaufman hit little girls on stage for singing the wrong note, made grown men piss in their pants, and made a very shameful public show out of a quarrel with an ex-girlfriend. Not many people seemed to be minding the fact that these perturbing events were actually set-ups aimed at shocking the unsuspecting spectators out of their seats. Similarly, at least some of Baron-Cohen's tricks are staged. Still, he insolently pushes the limits of the audience's patience, whether by showing them the footage of a spinning penis (*Brüno*, 2009), making them watch the truly cringeworthy scene from *Da Ali G Show* (2004), in which Borat, a 'naïve' reporter from Kazakhstan, performs an anti-Semitic song at a U.S. country music festival, or presenting them, alongside the rightfully disgusted dinner hosts, with a bag of faeces at the table. The audience is left to guess who the spinning penis really belongs to, whether the people singing along to Borat's nasty opus truly realise what they are doing, and whether Baron-Cohen actually has enough pluck to bring human excrement into the dining room. With gonzo tricksters, one never knows whether the shit is real. This is what defines them.

The meaningless confusion between fantasy and reality is not a uniquely postmodern effect. It is the 'normal' state of the trickster. If anything, the carnivalesque spirit of postmodernity, with its mass popular entertainment, reality shows and impressive spectacles whose high entertaining quality is dependent on technology, is an 'improved' version of the medieval folk culture. In our rational, technologically advanced society slapstick still plays a crucial role, be it in the form of morning-slot talk shows, Big Brother or even Jeremy Paxman's pit bull fights which often turn BBC's *Newsnight* into a bloody arena of political gladiatoring. The absence of the fourth wall means that the art is both amateur and democratic; it is the kind of art in which performers and the audience are united in the ultimate liminal experience. We, the cruel viewers, wish to be entertained; we want to know that the actors' pain is real. Bakhtin writes in *Rabelais and His World* that carnival culture, the culture of the marketplace

> does not know footlights in the sense that it does not acknowledge any distinction between actors and spectators. Footlights would destroy a carnival, as the absence of footlights would destroy a theatrical performance. Carnival is not a spectacle seen by the people; they live in it, and everyone participates because its very idea embraces all the people. While carnival lasts, there is no other life outside it. During carnival time life is subject only to its laws, that is, the laws of its own freedom. It has universal spirit; it is a special condition of the entire world, the world's revival and renewal, in which all take part.
>
> (Bakhtin, 1984: 7)

Likewise, Kaufman's postmodern, avant-garde trickster and Baron-Cohen's deceptively fresh foreign characters are, in fact, perfectly viable versions of the ancient profession of the public buffoon. Their performances are deeply ludic in the sense that they place the loudness, unkemptness and messiness of the spectacle above the figure of the creator. Just like in Allen Funt's *Candid Camera* series and their numerous offspring, the participants and audience co-create the show. The resulting product may be unbeautiful, barbaric, offensive, badly organised – but it cannot be otherwise as it is not a fully controlled work of a single genius mind (even through it was pre-planned), but a collective co-production.

If the 'hidden camera' technique is one of the newer ludic genres, heavily dependent on technology and spawned by the media age, old-style public entertainment is still as popular as ever. Take stadium-gathering gladiator-style sports, for example. Kaufman's move into wrestling midway through his career was not accidental. Cage-fighting contains everything a gonzo trickster may dream of: cheap and loud showmanship, active audience participation, the sharpness of liminal anticipation and liminal happening, visual excess, faux heroism and clownish loserness – and the endless stream of humiliation and ridicule. Kaufman has pushed it even further over the edge by choosing to wrestle women and shouting 'Go to the kitchen where you belong, woman' in the process. The capabilities of wrestling matches to create liminal excess were also explored by Baron-Cohen in the climatic scene of *Brüno*, in which two 'gay men' (the title character Brüno and his lover Lutz) cage-wrestle in the town of Fort Smith, Arkansas. As Jon Gambrell writes in *Huffington Post*, instead of the 'old-fashioned hetero-fest' as promised by the wrestler named Straight Dave (Baron-Cohen) at the beginning of the show, the 1600 audience of the 'Blue Collar Brawlin' event was treated to the sight of two men embracing, kissing and undress-ing. The reaction was predictable, and similar to that received by Andy Kaufman after the release of the advertisement video for his wrestling match with Jerry Lawler. In that notorious video the prankster advised 'the people of the southern portion of the United States' on how to use soap, razor and toilet paper. Like Kaufman, Baron-Cohen had the audience consisting of real people, and a pre-arranged fight and escape plan. He and the actor Gustaf Hammarsten (Lutz) fled through a specially set-aside tunnel (*The Huffington Post*, 8 July 2008).

Although contemporary gonzo tricksters draw on the centuries of experi-ence provided by their ancient, medieval and modern predecessors, in a way they have to work harder than ever to retain the public's attention and to keep it entertained. Regardless of this fact, gonzo trickster in his natural postmodern, depthless, decentred habitat (which, as Fredric Jameson argues, has long ceased to shock urban audiences consisting of TV-zombied consumers, overfed with sensual stimuli and information, and numbed by the abundance of kaleidoscopic imagery) still manages to rock the social boat and cause a stir. He does it by using the traditional trickster technique – intruding into the no-go areas, which still abound in the morally unfet-tered society: private life, all facets of political correctness, the irresolvable and potentially explosive conflicts between different social, political and religious groups (such as the incompatibility of Islam and homosexuality). As such, even the cruel and erratic purposelessness of contemporary gonzo jokes contains an important social message: that no aspect of social life should be immune from criticism otherwise there is always the danger that the system will crumble under the weight of its own rigidity. The trickster does not take sides – its task is to regulate. True, criticism provided by the trickster is always of the destructive and absurd kind, but as a shock therapy it is very effective and no one can accuse, say, Andy Kaufman, that his public-baiting did not do its job.

The Life and Death of the Trickster: Andy Kaufman

Bob Zmuda describes his very first encounter with Andy Kaufman and his controversial art as an overwhelming experience. The act, which would later become the comedian's breakthrough, and, consequently, the foolproof show which would outgrow both its author and its perceived iconoclastic character, was based on the incredible transformation of a useless little foreigner with his 'emetations' into 'de Elbis Presley'. The 'emetations' of the guy from 'an island in Caspiar' would simply consist of saying 'I am Jimmy Carter', 'I am Ed Sullivan' or 'I am Johnny Cash' in a silly voice. When they were performed in front of a new audience, its members would either snore or get annoyed. When the silly-voiced comedian announced, as his concluding number, 'de Elbis Presley', audience members would brace themselves for the final train crash. What happened next, however, was a cleverly constructed deception of expectations. People had been carefully groomed to despise the sad exotic loser. Zmuda recalls his reaction when he saw the 'Presley' transformation for the first time at the Improv comedy club in New York:

> This poor little Iron Curtain comedian then fumbled around in a tired little valise, found a comb, and began raking his hair into an Elvis coif. He reached back and pulled out some props. [. . .]

> My jaw dropped. This was no impression, this *was* Elvis. Then, as the trademark lip twitch went out of control, he deadpanned, 'There's something wrong with mah lip'. That brought a big laugh, partly because it was funny, but probably more so because we were all still in a shock. [. . .]

> Suddenly lights began to flash, and he launched into 'Treat Me Like a Fool'. He was actually singing instead of lip-synching, and he was great. He followed that first number with a killer rendition of 'Jailhouse Rock' that brought the house down. At the end of the act, this person, whoever or whatever he was – I still wasn't sure – nodded politely, eyes agog, and said – 'Dank you veddy much'.

> He went off the stage, and everyone else in the place went nuts. Budd Friedman leaped up the stage and proudly announced: 'That was Andy Kaufman, ladies and gentlemen, Andy Kaufman!'. I just sat there, stunned, unable to clap, blink, or even close my mouth.
>
> (Zmuda, 1999: 25–26)

Jim Carrey, himself a big Kaufman fan, lovingly reproduced this scene in Milos Forman's biopic, *Man on the Moon* (1999). He had wanted the role badly, and found it exciting – albeit emotionally draining – to portray his guru. As Zmuda explained in an interview to Christopher Null for the online magazine *Filmcritic*, 'Jim Carrey is the biggest Andy Kaufman freak in the world. If he wasn't Jim Carrey, he could travel the country lecturing on Kaufmanism. He fought to get this role. He was born to play this role' (http://www.filmcritic.com, 9 November 1999). Carrey proved to be a good Kaufman disciple, demonstrating the difficult art of staying in character for long periods of time: 'Jim said, "How would Andy Kaufman approach this role?". Jim approached the role just as Andy would have. We shot for 85 days. Jim was only there for 2. The rest of the time he was Andy or Tony' (http://www.filmcritic.com, 9 November 1999).

Bob Zmuda, whose book about his co-trickster's life served as the narrative canvas for the film, was portrayed in the film by Paul Giamatti. In a way, biopic – the genre depicting events close to how they happened 'in real life' – is the total opposite of Kaufman's own creative method, which consisted of fictionalisation, medialisation and fragmentation of reality. But then again, Zmuda's chosen book format is totally in tune with his role as the stabiliser and organiser of Kaufman's unhinged imagination. His job as Kaufman's writer and best friend was to make sequences (unintelligible as they are) out of the comedian's brilliant flashes of inspiration. A trickster destroys, not creates – but with the help of a good writer he may well stay in the business for a decent period of time. In Kaufman's case, this period comprised roughly ten years. This is an extremely long career for someone who hated celebrity, despised fame, stubbornly retained creative independence and vehemently deconstructed his own accomplishments – so much so that the industry eventually gave up on him. This was the result he wanted to achieve. Or was it?

The Beginnings

In 1949, the year when the eccentric American comedian Andy Kaufman was born, only 2.3 per cent of American homes had televisions. By 1962, 90 per cent did. According to Oxford Reference Online, 'Despite the relatively high costs of the first sets, Americans purchased televisions regardless of income. And television quickly emerged as the most popular mass medium, with more Americans spending more time watching TV than consuming any other mass medium' (Television/The Oxford Companion to the United States History: http://www.oxfordreference.com). Television was a magically convenient and physically undemanding way of occupying children: 'For the post–World War II family, television, compared to moviegoing, was cost-efficient entertainment; parents and children could be entertained at home, without traveling to a theater or buying tickets' (Television/The Oxford Companion to the United States History: http://www.oxford reference.com).

Andy Kaufman's family was affluent enough to buy a TV set. In fact, his paternal grandfather ('Grandpa Paul') was the first to purchase a colour TV set among his friends, even though the pleasure of owning one set him back $3500. Born in New York into a Jewish business family specialising in old-style costume jewellery, Andy was both mismatched to his background and perfectly drew on his family's outlandishness and originality. He always wanted to be a performer. A first-generation TV zombie, little Andy liked to pretend that he had his own TV channel, which made him responsible for creating a motley bunch of programmes to fill the schedule. He remembers 'making' all kinds of shows:

> adventure shows, horror shows, old-time movies, cartoons. I would just run around the room playing all the parts. [. . .] I don't remember much of them. I remember one that was like an old-time silent movie show – 'cause in those days they showed a lot of silent movies instead of cartoons. I didn't understand what was going on in these movies – all I knew was that those people were walking around faster than usual, with music playing. So when I was re-creating them for myself, there wasn't any plot. It was just me for half hour walking around fast and doing all kinds of faces and falling down and stuff like that . . . My parents would say: 'Why don't you go out and play? And I would say: 'I can't! I'm putting on my shows!'
>
> (Zehme, 2001: 18)

His grandparents supported their first-born grandson's madcap creativity which was incessantly spewing up streams of chopped-up images, meaningless ideas and random citations. Grandpa Paul got Andy and his brother a movie projector, and with it reels of movies, shorts and features: 'funny cowgirls singing on stick ponies. The Little Rascals trapped in a spookhouse. Boris Karloff as the Mummy. The Creature from the Black Lagoon' (2001: 28). The grandfather also kept bringing new records and occasionally took the family to an amusement park where they could sing songs in the recording booth. Little Andy sang both his own compositions and hits of the day (2001: 28). Media and television have taken away Andy's sense of reality and replaced it with something infinitely more precious – a new perspective on life, a unique vision of things, an understanding that, in fact, there is *no* such thing as *reality* at all. His father Stanley recalls how sometimes Andy refused to accept the fact that there exists a 'correct' answer to a question. Once, after receiving a wrong reply during a conversation at the table, Stanley Kaufman asked his son whether, in his opinion, two and two was four. Andy's answer was 'Not necessarily'. The father was so baffled that he failed to offer his son a convincing riposte: '"I can't go any further! That's it!". He's a kid for crying out loud – eleven, twelve! Later on in life I learned that two and two maybe in Eskimo language does not make four. Two and two can be something else entirely. This was what he was getting at. He has a perception of life that was always questioning everything' (2001: 50).

Kaufman's early revelling in postmodern relativism and total defamiliarisation of reality included watching B-movies and monster shows. Andy watched horror films broadcast every Saturday night on local TV, and especially liked the ghoul Zacherle who introduced the movies. He and his friend used to act out *Frankenstein Meets Wolf Man*. Andy also loved playing the Mummy, wrapping himself in toilet paper and parodying the famous shuffling Mummy walk. Sometimes they created their own monster mash combinations, and 'staged' fights between Wolf Man and the Mummy (2001: 52). Liberated from narrative constraints and prescriptions, enhanced with new combinatorial possibilities offered by constantly advancing technology, the media provided them with creative freedom (although Jameson would called it the freedom to make pastiches) but failed to teach them to construct perceivable semantic bases to prop up their textual and visual materials. Semantic bases in Andy Kaufman's work had to take care of themselves.

The monsters were the 'other' whose incursion into the post-war media signified profound changes in the political, cultural and social processes in society. Monsters dragged 'the other' to the surface of society's consciousness from the depths of the collective unconscious even before the new wave of fresh-faced poststructuralist philosophers started discussing them in their semantically challenging works. Anyway, the first TV generation kids, despite the seeming futility of the process, kept creating, kept looking, kept searching and kept joining the bits of the code together in a playful, childish way. The elusive 'meaning' was now hidden in the process, not the result. Creativity, even in a monstrous (or tricksterish form) is still a divine activity because it stands for life and movement, not death and stagnation. It stands for God.

Kaufman's God

Andy Kaufman's creative efforts have been revolving around the slippery idea of 'God', dead or alive, single or multiple. From his meditation experiments and spiritual ventures as a student of Grahm Junior College in Boston in the late 1960s, this wonderful idea materialised itself, in various distorted, and often monstrous, shapes and guises into Andy's jokes and shows. One of his novels was entitled *God* and was, in fact, devoted to his childhood and lifelong idol, Elvis Presley. It was suitably disjointed, fragmented and lacking in narrative logic for it was a typical postmodern narrative embodying all the key elements of the genre, such as interest in metafiction and fragrant non-linearity. Kaufman's first ever review came from *The Simmons News* school paper shortly after his dramatic reading of *God* in the living room of a women's dormitory at Simmons College in Boston, Massachusetts. It said, among other things:

> Kaufman has created a fragmented funhouse fantasy. . . . [His] versatile improvisations carried the audience through incoherent passages until parallel events became interwoven. His expressive delivery

complete with sound effects and gestures did not lag during the two-hour reading; nor did his voice crack under the strain of five-minute tee-heeing and hummmmmmming. Kaufman's vitality controlled the event and the myriad of voices talking, gurgling and singing.

(Zehme, 2001: 99)

In fact, in all his future chaotic performances the aforementioned cocksure vitality would be the (rather shaky) skeleton holding together the edgy scraps of material that the comedian would be able to offer his public. Kaufman himself was a walking, talking, barely coherent, multifaceted, cleverly constructed postmodern narrative. He was metafiction personified. Shaped by the media's kaleidoscopic multi-perspectivism, it lacks consistency, taste, direction. Like his contemporaries, he made art by creating copies of copies of copies.

A postmodern artist, Andy was fishing for God in an endless pool of images and eventually discovering his most veritable incarnation in the one and only Elvis Presley. He even received personal blessings from his deity after patiently waiting for eight hours in a storage cupboard in Las Vegas Hilton, and jumping out at the crucial moment, the Book of Elvis clutched to his chest. 'I am going to be famous too' – he announced to Elvis. 'I am sure you will' – was the patronising reply of the King.

God and the Fool

Having received 'God's' blessing, Andy was now confident enough to push his career forward. The issue of the common man and his failure is closely linked to the problem of the validity of God's existence in Kaufman's art. Andy's anchor characters – Foreign Man and Tony Clifton – are 'lost' people courting social acceptance, celebrity and fame. However, being losers – one sad and quiet, the other burly and offensive – they find no such acceptance. Foreign Man, who later metamorphosed into the loveable car mechanic Latka Gravas in the American sitcom *Taxi* (ABC, 1978–1982), is not only shy – he is openly un-artistic and un-brilliant. He is hopelessly, scandalously ordinary. His 'emetations' are awful, and his jokes are perfectly unfunny. One such joke, documented in *Man on the Moon*, contained the lines 'take my wife, please. I love my wife but she don't [*sic*] know how to cook. Her cooking is terrible'. Another famous example is 'the story of the cannonball' from 'The Andy Kaufman Special' which was aired on ABC in 1979. It went like this:

I would like to tell you de story of de three people who was carrying the beegest cannon in the world to Spain! Eet was two boys and one girl. And dey had thees beeg cannon. You know, eet was feefty feet long!

And dey carried eet over the mountains and under the valleys. And one day dey get to the top of de highest mountain in Spain. So the first boy, he point this cannon toward this castle, you know, to shoot! You know, because he was de boss. You know, so he want to point it. And he turned to the second boy and he say, 'All right! Hand me the cannonball!'. And, you know, but de second boy, he say – 'Duh, I thought *you* had dem!'. [Audience laughs] Vait! Listen-listen-vait! So dey both – eh – dey both turned to de girl, and she say – 'Dooon't look eet me!' You know, you know, because dey forgot to bring the cannonball! You know! Dey have de cannon, but dey have no cannonball, dey could not shoot! Do you understand? Tenk you veddy much.

'De cannonball story', apart from being hopelessly inane, is also amazingly clever in its inanity. It is self-descriptive. The cannon failed to shoot because 'dey forgot to bring de cannonball', and so does the story. The story fails to explode, but this has been the point all along. The story is a failure. The man is a failure. The audience, too, are failures. They laugh at themselves. The story serves as a metaphor not only for the Foreign Man's life and his type of humour, but also for Kaufman's chosen method. It is a metaphor for the process of waiting. Kaufman's audience, consisting mostly of 'common people', can relate to the monotony of waiting for things to happen to you. A movement, like the seemingly progressing narrative of the joke, may in the end reveal itself to be false. Things may happen – or they may not.

Kaufman's trademark 'Mighty Mouse' routine, which famously (or infamously) consisted of playing a recording of the theme song from the 20th Century Fox cartoon *Mighty Mouse*, and lip-synching the line 'Here I come to save the day!', while patiently standing for the rest of the song, is a variation on the theme of waiting for the right moment. All this character can do is lip-synch, 'emetate', copy. However, he has perfected his copycat routine to the tee. Kaufman's (rather bitter and cruel) message is that within each loser there lurks a desire to become a superhero – even if it is just a superhero mouse from a silly cartoon. The little shy performer is assigned a role, and is waiting for his turn to lip-synch the words written by someone else for a cartoon character. Regardless of the mousy insignificance of the task, he feels like a star. The scene is not funny per se, but somehow Kaufman makes the process of waiting – *waiting for the punchline*, which is the metaphor for anticipating a happening – into a transformation, a heroic change. The audience is watching, mesmerised, because pretending to be a superhero is what they do in the privacy of their own homes, and here is this guy doing it on stage, brave in his idiocy. Secretly, the 'little people' want to get rid of the monotony of their lives. They want a liminal adventure, a life-changing transition. However, most of their existence is spent in tedious anticipation.

The Foreign Man

In fact, Andy Kaufman is not the inventor of comedy based on greenhorn experiences. The American journalist and author Jody Rosen, who has researched early twentieth century Jewish comedy and vaudeville, points out that the genre of dialect comedy is not new. It was already thriving during the first decade of the twentieth century, when 'American popular culture functioned as a kind of psychic clearinghouse for anxieties about the millions of new European immigrants and black Southern migrants flooding into the nation's big cities' (*Slate*, 3 November 2006). In dialect comedy immigrants found comical tools for assessing the levels of assimilation, measuring the degree of cultural preservation and determining the depth of identity crisis:

> By laughing along with songs that lampooned the struggle of Jewish greenhorns, the Jewish audience affirmed its own sophistication. By writing and singing dialect songs that partook of some of the worst Jewish stereotypes, the Jews of Tin Pan Alley and vaudeville performed their American-ness. To mock the 'Hebrew' was to cast one's parochialism, cleanse oneself of the Old World taint, and join the social majority.
>
> (Rosen, quoted in Koegel, 2009: 267)

The joke is about the border, the tension, the transition, and other satellites of the conflict between the liminal and the mainstream. The joke is about what Andrew Samuels calls 'a competitive tension between being *alike* (sharing in *one* set of psychological assumptions and cultural traditions) and being *unalike* (invested in a particular set out of *many* sets of psychological assumptions and cultural traditions)' (Samuels, 1993: 326). Kaufman seems to be drawing on the creative and controversial legacy of Jewish greenhorn humour, but the issues he discusses are wider than experiences of any given ethnic minority. His issues – exclusion, failure, drive for success – although based on immigrant marginality, are, in fact, universal. It is much harder for the immigrants to gain a position in society, but people in general are expected to fight for inclusion and acceptance.

The main lesson Jim Carrey seems to have learned from Andy Kaufman (apart from chatting gibberish, using the Elvis quiff strictly for comical purposes and pulling improbable faces while shouting insults *à la* Ace Ventura) is that 'the funny' is not hidden in the punchline. Instead, the funny covers everything that precedes the punchline, and then what goes after it. The truly funny and the really tragic in human life happen *before* and *after* van Gennep's uncertain period of 'transition'. These states exist outside the *limen* even though most human beings do not notice them until a reckless chance turns their existence upside down. In short, the funny and the tragic are part of everyday life. Two truly amusing things are the waiting and the aftertaste of failure; the realisation that things did not happen, or that they went the wrong way, or that the result was not as significant as expected. Some of Kaufman's characters – such as Tony Clifton – are unnaturally loud in their pursuit of being noticed.

Tony Clifton and the Celebrity Culture

As a character, Tony Clifton was meant to express the complex interaction between ordinariness and fame. He was a Frankenstein-esque creation comprising bits of the repulsive Mr. X, whose reality-defying creative methods fascinated Andy, and Andy's own 'dark heart' (Zmuda, 1999: 51). This ugly, chain-smoking, heavy-drinking, foul-mouthed lounge singer was a grotesque depiction of fame and stardom. An anti-celebrity, Tony was created purely to annoy the viewers and unwitting participants in his pranks. The aim was not to get acceptance, but to get rejected, to get thrown out. Clifton sang very badly, mumbled stupid things, did even stupider things and often appeared in public (and on stage) accessorised by 'whores'. In many ways, he was the ultimate alter-ego of the yoga-practising and teetotal Andy Kaufman. So much different was he from his author that Andy had to perform a special elaborate stomach-cleansing procedure after each night of drinking, smoking and every other kind of excess inflicted on him by his creation.

Tony was played both by Kaufman and Zmuda, and thanks to the professionally done prosthetics and make-up the two Cliftons were visually indistinguishable. Although he was 'composed' of two actors who took turns to portray him, Tony always had a separate contract as if he were a real performer. Having a separate contract helped when Tony behaved especially badly – like the time when he arrived on the set of *Taxi* with two hookers, messed up the rehearsal (he was booked to appear in a Christmas episode as a degenerate Vegas gambler), insulted the crew and the actors, and was duly shown out of the door. Or rather, thrown out of the door by security – and, perversely, that was his own request (1999: 134–136).

Ugly as he was, Tony (alongside Elvis) was a good way to explore the shapes and guises of God in a society without the wholesome 'divine authority' which would be keeping the subject from fragmenting and providing him/her with a core and a meaning. The projection has gone into something else, or someone else. Kaufman, in his wild, hands-on gonzo experimentation, was trying to find the direction of the disappeared projection. Surely, God is not dead – he is alive – and he resides, say, in Elvis. Postmodern God has many faces. He is alive in culture-defining and mind-shaping celebrities whom the 'little insignificant people' (groupies, fans, idle onlookers) are trying to 'emetate'. Celebrities as deities make sense to the masses because, as Christopher Hauke explains, 'the fragmentation and "schizophrenia" of the postmodern subject can be viewed as arising out of the fragmentation of human qualities beyond any choice or control of the individual; the result is a fractured psyche, internally competing between its parts and seeking resolution and healing through projection onto such objects the culture offers' (Hauke, 2000: 70). To paraphrase Hauke (who is speaking here about the phenomenon known as 'the death of Princess Diana'), media and broadcasting coverage provide the public with a facilitated consumption of public images in whom the viewers, 'lost to their own fragmented sense of themselves', are seeking a range of condensed human qualities (2000: 68).

If Elvis was Kaufman's 'ideal' God, beautiful and unimpeachable, and therefore never 'emetated' in a silly way, Tony Clifton is the deconstruction of the phenomenon of celebrity and the demonstration of its powerful influence on the viewing public. Clifton was created in order to force the people to see the projection, and to reject it. It required the most hardcore of celebrity sycophants to fall in love with the character displaying all the possible abuses of cheap fame, from drugs and prostitutes to hysterical diva behaviour on sets of pop sitcoms. If anyone could actually *love* and '*emetate*' him, then the 'smallness' of such a person was beyond repair. Surrendering one's individuality to a star is the best material for gonzo trickster activities, and Kaufman could use it very well indeed.

Boundaries, Projections and Obsessions

In fact, during his short and intense career, Andy Kaufman managed to deeply explore all the contemporary facets of the age-old relationship between Man and God. God as Elvis. God as a famous swine with lots of money who believes he can do just about anything. God as Andy Kaufman. Andy Kaufman as Elvis as God. God as creator. The little powerless foreign man – little and foreign being the principal reasons for his power-lessness – who wants to 'emetate' God and become a creator too (for instance, he invents the story of 'de cannonball' or transforms into Elvis Presley). God as the author, the player, the actor; as the cruel manipulator of the audience. Andy Kaufman as the author shifting the responsibility for the performance onto the audience. The audience searching for God within themselves, and finding it in their own sublimated projection onto the figure on stage.

Kaufman brings the viewers round to themselves – or rather, uses shock therapy to wake them up – in his pursuit to show the dangers of mass projections which often become mass obsessions. The common man feels useless and lonely. He feels small and is looking for ways to elevate himself. In his pursuit to become bigger and stronger, he 'emetates' prominent people. Projection, especially a mass one, is a very effective method of becoming a hero. It is an overwhelming experience which has its dangers.

Jung never stopped warning the seemingly enlightened and independently thinking individual of the allure of the collective shadow:

> The mass is swayed by a *participation mystique*, which is nothing other than an unconscious identity. Supposing, for example, you go to the theatre: glance meets glance, everybody observes everybody else, so that all those who are present are caught up in an invisible web of mutual unconscious relationship. If this condition increases, one literally feels borne along by the universal wave of identity with others. It may be a pleasant thing – one sheep among ten thousand! Again, if I feel that this crowd is a great and wonderful unity, I am a hero, exalted along with the group. When I am myself again, I discover that I am Mr. So-and-So, and that I live in such and such a street, on the third floor. I also find that the whole affair was really most delightful, and I hope it will take place again tomorrow so that I may once more feel myself to be a whole nation, which is much better than being just plain Mr. X. Since this is such an easy and convenient way of raising one's personality to a more exalted rank, mankind has always formed groups which made collective experiences of transformation – often of an ecstatic nature – possible. The regressive identification with lower and more primitive states of consciousness is invariably accompanied by a heightened sense of life.
>
> (CW9/I: para. 226)

As Jim Carrey himself phrases it in the backword to Zmuda's book (predictably, the backword is done in the boundary-pushing mirror writing): 'Are you insulted, angry or even more bewildered than before? Good! That was always your purpose! You're still playing your parts brilliantly! After all, you were the stars of the show all along. Andy was the director and the audience. Enjoy your meal' (Zmuda, 1999: 295).

A true trickster never becomes embedded in his routine and never builds 'the fourth wall'. His entertaining power comes from 'the people'; its influence is in direct proportion to his psychical and psychological distance from the audience. The fourth wall only impedes the projection–introjection process, and the trickster, whose task is to stir up the trouble, to disturb the audience in a positive or a negative way, does not really need it.

Zmuda remembers that 99 per cent of Andy Kaufman's performances were never recorded or even seen by formal audiences because 'they took place on streets, in restaurants, and in myriad other public places'. Meanwhile, most of the witnesses 'did not know they were experiencing a performance, let alone that they had become an audience'. However, the 'live tricks' were as carefully planned as the time-weathered classics such as 'The Mighty Mouse' and 'The-Foreign-Man-turns-Elvis'. And they were as impressive (and, at times, pretty disturbing for the onlookers). One such mini-show, or 'psychodrama', as Zmuda terms it, designed to poke fun at celebrity and fame, was traditionally played by Kaufman, Zmuda and a female actor in restaurants. The two audience plants portrayed a happy couple. Andy would chat with them, flirting with the girl, and when the boyfriend left for the bathroom, Andy would ask the girl to go out with him, stressing the point that her fiancé is a *nobody* while he, Andy, is a star with bags of money. The baffled girl would eventually grasp the logic in her seducer's reasoning, and agree to leave with Andy immediately. Then the 'celebrity' and his new girlfriend would exit, leaving the cruelly discarded man (played by Bob Zmuda, whose acting training allowed him to be able to cry on cue) weeping at the table. This psychodrama never failed to wind up the entire restaurant. Of course, the shocked and outraged diners had no idea that they had been set up. 'Our restaurant "presentations"' – Zmuda reminisces – 'not only were amusing diversions, but also served as outlet for Andy's welling disgust over the nature of fame and the nearly mindless permission people would heap on someone just because they had seen the person on television or in the movies' (Zmuda, 1999: 185–187).

Another psychodrama about 'stars and losers' required, rather cruelly, that the entire Kaufman family flopped on stage. The show took place in a Catskills resort on Thanksgiving. Instead of doing his usual routine, Andy staged a family get-together, complete with grandmother's tales and family jokes. Andy's idea might be considered ground-breaking given that it was a prototype of reality television 20 years before its official birth. Unfortunately, the paying customers did not wish to listen to the Kaufman family chronicles, and got at first bored, and then angry. Andy was fascinated by his parents' failure in front of a big crowd of strangers, and did not even attempt to intervene for fear of ruining the smoothly-progressing gonzo spectacle entitled 'My Family Dies on Stage'. After the show the management ordered the Kaufman group to vacate the premises at once. Zmuda's interpretation of the incident accurately captures the spirit and psychology of the trickster principle. Neither flaccid conformity nor its ambitious alternative, vacuous and over-inflated fame, are the way forward for an individual:

> He was using his family as if they were a version of his Great Gatsby routine from the Improv. [. . .] Perhaps it was his pure rebellion against the ethos that informs the lives of most, that conformity and acceptance are immutable foundations of our daily society. Iconoclasm and revolution, on the other hand, though noble behaviour for historical figures, are merely disruptive and antisocial when exhibited by contemporaries.
>
> (1999: 180–181)

One may see Kaufman as a malicious prankster playing cruel practical jokes on unwitting victims. Another way to look at his undercover activities is to regard them as 'gifts' to his viewers. After all, it was his way of sharing his art with the people. His talent was to disturb and, by doing so, to make people question their reality. He was pretty generously paid for it. But money builds the wall between the performer and the audience, threatening to erode away the trickster's powers. Andy Kaufman never let it happen to him. Up until the very end he remained as scandalous, controversial, annoying and incomprehensible as at the beginning of his career.

The Dissolution and Resurrection of the Trickster

Kaufman truly embodied the trickster principle: he lived and died on stage, not discerning between 'the imaginary' and 'the real'. In the true trickster fashion, his shows were genuinely 'between good and evil' – they startled people, and the resultant shock made them think. When he announced, in 1984 at the age of just 35, that he had lung cancer, the media and even his closest friends kept suspecting the piece of news to be just another prank. After all, are not tricksters supposed to be immortal thanks to their transcendent qualities which have roots in their mercurial creativity? But Andy was also human, and the ultimate 'reality', the one that is physical, caught up with him.

Kaufman was right, however, in that there are many more different types of reality. One of them is the indubitable power of talent, originality, transgression and laughter. He has influenced the comedic philosophy of Robin Williams. He has anticipated reality TV. If you watch one of the several 'I am from Hollywood, I have the brains' clips created to boost the ticket sales for the forthcoming Kaufman–Lawler wrestling match, in which Kaufman is taunting the inhabitants 'of the southern portion of the United States' (including Jerry Lawler) by explaining to them all about their limited intellectual abilities, you can recognise the all-too-familiar goofing, provocation and face-pulling which would later become the hallmark of Carrey's early characters. Kaufman's rebellion, and his vision of the dichotomy between stardom and failure, are very much alive.

Finally, the audience of 'Tony Clifton Live', which took place on 16 May 1985, exactly one year after Andy's death, were treated to a miraculous happening: Andy's creation, the legendary debaucher, singer and individual nasty in every imaginable way, was resurrected from the ashes.[2] The venue, Zmuda recalls, was packed with entertainment-industry execs, artists, producers, fans, camera crews and comedians including Whoopi Goldberg, Rodney Dangerfield and Eddie Murphy. Other industry insiders, such as

---

2 Andy Kaufman sometimes joked about faking his death. Also, in the unpublished film script titled *The Tony Clifton Story*, Tony dies from lung cancer in the Cedars-Sinai hospital in Los Angeles where Andy would actually die some eight years later (Zehme, 2001: 264).

Steve Martin and Robin Williams, lent their names to the programme. Sitting in a corner was an unknown young comic named Jim Carrey (1999: 287). They were all shown clips from various disastrous Tony Clifton performances. Half-way through the song 'I Will Survive', however, the 'real' Tony Clifton suddenly emerged and picked up the song from where the projector left it. The audience, predictably, was hysterical, and the infamous anti-celebrity was given a standing ovation. Andy Kaufman, it seemed, has pulled his usual transcendental trick (was he not a fan of transcendental meditation?) of assisting the audience in crossing the border into the world of the uncanny, the supernatural, the abnormal and the absurd.

At the end of Tom Stoppard's play *Rosencrantz and Guildenstern Are Dead*, 'the little man' Guildenstern challenges the Player by telling him that acting is a profession specialising in deception, and that the actor, despite dying on stage so many times, in fact, knows nothing about death. But dying, the Player retorts, is what actors do best:

> They have to exploit whatever talent is given to them, and their talent is dying. They can die heroically, comically, ironically, slowly, suddenly, disgustingly, charmingly, or from a great height. My own talent is more general. I extract significance from melodrama, a significance which it does not in fact contain; but occasionally, from out of this matter, there escapes a thin beam of light that, seen at the right angle, can crack the shell of mortality.
>
> (Stoppard, 1991: 90)

The mortal man – actor – becomes immortal when he assumes another character. And although he has lost a sense of 'reality', he has mastered the art of transformation. He has mastered the invaluable art of liminal transition.

Sacha Baron-Cohen and the Problem of 'Otherness'

Baron-Cohen's creative path is very unusual. As Roland White writes in an article in *The Sunday Times*, Sacha's family has international roots: his maternal grandmother fled Nazi Germany for Israel, and his father, Gerald, is originally from Pontypridd, Wales. One of three brothers born into a middle-class Jewish family, he grew up in London where he attended Haberdashers' Aske's Boys' School. After a gap year, Baron-Cohen went on to read history at Christ's College, Cambridge, the topic for his dissertation being the role of Jewish people in the U.S. Civil Rights Movement (*The Sunday Times*, 21 January 2007).

At Cambridge Baron-Cohen joined the Cambridge University Amateur Dramatic Club. At the time he was also involved with Habonim Dror, the Socialist-Zionist youth movement. He attributes his interest in comedy to the influence of American actor and comedian Danny Kaye and British comedian Peter Sellers:

> There was a lot of emphasis on humour in my childhood. That's true for a lot of Jewish families, but in mine, I think there was even more. From a very young age, I was watching Sergeant Bilko and Danny Kaye comedies on TV. [. . .] And Peter Sellers was always an inspiration to me – I think I was seven when I first saw him as Inspector Clouseau, and I still remember how hilarious it was. Then, as I grew older and started seeing more of his films, I began to appreciate how amazing he really was. He managed to bridge comedy and satire – he was hilariously funny, and he also made some incredibly powerful comments on our society. And he had an extraordinary ability to inhabit his characters, which I admire.'
>
> ('Sacha Baron Cohen: It's So Sad, But I Have to Kill Off Brüno',
> *Mail Online*, 19 July 2009)

After graduating from Cambridge, to the disappointment of his parents, he decided against entering a serious profession (they wanted him to be a lawyer) and began his career of an original and outrageous comedian. After a number of jobs in fashion and on TV, he finally got his breakthrough in 1998 as Ali G on *The 11 O'Clock Show* on Channel 4.

Baron-Cohen seems to have always been interested in discourse wars, identity mix-ups, the barely veiled but highly explosive ideological tension between minority groups, and other manifestations of the postmodern loss of 'sameness'/God. His first truly successful gonzo character was a 'black' rapper and news interviewer Ali G who displayed a random and uneven mixture of gangsta rap and Jamaican black culture. Ali G resided in Staines, spoke in a faux-street dialect, dressed in a giant bright-coloured shellsuit, and wore yellow wraparound shades and a heavy gold chain. He originally appeared on Channel 4's *11 O'Clock Show* (1998–2000), then became the title character of Channel 4's *Da Ali G Show* (2000; 2003–2004), and finally became the hero of a feature-length film entitled *Ali G In Da House* (directed by Mark Mylod; 2002). The character was so incredibly kitsch that his overtrusting victims initially thought him to be a natural part of the postmodern landscape. Sacha's technique consisted of enticing public figures to do interviews, and then throwing at them rude and inappropriate questions in street slang. The result was highly embarrassing not only for the interviewee but also for the viewer.

Between Identity and Assimilation

Sacha's choice of black identity as a trickster mask is interesting. Ali G was his first successful trickster-foreigner who worked as a reporter. Sacha said of his early interest in black street culture: 'As a kid I was very into rap. I used to breakdance. Starting at the age of 12 my mother would take me and my crew in the back of her Volvo. We had the linoleum in the back, and she'd drive us to Covent Garden in the dead middle of winter. We'd pull out the lino and start breaking. Essentially we were middle-class Jewish boys who were adopting this culture, which we thought was very cool. That was sort of the origins of Ali G' (*The Sunday Times*, 21 January 2007). One of the inspirations for the Ali G character, Baron-Cohen explains, was a BBC Radio One hip-hop DJ named Tim Westwood: 'We used go to these hip-hop happenings, and even then he was kind of laughable. Once I found out that he was actually the son of a bishop, it became even more absurd. He was so keen to be presented as a gangsta' (*Rolling Stone*, 15 November 2006).

According to Patrick Goldstein, one link to his future interest in the intricate relationships between the minority groups on the one hand, and his creative–destructive emphasis on political and cultural oppression on the other, is his Cambridge undergraduate dissertation entitled *The Black–Jewish Allies: A Case of Mistaken Identity* (*Guardian*, 19 January 2007). The American psychologist specialising in interracial issues, Alvin F. Poussaint wrote in *Ebony* magazine in July 1974 that, although the relationship between the two groups has never been entirely smooth and trouble-free, having been tarnished by such shameful phenomena as black anti-Semitism and Jewish racism and complicated by the Arab–Israeli conflict, Jewish and Black communities in the US joined forces for the civil rights cause:

> The Jewish community has long been one of the strongest allies of blacks. More than any other white group, Jews helped to spearhead and support the civil rights movement. Members of the Jewish community gave a great deal of financial help to the chief civil rights organisations. Much more than that, at the height of the movement in the mid 60s, many Jews went South to man the battle lines. Many were injured and several died in the struggle for black equality. Two of the three civil rights workers murdered in Mississippi during the summer of '64, Michael Schwerner and Andrew Goodman, were Jews from New York. The third victim was James Earl Chaney, a black Mississippian. These three gave their lives because they believed in justice and equality for all men. Schwerner and Goodman were like many other Jews in their special allegiance to the black cause.
>
> (*Ebony*, July 1974, 120–128)

Baron-Cohen has his own angle on the issue:

> I was writing this at the time of the Crown Heights riots when the Jewish community was obsessed with black anti-semitism. And I argued that this obsession came out of Jews feeling betrayed by their

old blood brothers from the civil-rights movement. But while it was perceived in the Jewish community that Jews were disproportionately involved in civil rights, my conclusion was black Americans didn't see Jews as being more involved than any white Americans.

The Jewish kids were all there in the South, but because they were there as part of church organisations like the [Southern Christian Leadership Council], they weren't seen as Jews but as white liberals. So there was this deep irony that the Jewish establishment took martyrs like Andrew Goodman and Michael Schwerner – two civil-rights workers from New York who went to Mississippi to register black voters and were killed by the Ku Klux Klan and used them as symbols of a Jewish-black alliance when, in fact, they didn't really see themselves as Jews at all.

(*Guardian*, 19 January 2007)

Baron-Cohen's eventual transformation of the serious issues of identity, foreignness, assimilation and human rights into comedy form has been preceded both by the Jewish vaudeville tradition (Rosen in *Slate*, 3 November 2006) and Andy Kaufman's 'Foreign Man' sketches. Compare, for instance, Andy Kaufman's 'man from Caspiar' speech and Borat's introduction of his native country in the opening scene of *Borat: Cultural Learnings of America for Make Benefit Glorious Nation of Kazakhstan* (2006). Borat opens the film introducing his 'country of Kazakhstan' which 'locate between Tajikistan, Kyrgyzstan and assholes Uzbekistan'. He then goes on to describe the various inhabitants of his 'home town of Kuzcek': Urkin the 'naughty, naughty' town rapist; little children playing with weapons at the local kindergarten; Mukhtar Sakanov, simultaneously town mechanic and abortionist, etc. Borat himself works as a television reporter, which he immediately proves by showing his coverage of the annual 'running of the Jew' contest. According to the journalist, Kazakhstan is a glorious country which, unfortunately, is plagued by a number of major problems: 'economic, social and Jew'. The Ministry of Information has sent him, Borat, to the U.S. in the hope of gathering some lessons from 'the greatest country in the world' and to learn the American ways of dealing with these issues.

And Andy Kaufman:

I am from Caspiar. Eet ees an island. Eet's in the Mediterranean Sea and eet's a small island maybe many miles north of Tripoli, you know, in Africa. I know Tripoli because I know you have to go to Tripoli to get to Caspiar. We always get food from Tripoli so we always send to Tripoli. So you know eet's a small island not on the map. And we live, you know, not very many people. Mostly we fish. Just to eat. And food. And trees. I don't mean eat trees – but what grow on trees!

People think I am eating trees! No, fruit and vegetables! And we have bread, yah. But I wanted to be in show business, but I was going to stay on my island, but one day I go fishing and I go come back and my island ees not there. My island sink. Because eet's not there, I row de boat to Tripoli to go to United States to New York. Citizen I want to be. I want to be in show business.

(Zehme, 2001: 10)

Both these speeches explore the integration problem in the gonzo form. Both effectively defamiliarise the foreigner by making him sound exotic and backwards. He lives in a 'make-believe' country with barbaric customs (compare this to Baudrillard's untrustworthy nature of postmodern media), speaks in broken English and sees America as a land of freedom and a land of truth. The foreigner is the one who is incomplete, who has to learn how to become a proper human being by learning from more experienced nations. Moreover, he actually *wants* to learn. He wants to close the gap; to achieve the wonderful sense of completeness.

Kaufman's monologue, despite its perceived inanity, is very cleverly built. Of course, everyone knows what every non-native wants. They live in the middle of nowhere, they eat trees, they come to your country in boats, and they want to take away your jobs. Kaufman's foreigner is a combination of refugee and economic migrant. Undeniably, the best jobs are in show-business – that is why every fool, loser and daydreamer is trying to snatch a few crumbs from the Hollywood table. Baron-Cohen is also successfully playing on stereotypes, foregrounding them one by one: rape in this town has a status of official activity, the natives have appalling medical care (well, their mechanics also double up as abortionists), their nursery children play with Kalashnikoffs. All of Baron-Cohen's gonzo tricksters also aspire to 'make it big' in the media, doing all sorts of shameful stupidities on their way towards the breakthrough to fame.

'The foreigner' (or, to take a narrower path, the immigrant) is a perfect trickster disguise because it is a type of outsider, a creature strange and mysterious at best, and dangerous and scheming at worst. The foreigner comes 'from beyond' the cultural and geographical threshold, potentially bringing disorder and threatening the integrity of the receiving culture. The 'fear of the foreigner' is the phenomenon that has always been the dutiful satellite of humanity, sometimes hiding in the background, and sometimes eclipsing the light entirely (as it happened during the Holocaust). It has as many faces as there are types of cultural 'alien species'. The idealistic myth of cultural wholeness ruptured or eroded by the intruder gives birth to xenophobia and hostility. In fact, xenophobia, as defined by the European Parliament, is 'an attitude that goes before fascism or racism and can prepare the ground for them' (European Parliament, Evregenis, 1985, p. 60). From the perspective of social psychology, as Elisabeth Buk-Berge defines it, xenophobia is a 'categorisation in the form of stereotypes and prejudices, where one in-group attempts to enhance its *cohesion* through discrimination against an out-group'. In social sciences, it is seen as 'growing out of symbolic and normative systems that legitimate processes of *integration* and *exclusion*' (Buk-Berge in Moutsios, 2007: 183). In a way, xenophobia is a faithful servant of the *habitus* as it grows out of the fear of non-sameness and non-local, alien influences.

Psychologically, xenophobia mirrors the telltale nationalist metaphor of 'cleansing the wound', 'removing the parasites', and thus 'restoring' the national health. This metaphor is dangerously powerful and has a tendency to grow like a snowball, the little sprouts of uninformed enmity quickly becoming a fully-grown tree of hatred. Andrew Samuels writes, for instance, that Hitler was obsessed 'with a Jewish "spirit", functioning as a pestilential bacillus, undermining the very idea of nation' (Samuels, 1993: 319). In this extended (and extendable) metaphor, the 'invaders' and 'parasites' are either presented as burrowing under the skin of society and causing damage, or as living on the margins in terrible conditions and planning an inevitable insurgency. The idea of 'smallness', which is the basis of the foreigner–insect metaphorical equation, can be seen by the perceiver either in a positive or a negative light. On the one hand, the 'smallness' and pitifulness of the immigrant qualifies him for charitable treatment and further enlightenment. On the other, the 'smallness' guarantees him invisibility and safety necessary to perform his 'evil deeds'. Sometimes, the foreigner/immigrant is the clumsy and endearing 'Paddington Bear from darkest Peru'; sometimes he is a terrorist plotting insurgency in his house in deepest suburbia. In any case, he is the alien 'other'.

Invasion fantasies are a very rich field for tricksterish exploration, and gonzo tricksters (actors and authors who choose to become the mouthpiece of the trickster principle) traditionally run amok with them. They mock every step of the 'invasion' process, from initial infiltration by 'the little man' to the 'destruction of the host culture from within'. Kaufman's transformation of the little Foreign Man into the great American cultural treasure that is Elvis is only shocking because initially the audience has low opinion of 'the poor Iron Curtain comedian' (as Zmuda called this character) and his 'emetation' abilities (Zmuda, 1999: 25). Kaufman prolongs the deception and deepens the sense of failure by doing 'emetation' after 'emetation' while the audience keeps watching, partly out of pity and partly out of the sense of superiority, with a certain dash of slapstick cruelty that any ludic event inevitably elicits from people. Kaufman's groundbreaking comedy was based on his ability to change the direction of the laughter. In the beginning of the act, the viewers were laughing at the 'visitor from afar'. When he fumbled in his little valise, extracted a comb, and proceeded to rake his hair into an Elvis coif, he won over his enemies in the audience. They began laughing *with* him. The hysterical laughter in the end of the

Elvis mini-concert was the laughter directed at themselves (1999: 25). The foreigner has set them up. He has deceived them. Or have they deceived themselves?

What does the little foreign man understand about 'de Elbis Presley' and other great American icons? The premise of the joke is that the guy who comes from across the border *just does not get* the host culture. And so the viewers, who accept this premise blindly, are lulled into the liminal trap. Baron-Cohen's gonzo-comedic 'experiments' are structured in a similar way, and have a comparable degree of rudeness and ruthlessness to them. He follows in Kaufman's footsteps not only conceptually but also geographically, travelling across Southern and Southwestern States, and playing havoc with American provincial conservatism.

Journalist as a Trickster

Baron-Cohen's invasion tactics are greatly facilitated by his tricksters' choice of profession. Journalism is a truly mercurial occupation in that it is 'beyond good and evil', geographically it is 'all over the place' and technologically it can reach vast numbers of people in a short period of time. Sacha's rude, pushy, all-permeating reporters and interviewers – Ali G, Borat and Brüno – aim their microphones and cameras at their victims' vulnerabilities and secrets. In this day and age, when privacy is undervalued and everyone wants to be on TV, it is relatively easy to trick people into 'doing an interview' and make them look like fools. 'Nobodies' want their 15 minutes of fame while famous people use every photo opportunity to top up their degree of public exposure. Even the most media aware of politicians, who have mighty PR machines supplying them with all the right words and moves, cannot completely control the self-image they project into the outside world. The media (especially in its internet form) is a trickster because, once it gets hold of a piece information, it transmits it across the world with unstoppable speed. Information in the technological age is truly mercurial.

A journalist *and* a foreigner is a doubly powerful con man. His oxymoronic nature – a person who *collects information* but has a *language problem* – gives him the licence to say pretty much anything. He is someone who defamiliarises and 'absurdises' the established reality of the host culture by pretending 'not to understand' and asking 'stupid questions'. Under the premise of 'reporting' and the promise of media exposure, Baron-Cohen's tricksters have successfully used and abused their interviewees' trust. In their hands, any serious issue, be it abortion, anti-Semitism or slavery, acquires recognisable slapstick hues and turns into a comical public beating. Ali G asked representatives of different religions whether God can do better stuff than David Blaine (Season 1: 2003, Episode 2). He angered the grammar-freak Andy Rooney with the question 'does you think the media has change' (Season 2: 2004, Episode 12). He shocked the animal rights activists during a roundtable 'discushen' by inquiring whether it is illegal to experiment on animals in the privacy of your own home (Series 1: 2000, Episode 1). Thanks to his thick foreign masks, he remains blameless and unpunishable. As Patrick Goldstein rightfully notes in *The Guardian*, Sacha found a secure way of transgressing the stringent boundaries of political correctness: 'In an era when entertainers have to apologise for any sort of intemperate remark, Cohen cleverly created a comic character that provided him free passage for all sorts of outrageous behaviour, be it lewd remarks about women, mocking of worshippers at a Pentecostal church or a visit to a gun shop where he asked the proprietor, "What is best gun to defend against Jew?"' (*The Guardian*, 19 January 2007).

Waking Up the Collective Shadow

Borat's infamous song, *In My Country There is a Problem*, is one of the most outrageous examples of deceiving the audience's expectations and turning viewers into the object of derision instead of the more obvious target – the 'little foreigner'. In fact, Baron-Cohen's foreigner is a rather big, bulky and moustachioed Kazakh man. It is not his physical frame that is *little* – it is his views that are *narrow*. In the final segment of *Da Ali G Show* (originally shown on HBO on August 1, 2004), Borat arrives with his 'Cowboy-Astana band' in Tucson, Arizona, to participate in a country music festival at the Country West music club. The name of Borat's band itself is pretty Kaufmanesque in that it combines the name of Kazakhstan's second largest city Astana (former Tselinograd) with American heroic mythology. Wearing the full cowboy attire, hat, boots and all, Borat from a shabby ex-Soviet republic has clearly come to 'emetate' the great culture. He is fascinated by the United States; he wants to sing their songs; he wants to think and behave like the people of the 'U S and A'.

Borat's 'emetation', as the gonzo tradition demands, starts off as a poor and lacklustre spectacle, with him badly playing the basic G-C-D chord progression and singing (also badly) that Kazakhstan's 'transpOrt' (the last syllable being made spondaic instead of trochaic for comical effect) should be thrown 'down the well' so his 'country can be free'. With his white jeans, horrendous rhymes, silly metrical deviations and terrible singing, it is clear to the audience that the guy is a loser. After the first quatrain and catchy 'throw down the well' refrain, the audience, just like the people from Zmuda's Improv story, gradually begins to get involved and starts singing along. And then, keeping to the same structure and set of repetitions, the song takes a very dark turn, and cunningly takes the audience, who is no longer on alert, along with it. It transpires that another problem plaguing Kazakhstan is the mytho-metonymic 'Jew', who has 'horns' and 'teeth' and 'takes everybody's money' without 'giving it back'. Therefore, Borat proposes in his song, the Jew, who by the third quatrain has a full set of monstrous attributes as per popular anti-Semitic mythology, should be 'thrown down the well' for the sake of the country's freedom, after which action everyone will have 'a big partY' (another misplaced spondee). By the end of the song, the viewers are happily cheering, singing, and even visually illustrating the song's content ('you must grab him by his horns'). Their applause demonstrates that they really enjoyed Borat's performance. The edge of the joke, originally aimed at the moustachioed loser from the middle of nowhere, has turned against them. What aspects of this culture did the foreigner eventually 'emetate'? Its racism and intolerance.

Playing on the worst stereotypes in a deceptively safe environment, Baron-Cohen creates a ludic space in which Jung's *participation mystique*, amplified by the carnivalesque atmosphere, turns people into a merry mob, either unconcerned about the song's violent content or secretly relishing it. In any case, one can always blame the mirror (i.e., Borat) by saying that it was *he* who started it, and it was *he* who pronounced all these words on stage. The participants do not spot the liminal threshold, where the universal problem of 'transport' (or even transpOrt) metamorphoses into the equally universal 'problem with the Jew'. Now the foreigner Borat, alongside his author, the foreigner Baron-Cohen, truly deserve to be hated by the 'host culture' for infiltrating their flanks, congealing them into a group with one brain, and making them (unconsciously, semi-consciously, unwittingly) say and do dumb things. The trickster willingly takes on the projection and morphs into the shadow of the crowd's choice, but the blame, like the birthplace of the projection, always lies with the audience.

There are conceptually similar episodes in other Baron-Cohen projects, *Borat: Cultural Learnings of America for Make Benefit Glorious Nation of Kazakhstan* and *Brüno*. The legal might of Hollywood was prepared to sustain any blows from Sacha's unwitting co-actors. One such lawsuit came from two college fraternity brothers who, under the influence of alcohol, made a number of racist and sexist remarks in one of the scenes of the *Borat* 'moviefilm'. The boys argued that the production crew took them to a bar where they were plied with drinks, promised that the documentary would only be shown outside of the United States, and asked to sign a release form ('Humiliated Frat Boys Sue Borat', *USA Today*, 15 November 2006). Their case was dismissed.

It appears that the audience of the 'Blue Collar Brawling' event at the local convention centre in the town of Fort Smith, during which Brüno's appeasement with his long-suffering lover Lutz took place, was also offered cheap beer and even asked to wear T-shirts with homophobic slogans on them. Karin Hobbs, the centre's director, explains that the event was very aggressively advertised, with promises of 'hot chicks' and 'hardcore fights'. Tickets cost $5 in advance, $10 at the door, and the flyer urged the viewers to buy beer early as possible because it would cost $1 during the first hour only. In reality, the price remained the same but the crowd, which did not know that it would, was spurned into buying and consuming vast amounts of alcohol ('How Real Is *Brüno*?', *Newsweek*, 9 July 2009). The result of this elaborate planning and audience-bating was the homophobic catastrophe which became the climax of *Brüno*. The viewers became one raging sea, and started throwing various objects, including beer cups and a chair, at the 'gay men'.

Scenes like this are controversial as it could be argued that Baron-Cohen's tricksters dupe their victims into doing outrageous things. Or do they simply lower the threshold and give the people the licence to do what they would have secretly wanted to do anyway? In his own words,

> Borat essentially works as a tool. By himself being anti-Semitic, he lets people lower their guard and expose their own prejudice, whether it's anti-Semitism or an acceptance of anti-Semitism. *Throw the Jew Down the Well* was a very controversial sketch, and some members of the Jewish community thought that it was actually going to encourage anti-Semitism. But to me it revealed something about that bar in Tucson. And the question is: Did it reveal that they were anti-Semitic? Perhaps. But maybe it just revealed that they were indifferent to anti-Semitism.
> (*The Rolling Stone*, 15 November 2006)

Sacha's stratagems are geared up at teasing out the person's shadow for the purpose of using this shadow for entertainment purposes. Racist, sexist and homophobic people making fools of themselves in front of the camera, when montaged into a cross-country road-trip or a spoof documentary, generally make for a hilarious scene. Sacha acts like Stoppard's tricksterish player who watches for 'the most . . . private . . . secret . . . intimate' things that people do 'secure in the knowledge of their privacy', records them, and then broadcasts them for the entire world to scrutinise and laugh about.

Gonzo Trickster and His Moral Nihilism

With his dissertation about the Civil Rights movement and his reputation as a spokesperson (albeit a controversial one) for oppressed minority groups, surely Baron-Cohen should be considered an upright cultural insurrectionist bashing screeching intolerant bigots left, right and centre. However, far from calling Baron-Cohen's art 'the great leveller', some journalists put in a counterclaim, and label him a bourgeois bully who oppresses those who are socially disadvantaged. For instance, David Brooks writes in *The New York Times* that *Borat* is 'an explosively funny rube-baiting session orchestrated by a hilarious bully'. Brooks accuses Baron-Cohen of bourgeois morality and malicious middle-classlessness – a 'crime' absolutely incompatible with the trickster principle:

> The genius of Sacha Baron Cohen's performance is his sycophantic reverence for his audience, his refusal to challenge the sacred cows of the educated bourgeoisie. During the movie, Borat ridicules Pentecostals, gun owners, car dealers, hicks, humorless feminists, the Southern gentry, Southern frat boys, and rodeo cowboys. A safer list it is impossible to imagine. [. . .]
>
> Cohen also knows how to rig an unfair fight, and to then wring maximum humiliation and humor out of each situation. The core of his movie is that he and his audience know he is playing a role, and this gives him, and them, power over the less-sophisticated stooges who don't. The world becomes divided between the club of those who are in on the joke, and the excluded rubes who aren't. [. . .]
>
> (*The New York Times*, 16 November 2006)

Brooks puts Baron-Cohen next to other moguls of 'condescension media' (authors and producers of reality shows such as *American Idol* and *The Apprentice*, which are built on the bones of underprivileged participants) and accuses the Cambridge-educated trickster of 'democratised snobbery' which turns louts' antics into a consumption item for the vast educated class.

Some of Baron-Cohen's victims are actually middle-class. They did not display any 'louts' antics' and yet were drawn, with devastating results, into Baron-Cohen's productions. Baron-Cohen, they argue, has no respect for other people's dignity and privacy. One of such 'middle class fools' is TV producer Dharma Arthur who invited Borat for an interview on a morning show segment on WAPT in Jackson, Miss. She believed him to be a genuine Kazakh news correspondent ('Borat Victims Upset at Being Duped', *USA Today*, 2 November 2006). During the interview Borat stood out of frame, made rude remarks, kissed the male anchor, announced that he had to 'go urine', and ended up hugging the weatherman. The outcome of this interview for Arthur was deep depression and eventual job loss ('Borat Victims Upset at Being Duped', *USA Today*, 2 November 2006). Another of Borat's targets, an etiquette coach Kathie Martin from Birmingham, Ala., also feels left out of the joke: 'Unless you can figure it out for yourself, you have no way of knowing you have been tricked into being part of a childish prank with an R rating attached. And even if you figure it out, you've signed a release that Mr. Cohen's people say relinquishes any rights on your part to take action against them' ('Borat Victims Upset at Being Duped', *USA Today*, 2 November, 2006).

True to the immoral and edgy trickster spirit, Baron-Cohen's jokesters actively engage in culture wars, overstepping or nearly overstepping the safety line. As a wearer of the trickster's mask, Sacha is not required to create, moralise and teach – only destroy – but sometimes his postmodern annihilation of core moral principles hurts real people in a very palpable manner. In his Wexlerian belief that reality is constructed, reconstructed and endlessly manipulated, he seems to place a lot of faith in the legal might of the Hollywood machine which can crush those unwitting playmates of Borat and Brüno who have little or no economic or legal power.

The journalist Melik Kaylan called Sacha's style of comedy 'bullying nihilism' overflowing with 'Rabelaisian obscenity' (*Forbes*, 14 July 2009). Postmodern culture wars as executed and directed by the gonzo trickster may well expose the fact that (to paraphrase Kaylan) the different minority groups wouldn't hold together long if they faced the ugly truth about each other, but this exposure of 'godlessness', psycho-cultural fragmentedness and groundlessness does not in any way help to repair the split.

A gonzo trickster exposes the veiled wounds of society whose surface is relatively, and *pretentiously*, calm, but can his wound-disturbing activities play an important social role? How about staging a clash between an outrageously flamboyant gay man and a talk show audience consisting predominantly of overweight African-American women? What if he accuses them of racism – how does this expose the insane, fragile and artificial nature of political correctness? Or let us go ever further, and imagine a multiple culture war transgression. It will take place not in the superficially smooth Western society but in the place with real wounds – the Middle East. How about a Jewish comedian dressed up as a gay reporter interviewing a Muslim terrorist about the Israeli–Palestinian conflict and telling him that 'al-Qaida is so 2001'? Surely, this will have an explosive political effect and will reveal the absurd nature of the conflict.

As Rachel Shabi reports in *The Guardian*, Ayman Abu Aita, the 'terrorist group leader' and member of 'al-Aqsa Martyrs Brigade' is, in fact, a Christian peace activist who was not amused by the manner his image was manipulated in the film. As in Kathie Martin's case, the joke had serious consequences for him. Reality might not exist for gonzo tricksters, but it does for those they deceive. Aita claims that the film diminished his chances of winning the 2010 Palestinian Parliamentary elections and angered his neighbours: 'They are angry that I have embarrassed the Palestinian people, because we are being presented in this false, disgusting way. [. . .] Brüno can make jokes about anything he wants, but this is not a joke. Calling me a terrorist is not funny – it is lying' (*The Guardian*, 31 July 2009).

One might even accuse Baron-Cohen himself of being racist, sexist, elitist, exploitative or bourgeois-condescending. The inhabitants of the impoverished village of Glod in the Dambovita region of Romania, which is presented as Borat's 'native village', were particularly incensed by the way they were depicted in the film. Villagers were allegedly paid £3 each for their respective 'parts' in the opening scenes of *Borat* in which they are portrayed as the cultural 'other' – weird, barbaric and ignorant. The settlement is home to 'number four prostitute in all of Kazakhstan' (who is also Borat's sister), local children are running around playing with Kalashnikoffs, and the main means of transport is a dilapidated Dacia car driven by horses. Baron-Cohen is carefully mixing fiction with reality, for instance, by filming the shabby interiors of impoverished houses and building his stories around them. According to Bojan Pancevski and Carmiola Ionescu's report, the disabled man Nicu Tudorache, who was asked by the crew to wear a rubber sex toy on his stump, had no idea what the final result would look like:

> Someone from the council said these Americans need a man with no arm for some scenes. I said yes but I never imagined the whole country, or even the whole world, will see me in the cinemas ridiculed in this way. This is disgusting. [. . .] Our region is very poor, and everyone is trying hard to get out of this misery. It is outrageous to exploit people's misfortune like this to laugh at them.
>
> (*Mail On Sunday*, 11 November 2006)

Trickster has traditionally been associated with scatological jokes, and Sacha's characters, predictably, are full of them (the best probably being Borat bringing a bag of faeces into the dining room of an etiquette coach in Birmingham, Ala.). But one thing is to laugh at scatological jokes, and another is to clean your house after four days of filming during which a live cow was brought into your living room (which also triples up as bedroom and kitchen), and for which you were paid $30. To ensure his safety in the poor gypsy region, Sacha allegedly protected himself with bodyguards and stayed in a hotel in Sinaia, a nearby ski resort, while the rest of the crew enjoyed the village motel: 'He would come to the village every morning to do "weird things"' – the locals reminisce – 'such as bringing animals inside the run-down homes, or have the village children filmed holding weapons' (*Mail On Sunday*, 11 November 2006). There has been no compensation for the villagers of Glod as their lawsuit failed due to shortage of 'more specific allegations' ('Village "Humiliated" by Borat Satire', *BBC News*, 26 October 2008). The nearest cinema is 20 miles away, which explains their slow reaction to *Borat* (*Mail On Sunday*, 11 November 2006).

Can Sacha's treatment of Glod be considered chauvinistic and exploitative? Or did he deliberately overstep the boundary to show that, in this fragmented world and on this cultural minefield, every step is a potentially explosive venture with possible dire consequences? That modernity, with its mass migrations, tragic 'unsettlings' and 'uprootings', made it easier to find a scapegoat for one's cultural shadow? Village of Glod aside, Sacha's targeting of the nation of Kazakhstan is in itself a rather chauvinistic venture. It may not look so to a Western observer who, as an *outsider*, does not mind the taunting of a small ex-Soviet nation as long as the target is not one of the Western cultural minorities. The film was banned in Kazakhstan and was refused a distribution licence in Russia because, to a Russian person, the mockumentary is not a ground-breaking revelation about the fragile state of the postmodern truce between alienated peoples. It is simply an open derision of a central Asian ethnic minority.

In an interview to Arifa Akbar for *The Independent*, Sacha defends himself by saying that the joke is not on Kazakhstan:

> the reason we chose Kazakhstan was because it was a country that no one had heard anything about, so we could essentially play on stereo-types they might have about this ex-Soviet backwater. The joke is not on Kazakhstan. I think the joke is on people who can believe that the Kazakhstan that I describe can exist – who believe that there's a country where homosexuals wear blue hats and the women live in cages and they drink fermented horse urine and the age of consent has been raised to nine years old . . . I've been in a bizarre situation, where a country has declared me as its number one enemy. It's inherently a comic situation.
>
> (*The Independent*, 17 November 2006)

And although the joke 'is not on Kazakhstan', and not even on Glod, fictionalising reality for the purpose of educating people in the devastating effects of narrow-mindedness is always going to offend those whose image has been usurped by the trickster. Meanwhile, the person inside this destructive machine is well protected by the thick, almost indestructible, armour of fake identity fortified by the Fox's legal might.

Gypsies are the main ethnic group in the Dambovita County of Romania. A major minority in the country, gypsies are socially and econ-omically disadvantaged and suffer from racial discrimination. When Petre Buzea, the deputy mayor of a group of villages including Glod, was asked his opinion about the locals' reaction to *Borat*, he replied: 'They got paid so I am sure they are happy. These gipsies will even kill their own father for money' (*Mail On Sunday*, 11 November 2006).

Oh well. You have won, Sacha Baron-Cohen. Clearly, in Mr. Buzea's country there is a problem, and this problem is the Gypsy. Human nature prefers similarity to difference. It is geared up at spotting shadowy scape-goats and throwing them down the well, while the scapegoats themselves (to the best of their 'emetation' abilities) are trying to emulate the majority. Booyakasha and dzienkuje to you, Sacha.

Reality versus Rude Art: Sachsgate

On Saturday 18 October 2008 a serious ethical row erupted at the BBC. An episode of *The Russell Brand Show* was broadcast on BBC Radio 2 featuring two famous entertainers, Russell Brand and Jonathan Ross, leaving a number of offensive voice messages on the answering machine of the British veteran actor Andrew Sachs. The episode was advance-recorded and approved by the BBC controllers. The original idea was to interview Sachs on the show, but he failed to answer the telephone. Suddenly inspired, Brand and Ross began to discuss Sachs' granddaughter, Georgina Baillie, a burlesque dancer with the troupe called 'The Satanic Sluts', with Brand claiming that he had had a sexual relationship with Georgina, and Ross shouting out 'he fucked your granddaughter'. Brand went on to discuss the nature of the sexual relationship and added a number of intimate details. The ill-fated prank initially went almost unnoticed, but eventually snowballed into a monumental media scandal. The aftermath of the scandal was devastating for a number of established careers. Lesley Douglas, controller of Radio 2, resigned; Russell Brand quit his Radio 2 show. Ross was suspended without pay for 12 weeks, and was subsequently asked to accept a 50 per cent pay cut. He eventually made the decision not to pursue the renewal of his contract with the BBC.

Sachsgate was not the only (or even the first) example of 'serious trickster misconduct' in front of a large audience. In February 2002 BBC issued an official apology after Baron-Cohen's first professional alter-ego, the rapper Ali G, used very strong language in a live interview on BBC Radio 1. The shocked DJ Sara Cox twice apologised to listeners – during and after the show. Ali G also announced in the interview that he had smuggled drugs from Jamaica in his body, and 'referred in colloquial terms to having been intimate with singer J-Lo' ('Radio 1 Apologises for Ali G Outburst', *BBC News*, 18 February 2002). As expected, a number of public complaints ensued. Reacting to the event, the spokesman for BBC Radio 1 said: 'We are very sorry for any offence caused to our listeners. It is not something we take lightly. Everybody who come on to our shows is made aware of our content guidelines' ('Radio 1 Apologises for Ali G Outburst', *BBC News*, 18 February 2002).

In the world dominated by political correctness, only a mask as thick as Sacha's can protect you from controversy, lawsuits and awkward apologising. In order to say what you want, you need to have a character (Tony Clifton, Borat) who will take the blows and use the might of Hollywood to protect their inventors. Ross, whose poisonous tricksterism approaches those of Borat or Brüno, has none of these safety nets. His transgressive remarks provoke discourse clashes but, because he pronounces them 'as himself', he is responsible for the consequences. Ross's examples of deliberate political incorrectness include congratulating Madonna on 'her little lovely black baby David' when he hosted the 2006 British Comedy Awards ('Are you stopping there or getting more? When I went to Africa, all I got was a wallet') and wondering whether Heather Mills McCartney actually has two legs at the annual awards ceremony by the music magazine *Q* in London in 2006. His jokes were meant to be ludic, public, ruthless. Ross *meant* to cross the line.

Crossing the line, delivering a roughed-up ludic moment, courting controversy and driving the audience to the edge are all natural behaviours for the entertainer who embodies the eternally rude trickster principle. Making art out of fragments of real human lives is also what tricksters do – especially gonzo tricksters, those postmodern creatures whose task it is to emphasise the transience of reality and the truthfulness of fiction. If the truth is a false idea, then creative defamation is a legitimate craft because everything is the invention of the media – 'the war did not happen', Andy Kaufman did not die, the cat is both dead and alive. Instead of the conclusion that chaos is the father of everything, and the trickster is its bastard son who makes sure that things in this world are eternally moving, transforming, adapting, I will quote Tom Stoppard again:

> *Guildenstern:*
> We only know what we're told, and that's little enough. And for all we know it isn't even true.
>
> *Player:*
> For all anyone knows, nothing is. Everything has to be taken on trust; truth is only that which is taken to be true. It's the currency of living. There may be nothing behind it, but it doesn't make any difference so long as it is honoured.
>
> (Stoppard, 1991: 91)

A given reality exists for a given individual. Gonzo insurrectionists attack personal choice in order to emphasise the postmodern split. However, it is important to remember that each individual truth is fragile and easily broken. Each individual God must be honoured.

Conclusion

'Now, really, Fanny my dear,' said the sister-in-law, altering her position, and speaking less confidently, and more earnestly, in spite of
herself, 'I shall have to be quite cross with you, if you don't rouse
yourself. It's necessary for you to make an effort, and perhaps a very
great and painful effort which you are not disposed to make; but this
is a world of effort you know, Fanny, and we must never yield, when
so much depends upon us. Come! Try! I must really scold you if
you don't!'

(Charles Dickens, *Dombey and Son*)

It is probably cruel of me to use this passage from Dickens's monolithic
assessment of capitalist ethic and the effect of progress on human life in the
book about the anthropology and psychology of failure and success, for
'poor Fanny' is dying of complications shortly after giving birth to a male
baby, who is now the hope and future of his father's successful shipping
business, *Dombey and Son*. The speaker of the epigraph is Mr. Dombey's
sister, Louisa, who, like the cold-blooded and unemotional businessman
himself, believes in the superhuman philosophy of 'never yielding' – because,
in order to achieve anything in this 'world of effort', one must fight.

Much as he admired modernity and its 'efforts', Dickens was nevertheless
keen to show that sometimes human beings, even the most success-driven
and determined, fail. Failure is human – it is about hidden or overt
weakness. Sometimes they fail because, like Mr. Dombey, they neglect the
emotional side of human nature and because they refuse, or cannot,
'connect' (Mr. Dombey is cold towards his daughter Florence as she is no
use for the firm). But sometimes, like the little boy Paul, they are simply
weak human beings. They lose the survival game. The prospective head of
the tough business empire, Paul dies at the age of six because 'the effort' –
the competition, discipline, education – are too much for him. The system
(primarily in the form of his father) is punished for its own inflexibility. The
'other' – Nature, weakness, emotions – the 'uncivilised' binary opposite,
breaks both father and son. Is it bad to be a weak human being? Is one

allowed to fail – or should one fight to the end, in the hope to make one's voice heard, like various reckless rebels have done since the book of Job?

It is, of course, impossible to sum up the trickster principle – but trickster films show it as revolving around the concept of 'effort'. Lloyd Christmas and his dishevelled friend Harry, for once in their miserable lives, make a superhuman feat and travel to Aspen which, for them, is a place where all their dreams are bound to come true. Chronic losers, they cannot see luck even if it hits them in the face – like it did in the final scene of the film, when Harry and Lloyd turn down the chance of becoming 'oil boys' for a busful of bikini models. Looking at the disappearing bus with the naked girls, Lloyd says: 'Someday we'll get our break too, we've just got to keep our eyes open'. But the transformation has occurred: the two fools have moved from the dead point. They have made an effort.

On a more serious note – human representatives of the trickster principle often lose battles against oppressive regimes and seemingly insurmountable barriers to human freedom. The outcome of their rebellion is mixed. The truth-seeking efforts of Inspector Gittes in *Chinatown* lead to the death of the *femme fatale*. Steven Russell of *I Love You Phillip Morris* thinks up creative ways of escaping from jail but is invariably recaptured and returned to his cell. At the end of the film he is even placed into an ultra-secure lock-up from which he would not be able to abscond.

As far as 'effort' is concerned, political rebels in film fare even worse. Charlie Chaplin shows in his tragic-comic masterpieces that a human being fighting against the machine, be it fascist ideology, small-town conservative thinking or law enforcers, is always in a disadvantageous position. The machine is so methodical and well-organised that no insurrection, lest of all personal, can bring it to a halt. The best the carrier of the trickster principle can do, however, is plant the seeds of tricksterism in the mass psyche.

This is exactly what gonzo tricksters do – entertainers like Andy Kaufman and Sacha Baron-Cohen – they use shock tactics to drag people out of ideological or cultural stagnation and to challenge the (always local!) forms of 'normality'. Both have had quite a few human casualties to their name as neither seemed to care whether they hurt the very humans they were trying, so brutally, to force out of their narrow frame of mind. But, again, this is the essence of the trickster principle. Even with the word 'social' attached to it, the concept of the trickster always remains 'beyond good and evil' – and beyond morality. The trickster is pure movement; pure impulse; pure effort.

By contrast, those film protagonists who make 'too much effort' are 'asked' to cut down on it. Sandler's overworked, overtired characters (Dave Buznik in *Anger Management*, Michael Newman in *Click*), Jim Carrey's hyper-ambitious businessmen (Fletcher Reede in *Liar Liar*, Dick Harper in *Fun With Dick and Jane*), Stanley Ipkiss in *The Mask*, Erica Barry in *Something's Gotta Give* are all challenged by a metaphorical spokesperson for some 'universal disorder'. Workaholism at the expense of emotional life is also a form of prison. It suppresses that part of the psyche which is most unpredictable – but also most creative. As Jung writes, 'In the same way that the State has caught the individual, the individual imagines that he has caught the psyche and holds her in the hollow of his hand. [. . .] In reality the psyche is the mother and the maker, the subject and even the possibility of consciousness itself' (CW11: para. 141). In other words, individuals can also develop oppressive systems within themselves. When the system becomes too stagnant, the trickster arrives to shake its walls.

Our Western consciousness is as heroic as it is broken. Occasionally, in Jung's romantic attitude towards the unconscious one can glimpse the warning about the dangers of 'too much effort'. The foolishly Promethean pride of consciousness, which seems to think that nature can be driven away by hard work, technology, science and what not, is sooner or later going to result in a profound sense of guilt and fear of divine retribution for causing 'Ragnarök' – the conflict that dwells at the heart of the capitalist system. But why then, Jung asks, does consciousness exist at all, if its activities result, metaphorically speaking, in stealing fire from the gods? Why give birth to a potentially independent-thinking creature and then keep nagging him, trickster-way, about the dangers of too-much-working, too-much-rationalising, too-much-effort? Is it not foolish of nature to create its own enemy, to work against itself?

One clumsy answer is that, without consciousness, 'things go less well' (CW8: para. 695). Another, less clumsy answer of Jung's is that 'anything psychic is Janus-faced: it looks both backwards and forwards. Because it is evolving, it is also preparing the future. Were this not so, intentions, aims, plans, calculations, predictions, and premonitions would be psychological impossibilities' (CW6: para. 717f). This explains why the mythological trickster is both a backwards, instinctual creature, and the one causing the doom of the gods by his tireless activity. Consciousness lives by this impulse as well as restrained by it. It keeps it in balance. There is a third conclusion as well (both epistemological-idealistic and romantic), to which Jung arrived while he was standing on a hill in the Athi plains of East Africa: 'All Nature seeks this goal [attainment of consciousness] and finds it fulfilled in man' (CW9/I: para. 177).

Well, according to trickster film, nature seeks this goal, finds it in man, and makes man work very hard for it. Even the birth process can be regarded as a trickster event, and certainly a major liminal happening: human beings begin their existence by making an effort, by breaking free. Throughout their lives they keep their consciousness alive by overcoming obstacles, periods of stagnation, by rebelling against mass thinking. An effort does not come cheap and it does not always bring desired results. But, as Randall Patrick McMurphy says after failing to lift the hydro-therapy console: 'But I *tried*, didn't I goddamnit, at least I did that.'

Bibliography

Akbar, Arifa, 'Baron-Cohen Comes out of Character to Defend Borat', *The Independent*, 17 November 2006.

Babcock-Abrahams, B. (1975) 'A Tolerated Margin of the Mess: The Trickster and his Tales Reconsidered', *Journal of the Folklore Institute*, 11, 147–186.

Bakhtin, Mikhail (1984) *Rabelais and His World*, Bloomington, IN: Indiana University Press.

—— (1997) *The Dialogic Imagination: Four Essays*, Austin, TX: University of Texas Press.

Bateson, Gregory (1936) *Naven: A Survey of the Problems Suggested by a Composite Picture of the Culture of a New Guinea Tribe Drawn From Three Points of View*, Chicago, IL: Stanford University Press.

Baudrillard, Jean (2000) *Simulacra and Simulation*, London: Routledge.

Bauman, Zygmunt (1989) *Modernity and the Holocaust*, Oxford: Polity Press.

—— (2000) *Liquid Modernity*, Cambridge: Polity Press.

—— (2001) *Community: Seeking Safety in an Insecure World*, Cambridge: Polity Press.

Beaumarchais, Pierre-Augustin (2008; 1773) *The Figaro Trilogy: The Barber of Seville, The Marriage of Figaro, The Guilty Mother*, Oxford: Oxford University Press.

Benko, Georges and Strohmayer, Ulf (1997) *Space and Social Theory: Interpreting Modernity and Postmodernity*, San Francisco, CA and Indianapolis, IN: Wiley-Blackwell.

Berman, Marshall (1983) *All That Is Solid Melts into Air: The Experience of Modernity*, London: Verso.

Bloom, Harold (ed.) (2008) *Ken Kesey's One Flew Over the Cuckoo's Nest*, New York: Chelsea House Publishers.

Boas, F. (1898) 'Introduction', in J. A. Teit, *Traditions of the Thompson River Indians of British Columbia*, Boston, MA: Houghton Mifflin.

Booth, Robert and Siddique, Haroon (2010) 'How WikiLeaks Altered the Way We See the World in Just a Week', in *The Guardian*, 4 December.

Bourdieu, Pierre (2003; 1992) *The Logic of Practice*, Cambridge: Polity Press.

Brooks, David (2006) 'The Heyday of Snobbery', in *The New York Times*, 16 November.

Buk-Berge, Elisabeth (2007) 'Xenophibia Between Adolescents in Europe', in

Stavros Moutsios (ed.) *Educational Policies in Europe: Economy, Citizenship, Diversity*, Munster: Waxmann Verlag, pp. 181–197.

Campbell, Joseph (1959) *The Masks of Gods: Primitive Mythology*, New York: Viking.

—— (2008; 1968) *The Hero with a Thousand Faces*, Novato, CA: New World Library.

Chaplin, Charles (2003; 1964) *My Autobiography*, London: Penguin.

Coman, Mihai (2008) 'Social Drama in a Mediatized World', in Graham St John (ed.) *Victor Turner and Contemporary Cultural Performance*, New York: Berghahn Books, pp. 109–134.

Defoe, Daniel (1993; 1722) *Moll Flanders*, Ware, Hertfordshire: Wordsworth Editions.

Diamond, Stephen (1991) 'Redeeming our Demons and Devils', in Jeremiah Abrams and Connie Zweig (eds.) (1991) *Meeting the Shadow: The Hidden Power of the Dark Side of Human*, pp. 180–186.

Dickens, Charles (1846–1848; 2006) *Dombey and Son*, London: Penguin.

Doueihi, Anne (1993) 'Inhabiting the Space Between Discourse and Story in Trickster Narratives', in W. J. Hynes and W. Doty (eds.) (1993) *Mythical Trickster Figures: Contours, Contexts*, Tuscaloosa, AL and London: University of Alabama Press, pp. 46–65.

Douglas, Mary (1968; 1996) *Purity and Danger: An Analysis of the Concepts of Pollution and Taboo*, London: Routledge.

Douglas, Mary and Isherwood, Baron C. (1996) *The World of Goods: Towards an Anthropology of Consumption*, London: Routledge.

Durkheim, Emile (1893; 1964) *The Division of Labour in Society*, New York: The Free Press.

Eagleton, Terry (1997; 1996) *The Illusions of Postmodernism*, Oxford: Blackwell.

Easterling, P. E and Hall, Edith (2002) *Greek and Roman Actors: Aspects of the Ancient Profession*, Cambridge: Cambridge University Press.

Eliot, T. S. (2011; 1922) *The Waste Land*, London: Faber and Faber.

Evans-Pritchard, E. E. (1967) *The Zande Trickster*, Oxford: Clarendon.

Evregenis, M. D. (1985) 'Report Drawn up on Behalf of the Committee of Inquiry into the Rise of Facism and Racism in Europe on the Findings of the Committee of Inquiry', PE DOC A 2-160/85. Brussels, 25 November.

Flom, Eric L. (1997) *Chaplin in the Sound Era: An Analysis of Seven Talkies*, Jefferson, NC: McFarland Publishing.

Forster, E. M. (1910; 1969) *Howards End*, London: Edward Arnold.

Fox, Loren (2003) *Enron: The Rise and Fall*, Chichester: John Wiley and Sons.

Fraga, Kristian (ed.) (2005) *Tim Burton Interviews*, Jackson, MI: University Press of Mississippi.

Franklin, Bob (2005) *Key Concepts in Journalism*, Thousand Oaks, CA: Sage Publications.

Freud, Sigmund (1975; 1905) *Jokes and Their Relation to the Unconscious*, London: Hogarth Press.

—— (1928) 'Humor', *International Journal of Psychoanalysis*, 9, 1–60.

Gambrell, Jon (2008) 'Brüno's Prank: Arkansas Cage Fights Turn Gay, Crowd Goes Crazy', in *The Huffington Post*, 8 July.

Geertz, Clifford (1975) *The Interpretation of Cultures*, London: Hutchinson.

Goethals, Gregor T. (1981) *The TV Ritual: Worship at the Video Altar*, Boston, MA: Beacon Press.

Goldman, Lawrence R. (1998) 'A Trickster For All Seasons: The Huli Iba Tiri', in L. R. Goldman and C. Ballard (eds.) *Fluid Ontologies: Myth, Ritual and Philosophy in the Highlands of Papua New Guinea*, Westport, CT: Bergin and Carvey, pp. 87–124.

Goldstein, Patrick (2007) 'Police, Camera, Action', in *The Guardian*, 19 January.

Harris, Mark (2010) 'Inventing Facebook', in *The New York Magazine*, 17 September.

Hauke, Christopher (2000) *Jung and the Postmodern: The Interpretation of Realities*, London and Philadelphia, PA: Routledge.

—— (2005) *Human Being Human: Culture and the Soul*, London: Routledge.

Headrick, Daniel R. (1988) *The Tentacles of Progress: Technology Transfer in the Age of Imperialism, 1840–1950*. New York: OUP.

Heller, Nathan (2010) 'You Can't Handle the Veritas: What Aaron Sorkin and David Fincher Get Wrong About Harvard – and Facebook', in *Slate*, 30 September.

Hesiod (2004), translated by Apostolos N. Athanassakis, *Theogony; Works and Days; Shield*, Baltimore, MD: JHU Press.

Hockley, Luke (2007) *Frames of Mind: A Post-Jungian Look at Cinema, Television and Technology*, Bristol and Chicago, IL: Intellect.

Hoffman, E. T. A. (2006; 1819–1921) *The Life and Opinions of the Tomcat Murr*, London: Penguin.

Hyers, Conrad (1996) *The Spirituality of Comedy: Comic Heroism in a Tragic World*, New Brunswick, NJ and London: Transaction Publishers.

Hynes, William (1993a) 'Mapping the Characteristics of Mythic Tricksters: A Heuristic Guide', in W. J. Hynes and W. Doty (eds.) *Mythical Trickster Figures: Contours, Contexts*, Tuscaloosa, AL and London: University of Alabama Press, pp. 33–45.

—— (1993b) 'Inconclusive Conclusions: Tricksters – Metaplayers and Revealers', in W. J. Hynes and W. Doty (eds.) (1993) *Mythical Trickster Figures: Contours, Contexts*, Tuscaloosa and London: University of Alabama Press, pp. 202–218.

Hynes, W. J and Doty, W. (eds.) (1993) *Mythical Trickster Figures: Contours, Contexts*, Tuscaloosa, AL and London: University of Alabama Press.

Jacobi, Jolande (1973; 1942) *The Psychology of C. G. Jung* (eighth edition), trans. Ralph Manheim, New Haven, CT and London: Yale University Press.

Jameson, Fredric (1991) *Postmodernism, or The Cultural Logic of Late Capitalism*, London: Verso.

Joyce, James (2000; 1922) *Ulysses*, London: Penguin Classics.

Jung C. G. Except where a different publication was used, all references are to the hardback edition of C. G. Jung, *The Collected Works* (CW), edited by Sir Herbert Read, Dr. Michael Fordham and Dr. Gerhardt Adler, and translated by R. F. C. Hull, London: Routledge.

Jung, Carl Gustav and Kerényi, Karl (2002) *Science of Mythology: Essays on the Mythology of the Child and the Mysteries of Eleusis*, London: Routledge.

Jung, Carl Gustav and von Franz, M.-L. (eds.) (1978; 1964) *Man and His Symbols*, London: Picador.

Kaylan, Melik (2009) 'Brüno Examines the Ugly Truth', in *Forbes*, 14 July.

Kerényi, Karl (1956) 'The Trickster in Relation to Greek Mythology', in Paul

Radin, *The Trickster: A Study in American Indian Mythology*, New York: Schocken Books.

Kesey, Ken (1962) *One Flew Over the Cuckoo's Nest*, New York: Viking Press.

Klinger, Scott and Sklar, Holly (2002) 'Titans of the Enron Economy', in *The Nation*, 18 July.

Knight, J. and Lacey, H. (1825) *Lambeth and the Vatican: Or, Anecdotes of the Church of Rome, of the Reformed Churches, and of Sects and Sectaries, Volume 2*, London.

Koegel, John (2009) *Music in German Immigrant Theater: New York City, 1840–1940*, London: University of Rochester Press.

Kohn, Ingeborg (2005) *Charlie Chaplin, Brightest Star of Silent Films*, Rome: Portaparole.

Kopp, Sheldon (1974) *The Hanged Man: Psychotherapy and the Forces of Darkness*, Palo Alto, CA: Science and Behavior Books.

Maier, Sonja (2010) *The Death of A Dream – Hunter S. Thompson and the American Dream*, München: GRIN Verlag.

Makarius, Laura (1993) 'The Myth of the Trickster: The Necessary Breaker of Taboos', in W. J. Hynes and W. Doty (eds.) (1993) *Mythical Trickster Figures: Contours, Contexts*, Tuscaloosa, AL and London: University of Alabama Press, pp. 46–65.

Malpas, Simon (ed.) (2001) *Postmodern Debates*, London: Palgrave.

Mann, Thomas (1992; 1936) *Confessions of Felix Krull, Confidence Man*, London: Vintage Books.

Martin, Rod A. (2007) *The Psychology of Humour: An Integrative Approach*, Burlington, MA and London: Elsevier.

McCaughrean, Geraldine (1999) *One Thousand and One Arabian Nights*, Oxford: Oxford University Press.

McCreadie, Marsha (2008) *Documentary Superstars: How Today's Filmmakers Are Reinventing the Form*, New York: Allworth Communications, Inc.

Mezrich, Ben (2009) *The Accidental Billionaires: The Founding of Facebook: A Tale of Sex, Money, Genius and Betrayal*, New York: Doubleday.

Miller, J. C. (2004) *The Transcendent Function: Jung's Model of Psychological Growth Through Dialogue With the Unconscious*, New York: State University of New York Press.

Moutsios, Stavros (ed.) (2007) *Educational Policies in Europe: Economy, Citizenship, Diversity*, Munster: Waxmann Verlag.

Neumann, Erich (1974; 1959) *Art and the Creative Unconscious: Four Essays*, Princeton, NJ: Princeton University Press.

Nichols, John (2002) 'Enron's Global Crusade', in *The Nation*, 14 February.

Null, Christopher (1999) 'Ground Control to Major Bob: The Bob Zmuda Interview', in http://www.filmcritic.com, 9 November.

Pancevski, Bojan and Ionescu, Carmiola (2006) 'Borat Film "Tricked" Poor Village Actors', in *Mail on Sunday*, 11 November.

Pelton, Robert D. (1980) *The Trickster in West Africa: A Study of Mythic Irony and Sacred Delight*, Berkeley, CA: University of California Press.

Perry, Marvin, Chase, Myrna, Jacob, Margaret C. and Jacob, James, R. (2008) *Western Civilization: Ideas, Politics, and Society*, Florence, KY: Cengage Learning.

Poussaint, Alvin F. (1974) 'Blacks and Jews: An Appeal for Unity', in *Ebony*, 29(9), 120–124.

Rabelais, François (2006) *Gargantua and Pantagruel*, London: Penguin.

Radin, Paul (1972; 1956) *The Trickster: A Study in American Indian Mythology*, New York: Schocken Books.

Ricketts, Mac Linscott (1966) 'The North American Trickster', *History of Religion* 5(2), 327–350.

—— (1993) 'The Shaman and the Trickster', in W. J. Hynes and W. Doty (eds.) (1993) *Mythical Trickster Figures: Contours, Contexts*, Tuscaloosa, AL and London: University of Alabama Press, pp. 90–106.

Roberts, Timmons J. and Hite, Amy (2000) *From Modernization to Globalization: Perspectives on Development and Social Change*, Boston, MA: Wiley-Blackwell.

Rosen, Jody (2006) 'How Borat is Jewish Vaudeville', in *Slate*, 3 November.

Rosenberg, Donna (2001; 1994) *World Mythology: An Anthology of the Great Myths and Epics*, New York: McGraw-Hill.

Rowe, Sharon (2008) 'Modern Sports: Liminal Ritual or Liminoid Leisure?', in Graham St. John (ed.) *Victor Turner and Contemporary Cultural Performances*, New York: Berghahn Books, pp. 127–149

Samuels, Andrew (1993) *The Political Psyche*, London: Routledge.

—— (2001) *Politics on the Couch: Citizenship and the Internal Life*, London: Other Press.

Schickel, Richard (1996) 'Twisted Wire: Cable Guy is as Contorted as a Jim Carrey Face', *Time*, 17 June.

Schwartz, Vanessa and Przyblyski, Jeanne M. (eds.) (2004) *The Nineteenth-Century Visual Culture Reader*, London: Routledge.

Shabi, Rachel (2009) 'The Non-Profit Worker from Bethlehem Who Was Branded a Terrorist by Brüno', in *The Guardian*, 31 July.

Shakespeare, William (2007) *The Complete Works of William Shakespeare*, London: HarperCollins.

Silberman, Steve (2001) 'The Geek Syndrome', in *Wired*, 9 December.

Simmel, George (2004; 1903) 'The Metropolis and Mental Life', in Vanessa Schwartz and Jeannene M. Przyblyski (eds.) *The Nineteenth-Century Visual Culture Reader*, London: Routledge, pp. 51–55.

Skousen, Mark (2008) *The Making of Modern Economics: The Lives and Ideas of the Great Thinkers*, Armonk, NY: M. E. Sharpe Ltd.

Stein, Murray (1993) *In MidLife: A Jungian Perspective*, Dallas, TX: Spring Publications.

Stewart, Susan (1978) *Nonsense: Aspects of Intertextuality in Folklore and Literature*, Baltimore, MD and London: The Johns Hopkins University Press.

St. John, Graham (ed.) (2008) *Victor Turner and Contemporary Cultural Performance*, New York: Berghahn Books.

Stoppard, Tom (1991) *Rosencrantz and Guildenstern Are Dead*, New York: Grove Press.

Strauss, Neil (2006) 'The Real Borat Finally Speaks', in *The Rolling Stone Magazine*, 15 November.

Street, Brian (1972) 'The Trickster Theme: Winnebago and Azande', in Andre Singer and Brian Street (eds.) *Zande Themes: Essays Presented to Sir Edward Evans Pritchard*, Totowa, NJ: Rowman & Littlefield, pp. 82–104.

Tannen, Ricki Stefanie (2007) *The Female Trickster: The Mask that Reveals*, London: Routledge.

Thomas, Michael (1999) *Script Analysis for Writers, Directors and Designers*, Boston, MA: Focal Press.

Turner, Victor (1967) *The Forest of Symbols: Aspects of Ndembu Ritual*, Ithaca, NY: Cornell University Press.

—— (1975) *Revelation and Divination in Ndemby Ritual*, Ithaca, NY: Cornell University Press.

—— (1979) *Process, Performance and Pilgrimage*, New Delhi: Naurang Rai.

—— (1992) *Blazing the Trail: Way Marks in the Exploration of Symbols*, Tucson, AZ and London: The University of Arizona Press.

Van Gennep, Arnold (1909; 2004) *The Rites of Passage*, London: Routledge.

Varadarajan, Tunku (2010) 'What Does Julian Assange Want?', in *The Daily Beast*, 28 July.

Waddell, Terrie (2009) *Wild/Lives: Trickster, Place and Liminality on Screen*, London: Routledge.

Weber, Max (1930; 2005) *The Protestant Ethic and the Spirit of Capitalism*, London: Routledge.

Welsford, Enid (1936) *The Fool: His Social and Literary History*, London: Faber and Faber.

Willeford, William (1969) *The Fool and His Sceptre: A Study in Clowns and Jesters and Their Audience*, Evanston, IL: Northwestern University Press.

White, Roland (2007) 'Borat's Easy . . . Being Me is Odd', in *The Sunday Times*, 21 January.

Zehme, Bill (2001) *Lost in the Funhouse: The Life and Mind of Andy Kaufman*, New York: Random House Publishing.

Zmuda, Bob (1999) *Andy Kaufman Revealed! Best Friend Tells All*, New York and London: Little Brown Company.

Unauthored Articles

'Borat Victims Upset at Being Duped', in *USA Today*, 2 November 2006, http://www.usatoday.com/life/movies/news/2006-11-13-borat-fallout_x.htm

'How Real Is *Brüno*?, in *Newsweek*, 9 July, 2009, http://www.newsweek.com/2009/07/09/how-real-is-br-no.html

'Humiliated Frat Boys Sue Borat', in *USA Today*, 15 November 2006, http://www.usatoday.com/life/movies/news/2006-11-10-borat-lawsuit_x.htm

'Radio 1 Apologises for Ali G Outburst', in *BBC News*, 18 February 2002, http://news.bbc.co.uk/1/hi/entertainment/1827576.stm

'Sacha Baron Cohen: It's So Sad, But I Have to Kill Off Brüno', in *Mail Online*, 19 July 2009.

'Village "Humiliated" by Borat Satire', in *BBC News*, 26 October 2008, http://news.bbc.co.uk/1/hi/world/europe/7686885.stm

Dictionaries and Encyclopaedias

The Concise Oxford English Dictionary (1995) 9th Edition, Oxford: Oxford University Press.

The Oxford Companion to the United States History: http://www.oxfordreference.com

Film references

A Dog's Life (1918) Charlie Chaplin (director), First National Pictures, USA.

About Schmidt (2002) Alexander Payne (director), New Line Cinema and Avery Pix, USA.

Ace Ventura: Pet Detective (1994) Tom Shadyac (director), Morgan Creek Productions, USA.

Ace Ventura: When Nature Calls (1995) Steve Oedekerk (director), Morgan Creek Productions, USA.

Adam (2009) Max Mayer (director), Olympus Pictures, Deer Path Productions, Northwood Productions, Serenade Films, and Vox3 Films, USA.

Ali G Indahouse (2002) Mark Mylod (director),FilmFour, Kalima Productions GmbH, StudioCanal, TalkBack Productions, WT2 Productions, and Working Title Films, UK/Germany/France.

Anger Management (2003) Peter Segal (director), Revolution Studios, Happy Madison Productions, Anger Management LLC and Jack Giarraputo Productions, USA.

Batman (1989) Tim Burton (director), Warner Bros., Guber-Peters Company, and PolyGram Pictures, USA/UK.

Batman Forever (1995) Joel Schumacher (director), Warner Bros. and PolyGram Pictures, USA/UK.

Batman Returns (1992) Tim Burton (director), Warner Bros. and PolyGram Pictures, USA/UK.

Beetlejuice (1988) Tim Burton (director), The Geffen Company, USA.

Borat (2006) Larry Charles (director), Four by Two, Everyman Pictures, Dune Entertainment, Major Studio Partners, and One America, USA.

Bruce Almighty (2003) Tom Shadyac (director), Universal Pictures, Spyglass Entertainment, Shady Acres Entertainment, and Pit Bull Productions, USA.

Brüno (2009) Larry Charles (director), Universal Pictures, Media Rights Capital, Four by Two, and Everyman Pictures, USA.

Cabinet of Dr Caligari, The (1920) Robert Wiene (director), Decla-Bioscop AG, Germany.

Cable Guy, The (1996) Ben Stiller (director), Columbia Pictures and Licht/Mueller Film, USA.

Charlie and the Chocolate Factory (2005) Tim Burton (director), Warner Bros.,

Village Roadshow Pictures, The Zanuck Company, Plan B Entertainment, Theobald Film Productions, and Tim Burton Productions, USA/UK.

Chinatown (1974) Roman Polanski (director), Paramount Pictures, Penthouse, and Long Road Productions, USA.

City Lights (1931) Charles Chaplin (director), Charles Chaplin Productions, USA.

Click (2006) Frank Coraci (director), Columbia Pictures, Revolution Studios, Happy Madison Productions, and Original Film, USA.

Drop Dead Fred (1991) Ate de Jong (director), Polygram Filmed Entertainment and Working Title Films, UK.

Dumb and Dumber (1994) Peter Farrelly, Bobby Farrelly (directors), New Line Cinema and Motion Picture Corporation of America, USA.

Easy Rider (1969) Dennis Hopper (director), Columbia Pictures Corporation, Pando Company Inc. and Raybert Productions, USA.

Ed Wood (1994) Tim Burton (director), Touchstone Pictures, USA.

Edward Scissorhands (1990) Tim Burton (director), Twentieth Century Fox, USA.

Eternal Sunshine of the Spotless Mind (2004) Michael Gondry (director), Focus Features, Anonymous Content Productions, and This is That Productions, USA.

Exorcist, The (1973) William Friedkin (director), Warner Bros. and Hoya Productions, USA.

Fun With Dick and Jane (2005) Dean Parisot (director), Columbia Pictures Corporation, Imagine Entertainment, and JC 23 Entertainment, USA.

Gold Rush, The (1925) Charles Chaplin (director), Charles Chaplin Productions, USA.

Great Dictator, The (1940) Charles Chaplin (director), Charles Chaplin Productions, USA.

Hangover, The (2009) Todd Phillips (director), Warner Bros., Legendary Pictures, Green Hat Films, and IFP WestcoastErste, USA/Germany.

Heartbreak Kid, The (2007) Bobby Farrelly, Peter Farrelly (directors), DreamWorks Pictures, Radar Pictures, Davis Entertainment and Conundrum Entertainment, USA.

I Love You Phillip Morris (2009), Glenn Ficarra, John Requa (directors), EuropaCorp and Mad Chance, France/USA.

Immigrant, The (1917) Charles Chaplin, Edward Brewer (directors), edited by Charles Chaplin, distributed by Mutual Film, USA.

Liar Liar (1997) Tom Shadyac (director), Universal Pictures and Imagine Entertainment, USA.

Majestic, The (2001) Frank Darabont (director), Castle Rock Entertainment, Village Roadshow Pictures, NPV Entertainment, and Darkwoods Productions, USA.

Man on the Moon (1999) Milos Forman (director), Universal Pictures, Mutual Film Company, Jersey Films, Cinehaus, Shapiro/West Productions, Tele München-FernshProduktionsgesellschaft, BBC, Marubeni, and Toho-Towa, USA/Germany/UK/Japan.

Mask, The (1994) Chuck Russell (director), Dark Horse Entertainment and New Line Cinema, USA.

Me, Myself and Irene (2000) Bobby Farrelly, Peter Farrelly (directors), Twentieth Century Fox and Conundrum Entertainment, USA.

Metropolis (1927) Fritz Lang (director), Universum Film, Germany.

Modern Times (1936) Charles Chaplin (director), Charles Chaplin Productions, USA.

Nightmare Before Christmas, The (2003) Henry Selick (director), Touchstone Pictures, Skellington Productions, Inc., Tim Burton Productions, and Walt Disney Pictures [3D], USA.

Nosferatu (1922) F. W. Murnau (director), Jofa-Atelier Berlin-Johannisthal, and Prana-Film, Germany.

One Flew Over the Cuckoo's Nest (1975) Milos Forman (director), Fantasy Films, USA.

Pilgrim, The (1923) Charles Chaplin (writer), Charles Chaplin Productions, USA.

Psycho (1960) Alfred Hitchcock (director), Shamley Productions, USA.

Saturday Night Fever (1977) John Badham (director), Robert Stigwood Organization, USA.

Serpico (1973) Sidney Lumet (director), Artists Entertainment Complex and Produzioni De Laurentiis International Manufacturing Company, USA/Italy.

Shining, The (1980) Stanley Kubrick (director), Warner Bros., Hawk Films, Peregrine, and The Producers Circle Company, USA/UK.

Social Network, The (2010) David Fincher (director), Columbia Pictures, Relativity Media, Scott Rudin Productions, Michael De Luca Productions, and Trigger Street Productions, USA.

Something's Gotta Give (2003) Nancy Meyers (director), Columbia Pictures, Warner Bros., and Waverly Films, USA.

Vincent (1982) Tim Burton (director), Walt Disney Productions, USA.

Witches of Eastwick, The (1987) George Miller (director), Warner Bros., The Guber-Peters Company, and Kennedy Miller Productions, USA/Australia.

Yes Man (2003) Peyton Reed (director), Warner Bros., Village Roadshow Pictures, Heyday Films, The Zanuck Company, and Relativity Media, USA/UK.

Index

About Schmidt (Alexander Payne) 45, 56, 109, 136–38
Ace Ventura: Pet Detective (Tom Shadyak) 31, 139
AceVentura: When Nature Calls (Steve Oedekerk) 31, 46, 139
Ali G In Da House (Mark Mylod) 164
Alpha male 41, 87, 107–8, 117
Analytical psychology *see* Jungian psychology
Anger 4, 18, 21, 41, 45, 56, 57, 68, 76, 109, 112–17
Anger Management (Peter Segal) x, 4, 20, 37, 41, 48, 56, 63, 68, 109, 112–16, 132–33, 180
Anti-Semitism 165, 169, 172
Archetypes *see* Jungian Psychology
Aristophanes 6, 40
Aristotle 41
Asperger's Syndrome 79
Assange, Julian ix, 80–1

Babcock-Abrahams, Barbara 5, 7
Bakhtin, Mikhail x, 21–2, 43, 54, 68–9, 71–2, 88–90, 92–3, 98, 149
Balder (mythology) 25
The Barber of Seville (Rossini) 90
Bateson, Gregory 8
Baudrillard, Jean 65, 145, 167
Baron-Cohen, Sacha ix, 4, 55, 79, 143, 145–50, 163–77, 180
  Borat x, 4, 146, 148, 166–78
  Brüno 4, 79, 146, 148, 150, 164, 169, 171, 172–4
  Batman (Tim Burton) 4, 19, 31, 33, 36, 55, 74–6, 87, 99–102
  Batman Returns (Tim Burton) 4, 74–77, 93, 99–101

Bauman, Zygmunt x, 3, 48–9, 51, 55, 66, 73, 76, 87, 113, 116, 122–3
Beaumarchais, Pierre-Augustin 26, 90
Berman, Marshall x, 3, 49–50, 121
Bernstein, Leonard 114
Blade Runner (Ridley Scott) 100
Boas, Frantz 5
Borat (Baron-Cohen) x, 4, 146, 148, 166–78
Bourdieu, Pierre: the habitus ix, 3, 9–11
Bourgeois individual subject 52
Brand, Russell 143, 177–8
Bruce Almighty ()
Bruno (Baron-Cohen) 4, 79, 146, 148, 150, 164, 169, 171, 172–4
Burton, Tim 4, 27, 31–2, 36, 44, 55, 74–7, 99–102
  Batman 4, 19, 31, 33, 36, 55, 74–6, 87, 99–102
  Batman Returns 4, 74–77, 93, 99–101
  Beetlejuice 27–33, 36, 120
  Edward Scissorhands 36
  Ed Wood 36
  Vincent 36

The Cabinet of Dr. Caligari (Wiene) 99
The Cable Guy (Stiller) x, 4, 26, 31, 37, 57, 62–71, 79, 102, 116–19
Campbell, Joseph 6, 12, 20
Capitalism ix, 3, 49, 53, 75, 80, 87, 90–1, 94, 97, 101, 103, 113, 145
The Carnivalesque (Bakhtin) 21–2, 24, 41, 44, 54, 68, 88, 98, 108, 149, 171
Carrey, Jim viii, x, 1–2, 4, 19–20, 27, 29, 31, 37, 41, 43, 46, 57, 62–69, 67, 74, 80, 87, 94, 96, 102–9, 116–19, 138–41, 151–2, 160, 180
  Ace Ventura: Pet Detective 31, 139

Ace Ventura: When Nature Calls 31, 46, 139
Bruce Almighty 102, 138, 140
Cable Guy, the x, 4, 26, 31, 37, 57, 62–9, 71, 79, 102, 116–19, 139
Dumb and Dumber viii, 1–2, 67, 102, 107, 121, 139
Fun With Dick and Jane 4, 87, 94, 102–5, 139, 180
The Majestic 139
The Mask viii, 4, 20, 31–33, 44, 47–8, 96, 107–9, 136–140, 180
Yes Man 29, 37, 56, 96, 106, 140
Castaneda, Carlos 6
Cates, Phoebe 27, 135–6
Celebrity 87, 152, 158–9, 161, 163
Chaplin, Charles viii, 2, 4, 29, 38, 87, 92–3, 96–9, 123–9, 180
Charlot *see* the Tramp
  City Lights 123
  A Dog's Life 5, 29, 38, 123–4
  The Immigrant 38
  The Gold Rush 123
  Modern Times viii, 93, 97–9, 123–4
  The Great Dictator 4, 98, 123, 125–9
  The Pilgrim 4, 29, 123–5
  The Tramp (character) 29, 38, 96–9, 123–9
Chinatown (Roman Polanski) 4, 43, 133–5, 180
City Lights (Charlie Chaplin) 123
The Civil Rights Movement 163, 165–6, 173
Click (Frank Coraci) x, 4, 37, 41, 46, 69–72, 109, 180
Clifton, Tony (character) 147, 155, 158–9, 163, 177
Collective shadow 15–16, 52, 66, 74–5, 100–1, 123, 128, 146–7, 160
Collective unconscious *see* Jungian Psychology
Commedia dell'arte 90
Communitas 17–18, 68
Complex *see* Jungian Psychology
Consumerism 50, 75, 118, 120
Coraci, Frank 4, 41
  Click x, 4, 37, 41, 46, 69–72, 109, 180
Creativity 8, 18, 28, 34–6, 44–6, 53, 58–61, 103, 146, 153–4, 162

Da Ali G Show 149, 164, 171
Daniels, Jeff 1

Defoe, Daniel 89
Determinable function 94–6
Dickens, Charles 69, 92, 179–80
Division of labour 94–6, 111
A Dog's Life (Charlie Chaplin) 5, 29, 38, 123–4
Dombey and Son (Dickens) 179–80
Doppelganger, *see* also *the double* and *the shadow* 15, 18–19, 64, 77, 93, 99, 102, 139
Doty, William 5–6, 8, 44, 53
The Double, *see* also *doppelganger* 15
Doueihi, Anne 6
Douglas, Mary 6, 70
Drop Dead Fred (Ate de Jong) x, 27–8, 32–3, 37, 41, 46, 109, 120, 135–6
Dumb and Dumber (Farrelly brothers) viii, 1–2, 67, 102, 107, 121, 139
Durkheim, Emile 94–6, 121–3

Eagleton, Terry 53, 120–1, 145
Easy Rider (Dennis Hopper) 38
Edward Scissorhands (Tim Burton) 36
Ed Wood (Tim Burton) 36
Eisenberg, Jesse 83
Eliot, Thomas Sterns 93
The Enlightenment 49, 77
Enron 102–5
Eshu (mythology) 6–7
Eternal Sunshine of the Spotless Mind (Michel Gondry) 120, 139
Evans-Pritchard, Edward 6

Facebook x, 82–5
Farrelly brothers 1–2, 42
Fascism 14, 125–9, 167
Faun 42
The Feast of the Ass 43
Felix Krull (Mann) 92
The Figaro trilogy 26, 90
The First Gulf War 145
The First World War 14, 48, 126
Forman, Milos 34, 129–33, 151
Fragmentation 51–6, 58, 78, 101, 145, 152, 159
Freud, Sigmund 10, 15, 54
Freytag, Gustav 20
Funt, Allen: Candid Camera 143, 149
Fun With Dick and Jane (Dean Parisot) 4, 87, 94, 102–5, 139, 180

Geek 77–85
Geertz, Clifford ix, 3, 11, 14, 51
German Expressionism 99
Globalisation 54
Goddard, Paulette 126
Goldman, Lawrence 6
Goldoni, Carlo 26
The Gold Rush (Charlie Chaplin) 123
Gonzo journalism 143–4, 146
The Great Dictator (Charlie Chaplin) 4,
    98, 123, 125–9
Greek Comedy 40

The Habitus ix, 9–11, 48, 51–2, 80, 85,
    121, 131–2, 141, 168
Hacktivism 80
Hamlet (Shakespeare) 28, 88, 106, 140
The Hangover (Todd Philipps) 26
Hanuman (mythology) 42
Harvard 83–5
Hauke, Christopher 3, 54–5, 79–80,
    122, 147, 158–9
The Heartbreak Kid (Farrelly brothers)
    42
Henderson, Joseph 5, 12–13, 32, 43, 139
Hermes (mythology) ix, 3, 6–7, 30, 91
Hesiod 25
Hitchcock, Alfred 63
Hockley, Luke 60
Hoffman, E.T.A 92
Holocaust, the 14, 48, 127, 143, 167
Homosexuality 150
Hyers, Conrad 98–9
Hynes, William 5–6, 8, 39, 44, 48

Identity 11–12, 15, 24, 31, 52–3, 64, 72,
    75–6, 78, 85, 107, 113, 121, 127, 157,
    164–9
I Feel Pretty (Leonard Bernstein) 114
I Love You Philip Morris (Glenn
    Ficarra, John Requa) 87, 94–5, 102,
    139–40, 180
The Immigrant (Charlie Chaplin) 38
Individualism 50, 58, 66, 75, 78, 88, 102,
    121
Individuation *see* Jungian Psychology
Information society 61

Jacobi, Jolande 13, 15, 41, 111
Jameson, Fredric 51–3, 78, 145, 150,
    154
Jinni (mythology) 25–7, 78

Joyce, James 59, 93
Jung, Carl Gustav viii, ix, x, xi, 3–5,
    7–8, 11–16, 24, 32, 34–6, 38–9,
    53–5, 58, 60, 66, 79, 93, 111, 121–2,
    132, 139–40, 160, 171, 181
Jungian psychology
    Archetypes 3, 18, 24
    Collective Shadow 15–16, 52, 66,
        74–5, 100–1, 123, 128, 146–7, 160
    Collective unconscious ix, 54, 60, 93,
        154
    Complex 34–5
    Individuation x, 11, 13–15, 23, 39,
        47–55, 66, 88, 120
    Participation mystique 15, 24, 52, 60,
        160, 171
    Persona 57, 66, 75, 111
    Post-Jungians ix, 3, 47–55
    Shadow x, 3, 14–15, 18–19, 33, 36–8,
        56, 64, 67, 69, 74, 78, 80, 91–3,
        99–101, 108, 115–6, 119, 127,
        172
    Trickster *see* Trickster
    The Unconscious viii, ix, 3, 10–11, 13,
        16, 19, 27, 29–30, 34, 38, 54–5,
        59, 131, 181

Kaufman, Andy ix, x, 4, 14, 86, 139,
    146–63, 166–70, 178, 180
Keaton, Buster 92
Keaton, Michael 31, 76
Kerényi, Karl 8
Kesey, Ken 129–30
Kopp, Sheldon 6, 56, 111
Kwaku Anansi (mythology) 6, 42

Lacan, Jacques 14
Lang, Fritz 98–9
Liar Liar (Tom Shadyac) 106, 180
The Life and Opinions of Tomcat Murr
    (Hoffman) 92
Liminality 3, 17–18, 58–61, 94
Liminoid 58–61, 117–18, 146, 148
Loki (mythology) 6–7, 25, 28, 38, 93,
    108

The Majestic (Frank Darabont) 139
Makarius, Laura 6
Mann, Thomas 92
Man on the Moon (Milos Forman) 139,
    151, 155
The Mask (Chuck Russell)

Mass media 14–15, 60–1, 100, 122
Marx, Carl 10, 120–1
Mayall, Rik x, 27, 135
Medieval jesters 42
Mezrich, Ben 82
Mercurius (mythology) 30
Metropolis (Lang) 98–100
Metropolis (city) 3, 37, 61–2, 110, 121
Middle class x, 4, 64, 90–3, 101–2, 109–19, 173
Modernism 59
Modernity ix, x, 2–3, 14, 21–2, 48–58, 61, 69, 73, 75–9, 88, 90, 92–3, 96, 98–100, 113–14, 117, 121, 123–4, 128, 130, 144–5, 147, 149, 175, 179
    And individualism 47–51
    And fragmentation 51–6
    And postmodernity 49, 58
Modern Times (Charlie Chaplin) viii, 93, 97–9, 123–4
Moll Flanders (Defoe) 89
Mr. X (Norman Wexler) 86
Murnau, Friedrich 99
Myth 4, 12, 43
    Hero myth 13, 140

Narrative
    Gustav Freytag 20
    Structure 3, 20, 25
    The role of the trickster 20, 25
Natural Community 14, 73, 85, 121
Neumann, Erich 58, 59
New Economy 102–6
Nicholson, Jack viii, 2, 4, 19–20, 33–4, 38, 41, 45, 56, 74, 100, 108, 112, 114, 129–34, 137
    About Schmidt 45, 56, 109, 136–38
    Batman 4, 19, 31, 33, 36, 55, 74–6, 87, 99–102
    Chinatown 4, 43, 133–5, 180
    One Flew Over the Cuckoo's Nest 34, 56, 129–33
    The Shining 19, 38
    Witches of Eastwick 19
Nietzsche, Friedrich 7
Non-places 113–14
Nosferatu (Murnau) 99

Odin (mythology) 25, 123
Odysseus (mythology) 24, 29, 138

One Flew Over the Cuckoo's Nest 34, 56, 129–33
One Flew Over the Cuckoo's Nest (Kesey) 130

Participation mystique *see* Jungian Psychology
Pastiche 52, 53, 154
Pelton, Robert 5, 7, 9
Personal space 2
Pfeiffer, Michelle 75
Phallus 40
Philipps, Todd 26
The Picaresque tradition 89–90
Picaro x, 88–90, 92
The Pilgrim (Charlie Chaplin) 4, 29, 123–5
Plautus, Titus Maccius 6, 26
Polanski, Roman 34, 133–34
Postmodernism/postmodernity
    And capitalism 3, 86–105, 109–12, 117, 179–80
    And communication breakdown 47–62
    And death of the subject 54
    And the Enlightenment project 49
    And identity 47–62, 76, 78, 85, 158–98
    And morality 172–78
    And pastiche 52, 53, 154
    And the problem of God 50–4, 65, 72, 77, 80, 154–9
    And relationships 47–62
    And the trickster 47–62
Pre-industrial society 94
Presley, Elvis 151, 154–5, 169
Projection viii, 18, 37, 57, 60, 99, 116, 127, 158–160, 171
Prometheus (mythology) 8, 25
Psychotherapy 6, 56–8, 70, 132
Psychopomp 30

Radin, Paul ix, 5–6, 8, 12–13, 31–2, 36, 39–40, 43, 45, 91
Ragnarök (mythology) 7, 85, 93, 181
Ramayana (mythology) 42
Rationality 3, 10, 15–16, 20, 74–5, 77, 93, 98–9, 113, 117, 121, 128, 130
Reductio ad absurdum 93–4, 97–9, 131
Ricketts, Mac Linscott 2, 5, 6, 8
Rites of passage 17
Romanticism 93

Rosencrantz and Guildenstern are Dead
    (Stoppard) 88, 140, 146, 163
Ross, Jonathan 177–8

Sachs, Andrew 177–8
Sachsgate 177–8
Samuels, Andrew ix, 3, 6, 9, 90–1, 142,
    157, 168, 186
Sandler, Adam x, 2, 20, 38, 41, 46, 48,
    69, 71, 87, 112, 180
    Anger Management 112–16
    Click 69–72
Saturday Night Fever (John Badham)
    86
Satyr 42
Schumacher, Joel 4, 77
Segal, Peter 4, 41
Serpico (Sidney Lumet) 86
Servus Callidus 26
The Shadow *see* Jungian Psychology;
    see also *The Double* and
    Doppelganger
Shakespeare, William 21, 88, 98, 106
The Shining (Stanley Kubrick) 19, 38
Simmel, Georg 61–2, 110–11
The Social Network (David Fincher) x,
    4, 79, 82–5
Something's Gotta Give (Nancy Meyers)
    34, 38, 41, 180
Sorkin, Aaron 82–5
The State 14–16, 120, 122, 128, 132,
    142
Stein, Murray 6
Stewart, Susan 6
St. John, Graham 58–60, 116
Sports 58–9, 61, 116–17, 132, 149
Stiller, Ben 4, 42, 48, 62, 116
The Cable Guy 116–19
Stoppard, Tom 140, 146–7, 163, 172,
    178

Tannen, Ricki Stephanie 6
The Tramp (character) 2, 29, 38, 87,
    96–9, 123–5, 127
Technology 2, 3, 15, 32, 36–7, 50, 60–1,
    65, 72–4, 78–80, 101, 122, 128, 149,
    154, 181
Television 14, 64–6, 77–9, 130, 145,
    152–4, 161, 166
The Trickster
    In African folklore 6, 42
    Animal Connection 42–4

Boundary crossing 29–31
And capitalism 86–107
In Chinese folklore 42
And creativity 34–6
In Christianity 43
The Feast of the Ass 43
In Greek mythology ix, 3, 6–7, 30,
    91
Inadvertent libertarian 8
In Japanese folklore 42
Journalist as 169–70
And liminality 3, 17–18, 58–61, 94
Licentiousness 39–42
Loss of control 43–7
The name 31–2
In Northern American folklore ix,
    5–6, 12–13, 31, 39, 140
And postmodernism/postmodernity
    47–62
As psychopomp 30
As psychotherapist 56–8
In Roman mythology 30
In Russian folklore
In Scandinavian folklore
Scatological references 44–6
And social class 90–9, 109–12,
    116–19
And the shadow 18–19
Technology as 72–4
And television 64–5, 152–4
The Truman Show (Peter Weir) 96, 120,
    139–40
Turner, Victor x, 3, 5–6, 16–18, 21, 29,
    38, 50–1, 58–60, 94, 116, 120, 146,
    148

Ulysses (Joyce) 93
The unconscious *see* Jungian
    Psychology
Urban environments 61, 110

Van Gennep, Arnold x, 3, 17, 24, 38,
    136, 157
Vincent (Tim Burton) 36
Virility 40
Von Franz, Marie-Louise 5, 13, 32,
    140

Waddell, Terrie 6, 39
Wakdjunkaga (mythology) 6, 12–13,
    31–2, 36, 39–40, 42, 45, 88, 139
Walken, Christopher 69

Warhol, Andy 146, 148
The Waste Land (T. S. Eliot) 93
Weber, Max 50–1
Welsford, Enid 5, 42, 98
Wexler, Norman *see* also Mr. X 86
Wiene, Robert 99
WikiLeaks ix, 74, 80–1
Willeford, William 5, 29, 42, 98, 106
Winnebago Trickster ix, 5–6, 12–13, 31, 39, 140
Witches of Eastwick (George Miller) 19

Workaholism 41, 70–1, 181
Wotan (mythology) 26

Yes Man (Peyton Reed) 29, 37, 56–7, 96, 106, 140

Zarathustra 14
Zeus (mythology) 25–6, 35, 123
Zmuda, Bob 86, 142, 147–52, 158, 160–2, 168, 170
Zuckerberg, Mark 79, 82–5